THE BUSINESS OF SPECIALTY COFFEE

MAXWELL DASHWOOD

Published by Maxwell Dashwood in Great Britain 2023
Colonna & Small's
6 Chapel Row
Bath BA1 1HN

Cover Design & Book Design: Ally Simpson
Copy Editor: Travis Riley

Printed and bound in China

ISBN 978-1-3999-5984-1

Introduction

How it Started 11

My Beginnings in the Business of Coffee 13

Why I am Writing the Book 14

Overview: How I Have Structured this Book 16

Part One. Overview of the Specialty Coffee Industry

Introduction to Part One 18

Specialty or Boutique 19

    Terminology and Culture

    Scoring and Flavour

A Sense of Scale 22

Seed to Cup - The Scope of Businesses Involved in Coffee 23

The Concept of Quality 25

    Consensus and Community

    Scoring in Context

    Quality for the Consumer

    The Future of Quality

Is it a Business? 30

The Business Fundamentals 33

The Size of the Market 38

Part Two. Operating a Business

Introduction to Part Two 42

Where is the "Value Add?" 43

To Grow or Not to Grow 46

Break-Even 50

Cost of Production 53

Deliverable Margin 56

Starting a Business in Coffee - Barrier to Entry 59

Risk 62

The Impact of Scale 64

Access to Finance - An Industry Built on Borrowed Money 67

Ownership, Investment and Valuation 71

Compliance 76

Customer Acquisition 78

Lifetime Value and Loyalty - Customer Range 80

Customer and Supplier Alignment 83

The Ingredient Versus the Finished Drink 85

The Sweet Spot - Volume and Price 87
Customer Relations 91
Customer Research 94
Teams, Roles and Structures 97
People and Progression in the Coffee Profession 101
Expertise and Talent 104
Marketing - Access to Market 108
Research and Development 111
Adversaries or Partners? 114
Race to the Bottom 116
Killing Things That Don't Work 118
Prioritisation and Resource Management 121
Unicorns Aren't the Norm - Winner Bias 122
"True" Profit 124

Part Three. Market Forces
Introduction to Part Three 126
Macroeconomics 126
Innovation 127
Intellectual Property 132
Technology 135
  Functional Technology in Coffee's Journey
  Limitations and Mistrust of Technology in Boutique Business
Weather, Terroir and Agriculture 140
Sudden Change - A Pandemic 145
The C-market - Differentials and Currency Value 148
Government Policy 154
Colonial and Imperial Legacy - Capitalism and Globalism 157
A Global Community 160
Market Differences 162
Timing and Trends 164

Part Four. Values
Introduction to Part Four 167
What is Ethical Coffee? 167
What is a Fair Price? 171
Transparency, Traceability and Direct Trade 174
Impact - Specialty Versus Commercial Coffee 181
Certifications 185

Sustainability in Coffee   189
Independent Business - Small, Local and Craft   194
Greenwashing   197
Equality, Equity & Diversity   200
Values Driven Initiatives Inside and Outside of Coffee   205
Burnout and Mental Health and Physical Health   207

Part Five. Branding and Marketing
Introduction to Part Five   210
Sticky Brands and Sensemaking   210
Physical Experiences - The Value of Bricks and Mortar   212
Expertise, Trust and Word of Mouth   215
Premium and Luxury Versus Craft and Local   219
Semiotics - Specialty as an Aesthetic   222
Design and Differentiation - The Chain of Independent Coffee Shops 227
Lifestyle and Merchandising Coffee Brands   231
B2B Branding   233

Part Six. Strategy
Introduction to Part Six   235
What is Your Why?   235
Porter's Business Strategies   239
  The Four Generic Strategies
  The Five Forces
Scale, Diversification & Vertical Integration   243
Growing a Business - Quick vs Slow Growth   246
Funding and Financing   249

Part Seven. Business by Business
Introduction to Part Seven   252
Growing and Processing Coffee   252
  Economics and Scale
  Diversification, Vertical Integration and Risk
  Communication, Connection and Access to Market
  Research and Development, and Access to Finance
  People, Expertise and Talent
  Government Policy, Sustainability and the Future
Green Trading, Importing and Exporting   263
  Economics, Scale and the Market

Finance and Risk
Relationship, People and Expertise
Government Policy, Sustainability and the Future

Roasters 270
The Growing Market
Diversification and Talent
Finance, Growth and Equipment
People and Expertise
Technology and Access
Traceability and Sustainability
Marketing, Merchandising and Lifestyle
Vertical Integration and the Future

Online 280
Deliverable Margin and Outsourcing
The Pandemic and Word of Mouth Marketing
Cost of Acquisition, Customer Relations and Online Advertising
Diversification in Bricks and Mortar
Lifestyle, Merchandising and Sales Models

Retail 286
Margins and Selling to the Multiples
Price Elasticity and Shelf Life in Specialty Boutique Coffee

Coffee Pods and Other Drink Formats 289
Coffee Pods - Cost and Barrier to Entry
Coffee Pods - Marketing and Strategy
Coffee Pods - Sustainability and the Future
Instant Coffee
Cold Brew and Other Formats

Coffee Shops 297
Location Access to Market and Customer Relations
Customer Feedback and Industry Perception
Bricks and Mortar Economics
People, Expertise and Multi-Site Models
Sustainability, Automation and Trends

HoReCa and Offices 306
Businesses that Orbit Coffee 310

Part Eight. Thoughts & Questions Posed
Introduction to Part Eight 315
Singing the Praises of Specialty Coffee 316

Lean Margin Frameworks   318
The 5th Wave, Can You Scale Quality?   320
Industry Trends   326
   A Flavour-Oriented Drink
   Brewing Technology
   The Branding Blur
   Innovation and Technology
   Sustainability
   New Experiences
   Specialty at Scale

Exits & Consolidation   331
The Price of a Cup of Coffee   336
Is There a Coming Divergence in Coffee?   341
The Holy Grail - Vision Plus Business   347

Acknowledgements   350
About the Author   351

Introduction

How it Started

In 2007 I became intrigued by and then quickly obsessed with coffee. I was smitten. I felt that I had found my calling. This unique drink, its culture, and the industry that surrounded it appealed to my curiosity and overlapped many of my interests. At that time coffee appeared to be at an exciting inflection point - it drew me in with how much there was to learn, experience and discover. As with all business, there was an element of timing.

If I am being honest, I didn't show a huge interest in the traditional business side of coffee at that time. I thought that as long as you could identify value, then the business would follow. To some degree, I still believe this. Finding and focusing on an offering that has value is definitely more likely to result in success than just a robust understanding of business structure and accounting. In a way this distinction is silly. It is easy to think of business as the boring bits of an endeavour, when in truth it is all part of a whole - concept and creation, relationships and marketing sit as equals to systems, numbers and compliance.

Before stumbling across coffee in Melbourne, I had already begun to build an appreciation that all pursuits (unless you have a very large pot of money to access at will) need to be sustainable as a business. My father is a sculptor, and growing up I saw the challenges of pursuing art as a business, even for a successful and well-known artist who exhibited around the world. Meanwhile, I had a collection of jobs as a teenager and found myself learning about how these businesses operated, from the shelves of the supermarket to the pumps of the petrol station.

My main learning was founded on a precocious questioning of how things were done. Much like a curious child I would ask "why" about everything. I often had strong opinions on how things

11

could be done better. In some cases I was correct, and in others I was missing insight that I would later learn through experience. However, there was nearly always a business argument for why something happened. I soon learned this to be the case, though in my opinion, these thoughts still often led to an inferior product or service to the customer.

At about the age of 20 I started selling and marketing my portraiture, whilst also working a job at a pub. This was my first real business, it went well, and I became quite busy. I learnt about networking and the basics of business. The reason my work sold, I discovered, was because it achieved a value that people were able to engage in. Portraiture is an easier business to get off the ground than most other artwork. We are all able to perceive the skill contained in art that is focused on the likeness of a person we know.

At the same time, I was developing a passion for hospitality. As I mentioned, I was working in a pub. This was a country pub in the New Forest, and it proved to be the perfect place to talk to regulars and find customers for the portraiture.

There came a point when I had to stop working in the pub to keep up with my commissions. Although I was very pleased with this, it also led to the realisation that I didn't want to do the artwork, which was a solitary and repetitive task. The daily interactions between the pub team, its customers and the pub environment were of more interest to me. The business felt very much alive on a daily basis.

I expect I was a mixed bag as an employee. I brought enthusiasm and passion to my work, I worked hard and diligently, but I also challenged and questioned the way things were done.

In a subsequent job, I butted heads with management whilst working part-time in a local cinema, and left the job on principle. I stand by my reason for resigning, which was in response to practices that I saw as discriminatory. The management was (clearly) not open to my perception. My desire to help create a better version of the cinema was not only misplaced but, for them, proved actively problematic. Management was seeking to achieve the minimum that was viable. In their remit, the business simply needed to do "enough". The area manager proudly told me that the cinema hit the best results in a ten-mile radius. He neglected to mention to me that they were the only cinema in a ten-mile radius.

My Beginnings in the Business of Coffee

I started my first coffee business with my partner. It was a mobile events business. We drove far and wide to set up a coffee bar and café experience in fields and venues around the UK.

As you would imagine, this was a seasonal business, and we soon learnt that the biggest profile event often didn't offer us the best business opportunity. An agricultural show could, for example, be more profitable than a headline music festival.

We then moved to Bath, in the South-West of the UK. to open a specialty concept coffee shop. It was in a tiny spot, on a side road, with room for only five seats. We lived in the flat above the shop to keep costs low. This allowed us to start off lean.

After 18 months, and with a growing following, we moved to a larger more prominent store 400-yards away. This store was presented as a concept store and, as of today, we still view it as a customer experience centre rather than just a café. The idea was to build the experience around a rotating, curated coffee menu, and to host customer experiences with a focus on dialogue and discussion. We tried to rethink our in-store layout and visual communication to allow us to break expectation and to build a different experience to a typical coffee shop of the time. Through this process we developed a destination coffee shop that has become a springboard for many of my other explorations in coffee.

During this time, I participated in numerous coffee competitions, and wrote a good number of blogs. These proved valuable ways of engaging in the boutique coffee community, and ultimately contributed to what we were building.

In 2014 we started a craft beer and coffee hybrid store. We killed this project quickly as the business partnership wasn't right, which was a shame, as the business showed promising topline numbers. In 2015 I co-authored Water For Coffee with Christopher H. Hendon, which we self-published and distributed around the world.

Introduction

This book was the culmination of years of collaborative research, and it presents an in-depth, science-heavy exploration of the impact of water science on coffee brewing, a subject which was overlooked at the time. This was followed by the Coffee Dictionary in 2017, which was published by Octopus, part of the Hachete group. This book is now available in five languages.

In 2016 we started a roastery based around the idea of rare, high-scoring coffee. We chose to utilise e-commerce as a significant aspect of our sales mechanism, and subsequently to put specialty coffee into Nespresso compatible pods. For this business we took on venture capital investment. The Think Better Group, who invested in Colonna, also funded and supported another business project of mine, Peak Water, which is a domestic water filter jug, developed and manufactured in the UK, that also received Innovate UK government funding.

Why I am Writing the Book

On a sunny February Sunday in Bath, I found myself discussing the business of coffee with Darcy Miller of Darcy's Kaffe in Copenhagen. Clearly my enthusiasm was showing, as he suggested that the topic for my next book may have just presented itself. Presuming that these words make it to print, I must thank you for that Darcy.

I, like many, have found myself journeying through the industry over time and learning about the business of coffee through exposure, rather than through a structured business learning course or process.

At times I've looked around and said, "how are they doing that?" Or "how does that business make money? What is a good price? What is the norm for this business type? How does scale affect margin?" and so on.

Although, during my time in coffee I have had the opportunity to consult for all sorts of companies, from boutique to larger, more commercial enterprises, there is also much in the world of coffee that I have not had the chance to do. So, this book cannot rest solely on my experiences to date.

Coffee, as we know, is complex, and the business of coffee is very much so. Add to this the many salient details regarding the workings of the industry that are not openly divulged (for obvious reasons) and you can see that it requires an investigative process to understand the businesses that make up a cup of specialty coffee. Building an accurate picture of this has been one of the central challenges in the journey of writing this book.

I have not undertaken any global surveys, neither have I utilised any data algorithms to map the commercials of the specialty industry. I have had to utilise available resources and assessment by others, combined with the asking of a great many probing questions. I am so very grateful to all the people throughout the coffee industry who have been so forthcoming and generous with both information and time.

Through curiosity I often find myself learning about and exploring areas of coffee that are either less well understood or not widely discussed and shared. I love learning and trying to get to the bottom of things.

The approach that I like to take starts with finding and talking with people who are directly involved in the area that I would like to learn about. I then combine these conversations with the study of available information and materials. Through this I build up a picture of how I think this chosen topic works. I then strive to seek out experts in that field and present my understanding to them. I am told this process is called expert foiling.

I wait to see what holes they poke in my understanding, which, if they do, will suggest that my theory may need some revisions. At this point, I should have reached a decent understanding on the topic. Of course, in subjects so new and complex there are often differing points of view and debate amongst experienced experts. In this book I will look to present both sides of the matter, as well as giving my take. This book is, in its own way, that process in action, and I am open to any hole that may exist in the understanding I present. One of my favourite sayings is that when one teaches, two learn.

For many of us, when we start a specialty coffee business, we are passionate about coffee, and have a vision for what we want to build. The business side is often not as deeply considered - but for a vision to flourish it also needs to be profitable. I hope that this book is able to offer insight in this regard. I hope that it can offer some understanding of the "levers" at play that I wish I had grasped much sooner.

Overview: How I Have Structured this Book

I went back and forth on what to title this book. This title was the first that came to mind, and whilst I explored many other concepts, I ended up back where I started. The reason I questioned the title was that this book is not a step-by-step guide on how to start a business in coffee. There is value in books that take this approach, but the value I saw in pursuing this book was not to prescribe to a given approach to running a business. I believe there are many different approaches to running successful businesses. I instead wanted to embark on a journalistic journey to understand the industry within a wider context. I still very much hope there is much to learn and contemplate within these pages which can feed into how you could run a business in coffee.

I have structured the book in eight parts. I start in *Part One* with some "high-level" perspectives. First to broadly define what the specialty industry is and the main businesses that it comprises, and then to set out an overview of the different business-types that play a part in coffee's seed to cup journey, with a basic profile for each.

In *Part Two* my goal is to dive into the nuts and bolts of doing business. I often think of the different mechanics at play in a business as the "levers" of business. These are all integral aspects of running businesses that can be manipulated either by external factors or by the people involved in the business. These "levers" are the same in most businesses, but there is a different emphasis and importance on each one depending on the workings of the specific business.

For each topic I look to touch on how the different businesses in coffee are impacted. Every section in this part is relevant to every business, albeit to varying degrees. In some cases, the volume has been turned up or down. A component of doing business is that something that is not really a priority for one business can be an absolute priority for another.

In *Part Three* I look at wider market forces and influences that ripple through all of the businesses in the seed to cup journey. Coffee is truly a global industry, and as is the case with all industries, there are large patterns at play that affect every individual business.

Part Four explores how values in specialty coffee are a part of business, and also how different value concepts do and don't flow through boutique business behaviour. I seek to understand what equality and equitability in coffee can look like, and where they are possible. I also wanted to take time to challenge and critique messaging in branding in coffee and consider greenwashing.

Part Five looks at branding and marketing in the space. The cynic may argue that specialty coffee is largely defined by branding and marketing.

Part Six is a high-level look at different strategies that are utilised in starting, growing and running specialty coffee businesses.

In *Part Seven* I circle back to the typical businesses in the coffee's journey, and look to apply the themes we have covered throughout the book to each case.

And, in the final part of the book, Part Eight, I aim to conclude my thoughts and understanding of the boutique market with some opinions on what the future may hold.

Part One. Overview of the Specialty Coffee Industry

Introduction to Part One.

What is specialty coffee? At what scale does an independent coffee business outgrow its independent status? Can a coffee business be independent, but not specialty?

These questions are ones that people working in coffee often tussle with. In this first part of the book, I hope to frame the part of the industry that I will be digging into over the coming pages.

Funnily enough, I no longer personally identify as working in "specialty coffee." I prefer to say that I work in coffee, with a focus on higher scoring coffees that display a certain set of attributes.

With passion for a topic, often comes a sense of ownership that is felt by the people working within the field. Especially if the field in question is at a pioneering moment. Workers may find themselves crusading, spreading the word of their product, how it is different, how they perceive it as better, maybe even exceptional.

This process results in a form of idealism, whereby businesses, individuals or collective groups, who all identify as sharing a passion and goal, create a movement. This movement doesn't have a headquarters and it doesn't have a formally agreed ideology, so it is more of a loose collective.

The shared interest is built on assumptions (either unspoken or passed by word of mouth) of what the product is about, or of what it "should" be trying to achieve.

Of course, each coffee business is entitled to pursue its vision of what it wishes to achieve (within the law and without misleading people). Often, however, this can result in a personal or business inclination to speak on behalf of the community. In the past I have been guilty of this and to some extent, I still am.

This sense of certainty over a singular vision or objective has the wind taken out of it when you see the competing ideas of what coffee, particularly specialty coffee, "should" be. It clearly can't be reduced down to a single neat sentence.

In *Part One* I aim to give an overview of what one may be referring to when using the term "specialty coffee," this will be a backdrop for the wider discourse of the book.

Specialty or Boutique
Terminology and Culture

When discussing business, I am often challenged on simple notions that I hold to be true but have never fully defined. This can be especially true when categorising a specific area of a market. Specialty coffee, as a term, has not only come to define a drink with certain attributes and qualities, but a whole scene, and for many, it also represents a system of values. So, what is a specialty coffee? A quick answer would be that there is no clear definition. However, the term is also plainly and regularly used - people say it all of the time - so it means something, even if that meaning is not clearly defined.

In this regard, specialty coffee has much the same challenge as craft beer. On the one hand, a consumer may identify craft beer as some more intense and interesting flavours in a beer that quite likely has funky packaging. On the other hand, they may define it as a product, produced by a company with a certain set of values; a certain spirit, a certain size and with a certain identity; and that it represents a rebellion against what had become the ingrained commercial norm.

I think it is fair to say that most customers have an idea of what a craft beer product ought to deliver in its resulting flavour experience. Much the same can be said for specialty coffee. A consumer might expect to have a "different" tasting coffee, with interesting flavours and more natural acidity, or they may associate the coffee with a certain value chain.

In the cases of both the beer and coffee there is a correlation between the businesses you expect behind the production, and the curation of the drink. The culinary delights being presented have been championed and pushed by a movement of smaller, independent, passionate businesses and individuals.

Much like a genre of music or a trend in fashion, these businesses start to band together in terms of both identity and product. This happens organically; there isn't a formalised, committed agreement decided at a town hall meeting. In the cases of craft beer and specialty coffee, this process can be seen at varying stages in different countries around the world.

This does not mean of course, that these movements have any ownership over their approach to the product, or more precisely to the flavour profiles that they champion and experiences they are trying to create. Later in the book I touch on the lack of intellectual property in coffee.

Just as it is very possible for a large brewery to make a beer that tastes "craft," a large-scale coffee roastery can buy and roast a nano-lot of experimental process Gesha, that is much more likely associated with the "specialty" movement. In fact, I think it often surprises people how much specialty coffee is sourced and sold by larger, commercial coffee businesses that don't fit the specialty mould, so to speak.

For this reason, this book focuses more on what I call boutique coffee. At this stage, the specialty movement could perhaps better be described as the "specialty boutique market." This term better encompasses the coffee that is championed and the type of businesses that typically populate the space, and in particular dominate the media narrative.

Scoring and Flavour

The topic of what exactly constitutes the specialty coffee movement could fill a book all on its own. Instead, in this book, I focus on the business practices of the movement, and on the sale of coffee that reaches the specialty scoring threshold of 80 points or above on the SCA's scoring system, which is the threshold for coffee to be termed "specialty."

For all of the unavoidable subjectivity in coffee, this scoring system works well as a way to understand the quality of a given coffee. Higher scores definitely correlate with flavour attributes that are prized over others.

Scoring also has drawbacks. For example, two 85 point coffees from different producers, varietals and processes are unlikely to taste the same. In this way the score does not provide a full picture of a coffee.

The arbitrary limit of 80 also is not helpful for the perception of coffee below the line, which is often termed "commercial" coffee, creating a perceived gulf between this and "specialty." A 79 point coffee clearly is not magnitudes worse than an 80, yet it feeds into the narrative that 80 points put you on the side of the Jedi and anything below is the realm of the Sith. There really is a perceived ethical difference here where one does not need to be. In reality the gradient is more gradual. I will explore in this book the notion that commercial coffee has an important place. It is certainly naive and inappropriate to categorise commercial coffee as wrong or evil.

When most coffee is scored, a lighter, though developed, roast is usually used to highlight a coffee's terroir and provenance. Specialty coffee has tended to promote and be aligned with roasting lighter. This makes sense as the approach to roasting can be viewed as an extension of the cupping and scoring protocols. However, at exactly what point a roast becomes too dark to be specialty is unclear, and perennially up for debate. Some may argue that you can roast as dark as you want, as this represents a point of subjective preference. While I agree that this decision is absolutely up to a company and its consumers, this will still raise a question about whether the value of the coffee can be fully captured and passed on in the process, and indeed where the true significance of this lies in our understanding of specialty coffee.

Roasting is, without a doubt, one of the biggest influences on the cup profile of a coffee. Putting aside all details of brewing, water science and other factors, the biggest choice a business (that is not a farmer/producer) makes to impact the flavour of the coffee is roast profile.

I used to try and illustrate the way any given cup of coffee tastes using a pie chart. In the chart I would give the green coffee (growing, harvesting and milling) more than half the chart, roast would come next, then water and lastly brewing. This hierarchy does not tend to sit well with baristas, but just because a slice is smaller, this does not mean that it can't be of consequence.

The thought experiment is more about possible impact. You can't overcome the limitations of the raw ingredient with processes further downstream. The same can be said for roasting, there's only so much that water and brewing can do to influence a predefined roast style.

This has moved the conversation into the area of origin and brewing taste theory, and fascinatingly these do also play into the business of specialty coffee, especially considering its ambitions in the arenas of quality and flavour. The exact breakdown of how much of the specialty moniker is down to coffee quality and brewing science rather than branding, experience and aesthetic is up for debate.

A Sense of Scale

In terms of gatekeeping, smaller boutique companies cannot stop a large commercial coffee company from buying specialty grade coffee if it chooses to do so. This, again, has an equivalency with the way a big brewery can make a hoppy or sour experimental beer if it so chooses.

Despite this, as a rule of thumb specialty coffee is almost always still associated with boutique businesses. In coffee's case, this is down to a combination of price and availability, and just as importantly, an emphasis on the concept of quality, which is perceived as a primary goal of a passion-led, smaller business.

As the coffee's score goes up and the scarcity increases, so the price goes up. Scoring in coffee often reflects scarcity as much as "quality," which means that the goalposts move over time. Larger companies generally require consistency of supply and flavour, and a price that suits their customers' appetite, making the innate attributes of high-scoring coffee undesirable.

As the customer base gets bigger, the company is not within a specialist niche, and has to respond to the broad demand for a lower cost product. A larger customer base also requires accessible and repeatable flavour profiles. What customers are signing up for when walking into a store or buying a bag of branded coffee will predetermine what is required by the coffee business.

This customer has a desire for coffee to taste familiar and defined, which is in opposition to the boutique coffee drinker's interest in a new and unusual flavour profile. This dichotomy in behaviour can be termed as the "comfort drinker" versus the "explorer," and will determine which coffee business a person patronises.

For these reasons, specialty coffee is likely to be associated with boutique, independent business, and we can see the experimental nature of current high-scoring coffees, and the demand for small lots of green coffee, affirming this.

However, the volume of specialty coffee scoring in the low to mid 80s is higher and can suit large companies. These coffees are not necessarily as distinct in flavour, allowing companies to brand them as "better" or "nicer" coffee, without too much further explanation required. Debatably, the 80 point mark could be moved higher, to make it more useful in determining a true differentiation. But, it is also fair to say we see great coffees being presented by a growing range of coffee companies with different identities, brands and sizes, and there is no exact point score that will ever resolve this discussion.

In many environments, specialty is also indicated by preparation method. I think it is fair to ask if an automated coffee experience (regardless of the quality of coffee) can be called specialty, just as you can ask whether a lower-scoring coffee made via small-scale, manual processes could be called specialty. I imagine it is now becoming quite apparent why it is difficult to pin specialty coffee down.

Throughout the book I will touch upon how specialty coffee plays across a variety of businesses, and how a variety of different businesses together make specialty coffee. Specialty coffee can be discussed in two main ways. Firstly and most simply, as coffees that score above 80 points on the SCA's scoring system, and secondly, as an identity and engagement theme found across customer experiences, brands, the business community and culture. This second definition is clearly more blurry.

In *Part Five* of the book in the chapter, *Sticky Brands - Sensemaking*, I continue to look at whether specialty coffee is defined as much by a type of engagement with coffee as it is by specific coffee products and flavours.

Seed to Cup - The Scope of Businesses Involved in Coffee

The seed to cup journey is a familiar tale. It is told on stage at barista competitions, by coffee brands to their customers, by educators and, well, by anyone explaining the basics of what coffee is.

This same fundamental coffee narrative can be seen through the prism of the businesses that sit behind each part of the supply chain.

Coffee as an industry, and especially the specialty segment, can be full of passion, so it is easy to forget that, for all involved in coffee, it is also a business transaction. The exception to this is of course the end user, the individual enjoying the drink, at a particular moment in their day.

The reason it is so useful to consider the supply chain of coffee in this way, is that it allows you to understand the whys and hows of each stage, as each business along the journey of the coffee transacts with one another. When you run a business, a lot of decision making is based around what makes good sense, and for any of the stages to be sustainable they need to be profitable. On the whole, excluding the odd loss-making project, you will only see things come to life (and stay alive) that are profitable and viable. There are exceptions, of course. More on that later.

When I first ventured into the world of coffee, I thought of the coffee supply chain as several distinctly different businesses sitting back-to-back. I now see that these businesses are all more similar than I realised, they are each made of the same core building blocks.

Each business may have to concern itself with one building block more than another, this is true, but the frameworks are similar. I often think of it as a volume dial. Different businesses have the volume turned up in different areas of business fundamentals. For example, one business may need to be much more concerned with cash flow, whilst another with variable operational costs.

For this reason, the structure of this book is based around the core business principles that run throughout the coffee industry. When addressing, for example, the cost of production, it will be clear to see the ways in which this is an essential tenet for all businesses in coffee, from a coffee farm, to a roaster or an online subscription business.

There are other "coffee businesses" that are part of the industry but do not directly handle coffee on its journey to the cup, such as coffee machine manufacturers, roaster manufacturers and software makers. There are others that would not consider themselves coffee companies at all, but rather see coffee as one of the markets that they service, such as water filtration system businesses and packaging companies. I will touch on some of these businesses in the book, but mainly I intend to focus on the journey of the coffee bean.

This journey is mainly situated in four well known and established industry types: agriculture, finance and logistics, food manufacturing and hospitality.

The Concept of Quality
Consensus and Community

"The standard of something as measured against other things of a similar kind, the degree of excellence of something." - Oxford English Dictionary

Debate about what specialty coffee encapsulates may abound, but it seems unambiguous to say that it is based upon pursuing, exploring and rewarding quality in coffee. Though, it must be acknowledged that if quality incorporates context, this lessens the simplicity of this definition a touch.

The notion of quality is something we are all familiar with. It pops up in conversation regularly in our everyday lives, which does not mean that it cannot also be a philosophical and challenging topic.

This book is not the place to delve into debates regarding how to quantify quality. Theorists have explored the philosophical notion of whether quality can be concrete, something the protagonist in Robert M. Pirsig's *Zen and the Art of Motorcycle Maintenance* strives to achieve.

For most, quality is highly contextual. The definition that begins the chapter alludes directly to this, by mentioning "[measuring] against other things". It is easy to say something is "excellent," but if excellence is defined as surpassing expectation in a positive way, then the expectation itself defines the capacity for something to excel.

In other words, it's a matter of opinion; a subjective evaluation. Quality in coffee is not absolute, however, when in the company of individuals or a community who have a highly-defined and agreed consensus on a given topic it can sometimes feel like it. Consensus is really what defines a statement of quality.

This consensus is relative to the group of people forming the accord. When you apply these musings to coffee, it could lead to a conclusion that all of coffee is subjective, that there are just different tastes, and there is no truth in quality, however, a surprisingly robust consensus can be found in coffee's scoring system. I have always thought that this demonstrates how a collection of subjective experiences can create a somewhat objective framework regarding taste.

There are some flavour defects in coffee that more or less no one likes, such as phenol, potato defect or mould. As human beings we seem to have some "built-in" preferences and we are programmed to struggle with certain extreme flavours, often due to survival and health reasons. But we also have an incredible diversity of possible diets, cultural preferences and tastes.

Taste is definitely in play in the long and ongoing debate around the level of fermented flavours in a coffee. These flavours are created by methods of processing used at origin. How much ferment is too much? Whilst there are some structures in place around perceived coffee taints and levels of acetic acid etc, this area isn't clearly agreed upon. In recent times, experiments making use of highly-controlled bacteria and yeast ferment procedures have created flavour profiles that push not only people's palates, but the boundaries of the coffee scoring framework.

These coffees are interesting, as their specific qualities can be tasted with less influence from roast, water and brewing, as the flavour is so distinct. This clearly has value. However the shock and awe of the upfront qualities often don't stand the test of time, and tasters report becoming saturated with the flavours quite quickly.

I was recently speaking to a Cup of Excellence judge who noted that maybe intensity was starting to be rewarded more than complexity. This debate can get heated, which shows that, no matter how ideologically linked a group or community is, there cannot always be an easy consensus.

Scoring in Context
As an industry, coffee has a widely used points scoring system which reaches 100 points - but nothing scores 100. In the *Specialty or*

Boutique section I wrote about the 80 point threshold. This arbitrary line has been chosen to denote "specialty" coffee in contrast with "commodity" grade coffee.

Anything under the 80 point threshold is typically referred to as commercial/commodity coffee and anything above is typically referred to as specialty coffee. There is a continuing gradient as the score gets higher. 90+ point scores are not commonly achieved, and are seen as a very significant landmark.

This score is directly tied into the commercials of all coffee, defining its potential monetary value, and its suitability for coffee businesses with different scales and ambitions.

Coffee is sold on both physical specification (screen size, lack of physical defects etc.) and sensory attributes. The sensory attributes are assessed on the cupping table. In this way, coffee's value through the whole supply chain is really reliant on peoples' mouths (and noses) and their individual assessment of a sensory experience.

A correlation can be shown between a coffee's cup profile and physical attributes, and the sorting of the coffee at dry mills and throughout the seed to cup journey. However, there is still much variation in flavour profile, and the exact approach to cup scoring around the world depends on cultivar, processing and terroir.

Scoring can be relatively effective across different stakeholders in the supply chain once it is in place. The conversation typically revolves around how to calibrate the individuals performing the tasting and the blind assessment of the coffee.

There is inherent variation and bias in coffee tasting, something which seems inevitable in all interpretative human assessment tasks. Sensory science regularly displays the limits of human capacity to act as a robust, analytical tasting tool. Humans are highly subjective and can have their experience swayed by a number of external and internal factors.

Scoring also, as I have mentioned, has a direct relationship with a coffee's commercial value. For these reasons blind tasting is often utilised in the supply chain to avoid cognitive bias as much as possible. It is advisable for everyone to taste blind in any case where a score is to be used seriously.

A sensory assessment is also documented at a moment in time by one or a group of individuals. Coffee is a raw ingredient, and has a changing and perishable nature. A coffee's pre-shipment score (still at the country of origin) and landed score (in the country where it has been sold) always differ to some degree. This becomes particularly pertinent as coffee ages further from harvest, sitting either in a warehouse or on a roasters' shelves, losing quality and therefore value.

Then of course there are questions surrounding the production of the coffee. Roast style would (if assessed) affect a coffee's cup score, and the same goes for the method of brewing, the water used, and on and on. It can feel like a dizzying array of variables that impact quality, creating intrigue and frustration, elation and disappointment.

When using scores week-to-week in a practical context it can become easy to start thinking of them as robust, but there will always be some variation across stakeholders on scores, some more generous and others more critical. There will be variation in context, and there is a running debate about how much one should "adjust" their scoring per origin and style.

Perhaps the bigger challenges come with coffee that sits outside of the currently agreed framework. The success of the Eugenioides species has been fascinating. This is an entirely different species of coffee to Arabica (the species upon which specialty coffee has been based up until now) and it tastes very different. As you may expect, it is presently judged using the Arabica framework, but that's difficult, and when people taste it they are often confused, you will hear honest professional cuppers say "I don't know how to score this."

The ongoing, relentless pursuit of not just quality but unique experiences in coffee means there will always be flavour trends and an evolving target. New profiles will enter the sphere of specialty coffee and the popularity of existing profiles may change.

Quality for the Consumer

I hope this chapter has been able to indicate that quality is intrinsically related to value in coffee, but that it is also not concrete or straightforward to assess. For a professional cup-taster, working at any point in the supply chain, the goal is both to build a good ability to assess coffee sensorily, and to be aware of the frameworks for quality, which will continue to evolve.

From a commercial point of view, larger companies often approach cup profiles with a question of their customers' expectations and preferences. Meanwhile, a boutique business is more likely to take the opposite tact, choosing to present what they find to be exceptional.

Quality is not simple and the highest scoring coffees, say, extremely floral, clean coffee, don't necessarily resonate with all (or even many) consumers. Specialty, boutique customers are a segment all to themselves.

I think that the microcosm of high-end coffee, sold at auction, and with distinctive and unique flavour profiles is niche, not just because the coffees are rare, (and expensive) but also because engagement with them is often demanding, and requires highly-interested individuals who really want to explore coffee. From a wider, commercial point of view, this shows the limitation and the true potential scalability of high-scoring specialty coffee.

When doing consumer research, there are many variables to dig into if you wish to really understand preference. Even when serving just one specific type of coffee, preference based around a coffee beverage's concentration will vary wildly. Some will prefer intense espresso, and some light, tea-like filter coffee, with many possibilities in-between. The addition of milk is equally key in understanding preference and enjoyment for coffee drinkers. However, as this is not the format in which coffee is scored, it does encourage questions around how relevant a coffee's given score is in all contexts.

The Future of Quality

Although I have pointed out a significant difference between commercial coffees and the most unusual of the high-scoring specialty lots, making them potentially inaccessible to the uninitiated coffee drinker, when talking with Spencer Hyman, founder of Cocoa Runners, he pointed out another way of looking at this. As he sees it, the "upgrade" to a higher quality coffee is not necessarily jarring. In the context of his product, he explained that to move someone from a commercial chocolate product to a bean-to-bar chocolate involves asking the customer to approach chocolate in a completely different way. Craft chocolate will be consumed at a different time, in a different way, for a different reason. Due to its delivery system, coffee is typically less divided in terms of the "switch" of context.

This is definitely true of a drink like the flat white, which has a strong resemblance across all areas of the industry, less so with a specialty style of filter coffee that might show a delicate flavour and tea-like consistency. Regardless, the bulk of the coffee sold by the businesses of specialty coffee lie in the low to mid-80 point mark, and are brewed in a way that is not miles away from non-specialist brews.

Paul Arnehpy, Roasting consultant was part of the global team who worked on the fourth edition of "The Coffee Guide" by the International Trade Centre. He mentored the ensuing debates around this challenging topic and how it pertains to the day-to-day business of coffee. Their conclusion was to question whether the 80-85 point range could really be called specialty.

I have spoken also to Stephen Morrissey, Chief Commercial Officer at the Specialty Coffee Association. He outlined how the organisation is completely re-thinking the scoring system. They have recently released a new scoring framework that prioritises attributes and contexts of coffees and addresses many of the failings of the current scoring system. It will be interesting to see if the framework in its entirety is widely adopted in place of the old but ingrained system.

The concept of quality is intrinsically baked into the business of coffee, and as we will see throughout the book, quality is part of the commercial considerations of all the businesses in the supply chain. Regardless of the challenge to completely and absolutely define quality it will always be there, and will retain a direct connection to a coffee's value.

Is it a Business?

"The activity of making, buying, selling, or supplying goods or services for money." - Oxford Dictionary

As per this definition, any transaction-based activity constitutes business. However, there is a good reason that people often question whether something is really a business or not. Sometimes this is done for rhetorical reasons or as a leading question. The subtext is that a "real" business is something that is profitable and viable, and that has a certain substance.

The title of this book is designed to elicit a response from boutique coffee minds, for whom thinking of specialty coffee as merely a business can be jarring. This stems from a person's origins and motivations to start a specialty coffee business or enter boutique coffee as a career. In a space where curiosity, quality, and transparency are valued, a purely commercial business approach falls short.

The quality coffee movement almost defines itself by its opposition to the pure, commercial enterprises of wider coffee. In this sector, you start a business to explore your enthusiasm for coffee. This may mean quitting another career or job, meaning that for a lot of independent businesses and entrepreneurs, the goal of the business is not to be as profitable as possible, but to provide a work life balance and allow for further exploration of coffee within a unique personal business and vision.

When approaching business from this perspective, there isn't a box to be ticked. Rather, there is a gradient on which the enterprise sits. There are examples of what might be called "hobby businesses" that work really well for the owners. These are often started with clearly defined ideas of the limitations of the business, what the founders want the activity to mean to them and how they want it to fit into their lives.

It is likely that many more businesses are started without a clear idea of how they will develop. This is natural, and I don't think you should hold this against anyone. A new business is always a learning experience. At some point the founders will be forced to think about the business as a business, at least to some extent. In boutique fields there is a conflict that can occur between running a business and pursuing a passion.

Often at the beginning of a "passion business" and for many years thereafter, the founders will work for very little and pour their time and energy into the project. This is something that I have personally experienced. For as long as the experiences are novel and interesting, the exchange feels rewarding. However, several years in, the enthusiasm for something that barely breaks even and can't wash its own face will likely dissolve, or at the very least, be diluted.

At this point a business owner will have to make a choice. It could be that they decide to box the business, making a few changes and keeping it, but in a more sustainable way that fits with their lives. They could also decide to shut it down. Or, they could focus on making the business something that is more profitable and structured - to take it beyond a simple, passion project.

The world of specialty coffee is full of all sorts of businesses that sit somewhere on this scale. It is useful when analysing the marketplace to consider this phenomenon. If a business is something someone is passionate about, they are likely to be happy for it to make less profit. "Enough" will be different for each person. It may go further though, and if a group of owners love the business enough, they may be happy to run it at a loss, if they are in a position to do so of course.

Although I think the highest density of coffee hobby businesses are at the roasting and café end of things, this concept can be applied throughout the coffee chain.

It would typically be more apt to use different terms in the farming context, such as "supplementary income," by which I mean growing coffee on the side and not as the main income focus for the stakeholders. It may not be as common as in wine but there are also coffee farms run as hobby or passion businesses. To my knowledge, this is not a phenomenon that occurs in exporting, trading and importing green coffee. The barrier to entry in these areas, especially regarding access to finance, makes this unlikely, but not impossible.

It is important to bear in mind the different meanings that sit behind the simple sounding word "business" when traversing the world of coffee.

Later in the book I look at the example of loss-making, aggressively funded models. This is deeply different from a passion project. Both of these business models can occupy the same market and influence the customer proposition. This context is important to remember. It feeds into a truer understanding of what works and how it works when you are trying to benchmark success.

The wider market is also impacted when these different models engage with each other and sell to a similar customer cohort. At the end of the book I will touch on how focusing on the underlying structure of your business can be key to actually progressing the vision of your passion-led business, these things do not have to be mutually exclusive.

The Business Fundamentals

Business is such a big topic that it can be easy to miss the wood for the trees. It can be useful to look at the many businesses of coffee in broad strokes, giving you a rough idea of how the supply chain and the wider market is shaped in terms of financials. In this chapter my goal is to answer a more basic question: how much net profit should a roastery aim to make? And for that matter, a producer, a trader or a coffee shop. What is the typical gross profit of each of these businesses? Where do the different running costs sit in each model? I guess you could call this the basic economics of the coffee supply chain.

These numbers are not usually made readily available. At all times, businesses and individuals in coffee are positioning themselves, and thinking about how they will be seen by another actor. Everyone is on display and everyone is selling a positive image of what they and their company are doing. It may sound cynical, but it's true, even if only through omission of the real numbers, the image presented is often rosier than reality.

This is not deceitful, rather a tactical position to build trust and paint a picture of where a business aspires to be. A stated net profit may be a goal or a one-off month, rather than the average. A given volume may be an anecdotal amount from a busy week. You get the picture.

It may also go the other way of course. A business may choose to lower their numbers. This phenomenon is more likely in boutique business, like specialty coffee, whereby seeking profit is an uncomfortable topic.

Part One. Overview of the Specialty Coffee Industry

The impression can be given that a boutique coffee company should be a charity of some kind, or at least modest in its commercial ambitions. There are associations between the size, success and profitability of a business and its inherent quality, something I touched on already when considering the definition of specialty and boutique in business terms.

The natural suspicion is as follows: if a coffee business is very profitable, it must have high gross profit and low costs. If the business isn't charging very high prices to customers, then how good can the ingredients be? And how fair is their supply chain?

This dynamic is very different in other areas of the business world. One of my clients was looking to implement a coffee programme in their business. Their coffee volume is quite low per site, and they don't want to spend lots of time on coffee preparation. Therefore, we went to visit a variety of leading bean to cup machine manufacturers and suppliers. In every case, the pitch by each company included reference to a healthy bottom line. The purpose of this is to give the client confidence that the company can deliver on its promise. For these companies, this part of the pitch demonstrates a lower risk to a potential business partner, mitigating for dramatic supply issues such as the company going out of business.

This isn't very common in the boutique part of the industry. I suspect that the rationale stems from specialty coffee's discussion over paying a "fair price" for coffee. The underlying subtext is that if a company appears overly profitable, then it cannot be fairly and equitably distributing wealth back through the supply chain.

This is a reasonable thought process, however, in my journey to understand the coffee industry's commercial mechanics I have noticed that it is rarely the case that someone else, somewhere in the chain, is creaming the profit. It is all a relatively lean marketplace relative to risk and complexity, with profit being derived through volume rather than a high percentage of profit per unit sold.

Boutique, specialty coffee should rarely be worried about being seen as "too" profitable, as the profits are almost never high enough to attract attention.

The business mechanics that underpin the coffee industry are pretty old school and comprise of agriculture, finance and logistics, food manufacturing and hospitality. There are many businesses in each of these sectors that don't work with coffee and you can benchmark each of these industries to get an idea for what the norms are. The goals for profitability in these industries typically range from mid-single digit to mid-teen percentages of pre-tax net profit.

At the time of writing this book, global inflation has caused most businesses to review their net profit goals with the expectation of a string of less successful years, whereby they will have a lower net profit. In a competitive market place, companies prioritise availability over profitability when costs rise. This means that they are prioritising customer retention rather than protecting profit, resulting in some periods of time with lower profits. If the increased costs hold, then the prices will be passed on to clients in the fullness of time.

Regarding the high-level view of the basic commercials that make up each of the businesses in the coffee supply chain, I wanted to provide some simple breakdowns of what a business in each part of the industry does and can look like based on mine and others research in this regard. Each of these examples is supposed to represent a realistic but ambitious target model. The actual industry averages will be lower as many businesses wont hit these targets. These are "good" results relative to the industry.

Specialty Coffee Farming
(cherry/cherry plus wet milling) farm
gate 3 hectare Latin American farm model

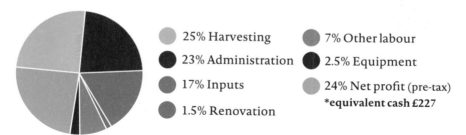

- 25% Harvesting
- 23% Administration
- 17% Inputs
- 1.5% Renovation
- 7% Other labour
- 2.5% Equipment
- 24% Net profit (pre-tax)
  *equivalent cash £227

These numbers utilise the Caravela white paper - A Study on the Cost of production in Latin America, and the article *Rich Farmer, Poor farmer*. Based on 30 bags per hectare.

Medium Specialty Coffee Producer
(including multiple farms, dry
milling & exporting) FOB

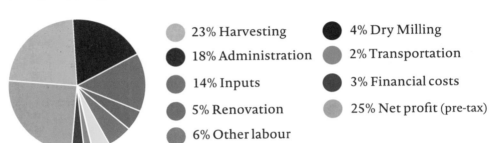

23% Harvesting

18% Administration

14% Inputs

5% Renovation

6% Other labour

4% Dry Milling

2% Transportation

3% Financial costs

25% Net profit (pre-tax)

Specialty Green Importers

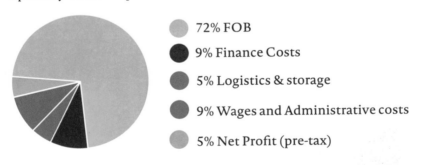

72% FOB

9% Finance Costs

5% Logistics & storage

9% Wages and Administrative costs

5% Net Profit (pre-tax)

Specialty Coffee Roastery

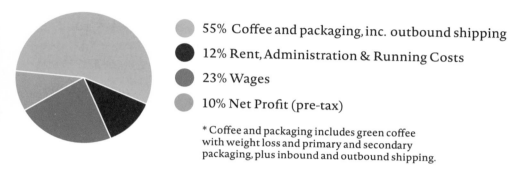

55% Coffee and packaging, inc. outbound shipping

12% Rent, Administration & Running Costs

23% Wages

10% Net Profit (pre-tax)

* Coffee and packaging includes green coffee
with weight loss and primary and secondary
packaging, plus inbound and outbound shipping.

Specialty Coffee Shops

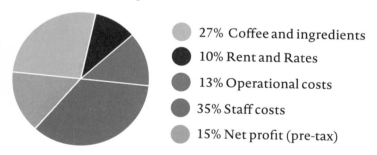

27% Coffee and ingredients

10% Rent and Rates

13% Operational costs

35% Staff costs

15% Net profit (pre-tax)

These overviews come with some very large contextual caveats. These are each the kind of goal you would see in an ambitious but realistic business model or forecast for boutique SME (small to medium business) versions of each business type. A small business can be defined as under 50 employees and a medium under 250 employees.

There are, in each case, examples where a company has managed to get many of the levers right and has created a brand and value proposition that allows them to surpass these profit models. This could be a farm that has optimised scale and quality and developed a strong in demand brand with access to market and low cost borrowing, or a small, low rent, high volume takeaway café.

As a counter to this there are also many many businesses that are never able to hit the profitability outlined in these examples. These would be businesses that struggle, as well as those that never get things to add up, and have to shut down. It should also be noted that the split of costs are also an average and can vary depending on the business.

A vital concept to bear in mind when looking at these numbers is that the value of a net profit percentage can only be understood in combination with the scale and revenue of the operation. The reason I added a monetary profit value into the smallholder coffee farming example is to help demonstrate that, although 24% is a high percentage, it will still only equate to a small cash profit in a business that is too small. It is not enough to make a one hectare farm work, for example.

The further upstream you are in any industry, the less value you realise for a given unit of product. This means that a given percentage profit equates to less monetary value upstream, than downstream per unit of coffee sold.

A green importer is an example of how the prices move around a lot depending on the cost of the green coffee. Storage and logistics are constant per kg regardless of green cost.

Another concept to bear in mind is that these numbers are averages across multiple trading years. The swing in coffee farming profits has the potential to be the most dramatic due to the impact of volatile markets and weather events.

The Size of the Market
At the time of writing this book, estimates (Statista) outline an expectation of 4.61% year on year growth between 2023 and 2028, for coffee globally. In the same time period, there are forecasts

(Businesswire) of a 11.3% growth rate for the specialty coffee market. As a reference, 9% would typically be considered good.

Getting precise numbers on how the market is split up from a supply point of view is challenging, but it is generally agreed that specialty is currently around 10% of supply. The monetary value created relative to volume is higher throughout the specialty supply chain. The global coffee market was estimated to be at a value of $126.38 billion in 2022 (Expert Market Research) and the specialty market was valued at $52.1 billion (Credence Research) at the same time.

Valuations of the specialty coffee market vary widely depending on how you categorise the companies that make up part of that market definition, and more specifically, whether they use exclusively specialty grade green coffee. Either way, this data supports a narrative around coffee as a value driven product that is growing, and specialty coffee is a key part of this market.

The specialty market is predicted to grow to a value of $102.3 billion (Credence Research) by 2028. A lot of the current market value and forecasted opportunity is driven by large companies and brands. In the last part of this book we consider the idea of quality at scale, looking at what is possible. However, boutique businesses in all markets flourish when the wider market is bigger and growing. The growth we have seen to date doesn't look set to slow down anytime soon, meaning that boutique specialty coffee businesses and concepts will continue to be part of an evolving marketplace with opportunity.

In the UK, green importers each report and see growth on the whole, though often this is based upon a growing range of clients, from pre-existing larger roasteries to a growing stream of micro-roasters. B2B (business to business) sales dominate the market with a 74.3% share (Businesswire). This categorisation refers to sales of coffee into cafés, restaurants, hotels and offices etc. Online sales and ready to drink formats have shown some of the highest growth.

Market sizing is a term commonly seen in a company's investment deck. Aside from sheer curiosity, the reason to try and evaluate a market's size is to be able to better gauge the market opportunity for a given business aiming to, or already operating in that market.

The idea is that you can backsolve from the big numbers to broadly ascertain the opportunity for the business in question. As ever, there is more to understand than what is on the surface. A big market does not necessarily mean lots of market opportunities. Knowledge of the industry can help to break these large numbers down and see what they are composed of.

A very large market may be quite saturated (which means that the volume of products available or companies working in the area is already at capacity), or it may be monopolised by a few big players, creating a shutout for those entering the market. Coffee doesn't typically display this characteristic, but it can occur in parts of the industry.

Countless other scenarios can impact the viability of a given market. A highly segmented marketplace with a lot of players, for example, may indicate the limitation of the opportunity of any given brand or company in the space to own or capitalise on the market as a whole. This scenario has some relevance to the boutique specialty space.

Businesses tussle with questions of how to understand and benefit from market opportunity all of the time, trying to figure out the answers to how they should strategically approach their marketplace. This is not just start-ups, but an ongoing process for established businesses as well.

Simply outlining a market's size, or its growth, is only a small piece of the puzzle. However, an understanding of the marketplace with context can produce an advantage, as long as it is combined with an open mind and the ability to see and react to change.

There are clearly limits to the amount of specialty coffee that can be grown, but just as key, is the limit on price elasticity in consumer buying behaviour. Specialty has in many cases been exploring the potential for differentiated value propositions in the marketplace, as well as what profitable sustainable business will look like. The industry will face many challenges but the market data suggest that an interest in specialty coffee is supported by indicators of overall market growth in the coming years. In the midterm we have the increasing impact of climate change and sustainability to consider and in the longer term we will, like all industries, encounter global population decline. Those scenarios are particularly hard to model accurately.

Part Two. Operating a Business

Introduction to Part Two

It is my observation and opinion that businesses in coffee all have a lot more in common than they may realise, and I believe that everyone, in each position in the coffee supply chain, can benefit from putting themselves in the shoes of the other businesses.

It can be easy to generalise or simplify something when looking at it from afar. It is only when you experience it for yourself, that you will realise that you had it wrong. You can begin to draw lots of parallels with experiences that you have had - creating lightbulb moments where you realise a thread of similarity and see things that you didn't see before.

When thinking about a supplier or a client, imagine you are in their shoes. Imagine that you are responsible for paying the salaries and achieving profit and planning out the year. I appreciate this is a much easier thing for someone who already runs a business to imagine, but I do believe everyone should be thinking this way to some degree.

As an employee in a business, working to understand how the business works overall, and how you fit into the wider business, will be valuable in helping you excel in your own role, whatever that role may be. There is of course the danger of making false assumptions, and thinking that you understand the business that you are a part of, better than you actually do.

In the second part of this book, I look to journey through the main levers of running businesses, whilst considering how these can vary in terms of their impact and importance through the seed to cup journey. My motivation behind focusing on levers is the huge variety of contexts that occur in any given part of coffee's supply chain. The realities of doing business in one country can be vastly different to another country, but the underlying levers will be the same. The difference will be how those levers are worked. This part of the book explores the microeconomic levers at play in the coffee industry.

Where is the "Value Add?"

The concept of value add in any industry is really a question of where it is "worth" doing business. This sounds very obvious. Of course, all essential links in the chain from seed to cup have a degree of value. The question often comes down to which parts of the chain you should undertake in your business, rather than outsourcing and working with another company. It also naturally leads to the question of vertical integration.

A good bit of advice for all of us as individuals is to play to our strengths. The same is true in business. If you are going to work on your weaknesses then prepare yourself for risk, and a difficult journey. This point is clearly contextual, and there are many examples where identifying and addressing a weakness can make for a better business. However, the point still stands, you need to know when to allow another company to provide a service or good for you. This is good business if it allows you to focus on facets of the business in which you can add value.

There will be aspects of producing a product in which there is no real value added if it is done in-house, rather than by a supplier. Conversely, it may be that someone else could achieve the task to a higher standard than you or your team's capabilities. At the same time there are also examples of where not doing something in house can hold your business back.

Milling coffee is a good example of this in practice. I spoke to Fernando Lima, a coffee producer in El Salvador, and he explained that wet milling is a value add that he wants to be in control of, and keep in house for his farms.

It adds value in multiple ways. It is an opportunity for him and his team to apply multiple processes to coffee and be fully flexible, regardless of the scale of the coffee lot. Their personal approach can add unique value to the products via improved or unique flavour, which feeds into their wider coffee brand. Additionally, there is a cost saving for him to wet mill, and the scale is right for him to coordinate the process in-house.

Dry milling, however, represents almost double the cost per carga (100lbs/45.4kg) than the price of outsourcing the task to a third-party milling operation. He struggles to see a reason why he would want to take on the dry milling. Of course, he needs the dry milling partner to do a good job, but he doesn't do it himself, as it doesn't add value.

I think in specialty, boutique coffee there can be a desire to carry out every potential process to generate a narrative of authenticity. Whilst this may be important for your business in key areas, it is not always the best option.

What is true for Fernando may not be true for others. I have seen this through my own coffee roastery. I can and do outsource to some companies available to supply me, however my company's requirements often do not fit the structure and offering of the potential suppliers, leaving me in a no-man's land, where I am not happy with the value proposition of the outsourced solutions. At this point I can't help but wonder whether we would be better to implement these specific processes ourselves.

Kyle Bellinger, founder of specialty coffee importer Osito coffee, gave me an example in his business in which this turned out to be the case. Kyle also runs an exporting office in Colombia. Kyle and his business partner in Colombia have elected to go down the route of investing in their own dry mill. The outsourced dry milling solutions available to them are either quality driven but with poor commercials and services, or highly efficient and commercial but without sufficient focus on quality.

The value add is therefore not an absolute but, as with many things in this book, a consideration within the context of each individual business. The question each business is asking itself is, is it worth doing it ourselves? Will it add value? This may not be a short -term consideration. It could be that what may not be achievable or valuable to do now could be worth it in the longer term.

This question often cannot be objectively and analytically addressed. I get it, sometimes you want to do it all yourself either because you're a control freak, or because it's what your customers want to see. I have often seen these dynamics in play when businesses working in other parts of the industry start roasting coffee. From a purely economic point of view, in many circumstances, the move to roasting coffee for a coffee brand that previously outsourced, rarely makes business sense. But for the coffee brand, it looks and feels like a natural progression.

It is very easy to make assumptions about how much money will be saved by bringing the roasting process in-house for a business that currently buys their coffee from a third party roasting business. This could be a group of cafés that look to bring roasting in house or a company that currently gets their roasting white labelled by a roaster. In nearly all these cases, a roastery at a reasonable scale will be able to provide a product at a price that won't be easily matched on a smaller scale, in-house.

Of course, there may be some legitimate reasons that are not simply cost-oriented, such as achieving the specific product flexibility you are after. Roasting in-house will avoid MOQ's. And, as is the case in Kyle's importing company, a quality need.

In doing so though, many other challenges become yours. Green coffee risk and cash flow need to be considered. An underlying capitalist theory states that with increased risk, comes the potential for increased reward.

In boutique coffee, the decisions are not all analytical business questions, but rather a business's pursuit of something in coffee that they started out to be involved with or to do in a certain way. It is natural and not uncommon for a curious, experience-led founder to take on new parts of the supply chain one-by-one as their business grows.

A valid branding and company authenticity argument can also be made here as these additional facets of the business also add value for customers. Although I rarely find these "value adds" to be as simple as their marketing, there is no denying that the decision to manage the coffee supply chain as a company is influenced by perception, and not just the desire to work the appropriate supply chain and best product solution. A coffee shop is an important example of adding value.

The mark-up on the cup of coffee in a café is typically one of the highest mark-ups in the industry. This is because the value add is not simply the cup of coffee but the experience offered to the end user. This experience has value, though it can cost a lot to provide.

Asking yourself the question of what your value add is, in a complex supply chain like coffee, is key. Your answer may change over time as the business grows or the market changes. Vertical integration is visible everywhere throughout the world of coffee, popping-up as companies seek to manage their value adds. This said, it is also true that in multiple scenarios companies choosing to focus on quality and specificity have been shown to be just as successful, whilst collaborating with partners and suppliers.

To Grow or Not to Grow
This question can be asked at the largest scale, but also at the micro scale for each individual business. It is often argued that growth is crucial for the long term survival of a business. Many benefits can follow business growth such as attracting new talent, funding projects, efficiencies, being competitive in the market, and driving the bottom line. This last example can often actually be harder to achieve when top line growth is sought, as this takes precedence over profitability. In growth models such as these, profitability can hopefully come later.

Growth is a key indicator for investors and shareholders in businesses, but growth isn't sought by everyone starting or running boutique and specialty coffee businesses. For independent, boutique businesses there are points in their journey where they can decide if growth is a suitable and desirable plan or not.

An independent coffee business is usually started with some capital from friends and family or from a bank loan or an angel investor. With limited finance, there is a vision to make something relatively confined. The business has a period of growth in the regard that it starts as an idea and becomes real and then has a period of time building up trade and optimising what it is doing.

In the case of cafés and farms, physical location creates a ceiling for the possible growth unless the business looks for more space.

For many other businesses there is less of a natural ceiling. A roaster may have a small machine but they can put in longer hours or contingency roast if the demand is there and they are able to find ways to increase sales and demand for their products and services. An exporter and importer will be seeking to secure access to finance to move more coffee if the demand is there. The barriers to growth are different depending on the business and these are only a few examples.

In the specialty boutique space there are a number of operator types with different motivations for starting a business. On the one hand there are those looking to start an independent business of their own, and be their own boss, most often in the sphere of cafés and roasters. This could be a barista or production roaster deciding to head off and start their own venture. A personal journey is feeding their choices. They may be driven to fulfil their creative desire to build a new environment, or to roast and engage with coffee in their own way.

These businesses are not big growth concepts. If they find success they may morph and evolve over time, and at this point they may make the decision to invest in more equipment or to open more sites. They may also make the decision to take on investors and dilute their ownership in the pursuit to build something bigger, with a higher aspiration for growth. However, these businesses may also remain small and focused for their duration. In fact, all boutique business, from the farming level downstream to the customer, is typically not overly growth orientated, as boutique businesses approach products and experiences in more confined and curated ways. Some of these boutique businesses will grow their value proposition and morph away from being a boutique company. For boutique businesses to generate high value they need a high product price. Of course, a boutique company can grow to be a bigger boutique company, and this is a question of context.

The question of how much a quality-driven operation can grow is different throughout the supply chain. A major challenge for many farming operations outside of Brazil is retaining quality at scale with the need for a large seasonal labour force for harvesting.

Growing by investing the profits from a small or even medium-sized independent business with moderate to lean profit is inherently slow going. Seeking funding through debt hurts the business model, as that debt repayment becomes part of the operational cost. This is often why equity is a desirable way to seek funding. The challenge with equity is the dilution of the shareholders relative to the company's valuation, and the return for everyone involved over time. More on this later in the book.

The route to growth is rarely straightforward, and this is particularly true in the coffee space. Growing any business is challenging and it typically comes with increased risk.

Investment cycles are an interesting aspect of growing many businesses. The different phases begin with investment, followed by optimisation, followed by further investment and so on. Joshua Dick took his small family coffee cleaning product business and grew it into a large market-leading company before selling up. He later wrote the book "Grow like a Lobster." In the book he uses the lobster analogy to explain his phenomenal success.

A lobster is a soft vulnerable animal that uses its shell for protection, but the shell doesn't expand. As the lobster grows it must cast off its shell, leaving it exposed whilst growing a new larger shell. The analogy is clear - a business creates its landscape and grows into it, but when it has maxed out the potential of its current environment it can either choose not to grow any further or enter into a period of increased challenges and vulnerability as it moves into the next stage.

The exact route taken by each company will be different and the tipping points around each phase will impact decision making and strategy. Heavily-funded businesses may look to skip over multiple organic growth phases and achieve scale quickly. It is a valid, capital-intensive strategy applied in hospitality regularly, often referred to as a "roll out", but it is risky for a number of reasons.

Large existing food and drink businesses will also approach growth in this way. By front-loading the new launch or brand, they are able to put the business everywhere all at once, and aim to hit critical mass from the outset. Challenger brands will start small and hope to make a dent against these bigger players.

Specialty boutique coffee has very much been an industry of challenger brands.

As the success of the space grows this is changing, and a variety of established larger businesses are looking to explore the specialty aesthetic and product approach, which before now may not have been deemed a big enough opportunity. The term "5th Wave," coined by Allegra strategies, is a continuation of the idea of the three waves that are often cited in an attempt to chronicle coffee culture and business as it has developed over time. The 4th wave, they propose, was investment in the science of coffee, and the 5th wave represents the business of quality coffee when executed at scale. We explore this idea in more detail in the last part of the book.

Whilst this growth of the boutique and premium coffee space is visible around the globe, there are also businesses who actively stay small, aiming for a size that optimises their story. This could be a premium coffee farm, a boutique importer or a specialist roastery. In each case, you could find examples of founders shooting for a size and then pressing the pause button. There are many reasons to consider keeping a business at a certain size. This could be a choice to optimise the current framework of the business without taking the risk of further growth, or it can be about maintaining scarcity and value.

Many operators in specialty coffee discuss the ability to maintain quality whilst growing. Much like the lobster analogy in commercial growth, quality has frameworks that allow for optimisation at different scales. I truly believe that the achievement of quality in coffee is always primarily driven by a passion to pursue excellence in the business, but the optimal size for quality isn't necessarily very small and it can equally become very difficult at large sizes. There are many benefits that come with size and that can help to increase the ability to focus on quality, however this will only be the case if quality is a core principle of the business.

In many smaller scale and independent business cases, the desire to halt growth and maintain a relatively fixed size is due to work life balance for the founders or owners. Growing a business is typically time-consuming and can be stressful depending on whether you can find enjoyment in the challenge.

There is also the slightly dramatic saying, "if you stop you die". Most businesses will have a "churn" of customers, and if they continue to grow within their means then they reduce long term risk. Only a very strong business can stay small and successful over a long period of time, they must be hitting a value sweet spot.

Later in part six in *Growing a Business. Quick vs Slow Growth*, we look at some of the strategic approaches to growing businesses in the market. Regardless of the strategy taken by a business, growth is a key part of how a business is viewed, and its approach to the other levers in the running of the business will be informed by the degree of ambition that exists for growth.

Break-Even

The "break-even" is a fundamental business concept. You need to know where this point is in a business at all times.

Business economics often appears to be discussed in terms of percentages, making it challenging to discuss a business as a per-unit sum. For example, we often discuss a coffee price "per-cup" or a cost of production as a percentage of a lb or kg of coffee, green or roasted, but what this actually tells us is very limited.

The problem with this approach is that it doesn't consider any fixed costs and importantly at what point break-even is actually achieved. Selling one cup of coffee in a day won't allow you to break even for the day, even if the margins on that cup are all perfectly figured out. Any discussion about where the revenue from a cup of coffee is spent in a business is based on assumptions of quantities of coffee sold relative to the size and running cost of the coffee business.

Granted, in a coffee shop, the ingredient costs are directly related to each drink, and are largely the same (excluding the fact that a shop with higher volume will likely achieve better per kilo coffee prices). If you use 15g of ground coffee, that cost stays the same per cup no matter whether you make 5 or 300 drinks, however, other costs are better understood in relation to daily or weekly revenue.

The rent will stay the same regardless of the amount of coffee sold and money made (unless you have a percentage of turnover deal with the landlord). The staff costs are not overly flexible either.

Yes you can increase or decrease the team's hours in response to busier times, but clearly you can't tell someone to hang around and only clock on when it's busy, and to clock off and not get paid when it goes quiet for fifteen minutes. This isn't good for the staff member or the quality of service that the business can offer.

All of these fixed costs mean that each business will have a break-even. The break-even is almost always a more critical number than the theoretical net profit.

For example at the time of writing, Colonna & Small's, our café in Bath, is targeting a 15% net profit. I explain to the team that for a £3.80 flat white, 27% of the price we charge comprises the coffee and milk cost. Following this, the labour cost goal is 35% and the rent and rates should roughly account for 11%, and so on. This outlines how all of the costs "should" break down per coffee in this specific business.

I could alternatively simply tell the team that the break-even for the day is approximately £900 of takings. This second way of "framing" our underlying cost mechanics is much more powerful. It is a superior way of communicating the basic commercials of opening the shop each and every day.

This is a benefit of the coffee shop format. Day-to-day visibility means that as long as you have saved your VAT ready for the quarterly bill, you shouldn't get any big surprises, and should have a relatively good idea of how the business is faring at any moment in time. A shop's biggest challenge regarding profitability will likely be seasonal changes in trade, and managing staff costs against varying revenue over time.

This is not the case for many of the other businesses in the supply chain who are all playing longer games, which means that break-even is harder to stay on top of.

In all cases, the break-even will be a mixture of fixed product costs, and other costs of doing business. The most profitable position for the business will be to achieve sales that surpass the break-even costs, and to maximise sales to a point whereby the costs required to deliver new and increased sales don't simply jump up and eat the newly acquired revenue.

To expand on this point, at some point a business needs to increase its costs in order to actually deliver on the increased sales. This is a common challenge for small and start-up businesses.

Often started by founders and a small team, you quickly figure out how much coffee you need to shift to pay the rent (you might not pay yourself to start) and then get into a rhythm where things are going quite well and there is some profit. However, the small number of resources means that the business will soon hit a limit, and it will become necessary to take on new costs. For a coffee shop this often presents itself in the form of more labour to meet demand. This also increases the break-even, and likely reduces profitability until the growth sustainably supports the increased labour costs.

The same applies to equipment and infrastructure in one way or another. The new assets are not part of the daily expenditure like wages, but they need to be paid for somehow, and often need paying back via debt, which also increases the monthly break-even.

When a farmer invests in agricultural inputs, such as pruning, managing coffee trees and buying fertiliser, they add to their break-even cost in the same way, but in doing this they intend to achieve a higher yield and quality, which will make the investment worthwhile. The variability surrounding the exact price that the coffee will achieve when harvested is hard to define and difficult to predict, which means that their business forecast is very challenging to accurately predict on a yearly basis. The breadth of different coffee qualities harvested can impact the farm's success along with the ability to sell the coffee at a profitable price that surpasses break-even.

The focus of lean, net profit business often turns to reducing the break-even. The challenge is to achieve the lower break-even without impacting opportunity or the quality of existing business. For example, you can cut costs in a way that reduces product quality or impact service and experience, which would put the business at risk of losing its existing client base and damaging its reputation and long term potential. On the other hand, it is imperative for a business to question whether it is producing its products and services in an efficient way.

Most businesses will find themselves going through phases

where they risk their break-even point in the pursuit of growth.

Cost of Production

Break-even is effectively a measure of the cost of production. It is, however, still relevant to talk about these two terms side-by-side, as cost of production is a term often mentioned when talking about the challenge of growing a coffee business profitably.

The major challenge to talking meaningfully about cost of production is that it is a unique figure to every business. Whilst there will be some similarities, and perhaps some useful averages to consider, the cost of production can and does vary dramatically. Often this is to do with scale, but it also relates to complexity, location and a myriad of other factors. Access to finance is a key element that is often not fully considered in coffee farming. Countries that have supported or subsidised access to finance provide an inherent advantage (as long as another of the key variables is not prohibitive in that country) as the farming business can be financed without the gross profit being impacted by interest.

In coffee parlance, it is common to hear discussion of transparency. This happens mostly at the consuming end, roasters and coffee brands make a point of championing transparent supply chains. I will look more specifically at the nature of transparency later in the book, however, when asking someone what their goal is in regards to transparency, the conversation will usually lead to the need for a "fair price". And when you ask what a fair price is, the answer is normally that it is a price that at the very least covers the cost of production and makes a sustainable profit.

A business is not, of course, sustainable without this. Ironically, the roaster or the coffee buyer looking to pay the cost of production doesn't know what this price is at a farming level. The only entity that truly knows the cost of production is the one making the thing. Actually, I should rephrase that, the only entity in a position to understand the cost of production is the one producing it.

A theme in this book is that small, boutique businesses are often light on the ground when it comes to detailed analysis of business metrics, decisions and calculations are often run more on feel. By this

I mean that many businesses don't have an accurate understanding of their costs.

Let's say that you are in a position to accurately define your cost of production, does that mean that this is an appropriate cost? It is rarely adequate in my opinion to say "things just cost what they cost". As a roastery and café operator, I have to question the costs that the businesses incur (and that will be passed on to the customer).

A small micro roastery with a 1kg roaster, will have a very high cost of production. This is due to the time it takes them to roast an amount of coffee versus a roastery with more capacity. The average price per kg of coffee sold in the market may not apply to them, they may feel that it needs to be more for them to make it work.

Likewise, a shop could create an elaborate approach to preparation and serving that requires double the number of staff. Their cost of producing a cup of coffee suddenly becomes much higher than a typical café.

In each case, are the businesses justified in charging the higher price to match the increased cost of production? I would say that the café is more likely able to charge a price that is elevated and covers the increased cost of production if (and only if) there is a value added to the consumer experience. In an open market, you cannot simply argue that your product has more cost at your end, the customer needs to recognise and place value on the difference.

This is most easy to debate at a coffee growing level, in which a nano coffee experiment (on a single plant for example) can yield something unique with scarcity that creates the demand for a higher price - in this case the value can flow through. But, you can bet that if the coffee doesn't display traits in the cup to back up the story, a high price tag will be difficult to achieve. Contrarily, it's pretty unrealistic to argue that you need to roast on a 1kg roaster to get a superior result, so in this case value is not derived from the process. The cost of production is simply too high.

It is fair to say a specialty boutique roaster can and should charge a higher price for the act of roasting, as they are smaller and more specialised, however, a one kilo roaster pushes that logic too far. When I spoke with Colin Harmon, founder of 3FE coffee, he termed this kind of practice to be "financially irresponsible." In reality, the infrastructure of a one kilo roaster is not sufficient to run a specialty coffee roasting business. The cost of production is simply unreasonably high, relative to the market place and the other businesses that are part of it.

The general discourse surrounding the cost of production at a farming level has a large amount of complexity. You have regional variances within one country, such as office location. The bigger differences though come via an open global market, where entire economies produce products that compete with one another.

The good news is that there is differentiation. Not all coffee tastes the same, and this is magnified by origin. The coffee market does have differentials per country. These differentials are not a documented market number like the C Market. Instead, this is a number that people hold in their minds in a given country - these end up being discussed as part of all contracts and sales prices for different qualities of coffee at any one moment in time. Later in the book we will talk about market pricing and the questions around the economic sustainability of growing coffee.

Specialty boutique coffee is typified by increased costs of production at every level. This is a key thing to note. A higher price for boutique coffee reflects a higher cost of production, not simply a higher price for the same product. This being said, the ability to hit a cost of production is on everyone's mind in the specialty boutique sector throughout the chain.

Limits on the price that can be asked of consumers, also limits the possibility of making a very small or high-cost operation sustainable.

As you can see, one of the complexities of the coffee business is that no one element can be taken in isolation. Cost of production ties closely to size and sales volumes. In each business model, throughout the supply chain, there is a point at which things aren't viable if they get too small, this is particularly clear in coffee farming where even with a sales cost that easily pass the cost of production, the volume created is simply too small to be sustainably profitable. This can be seen as the shift between a hobby or side project and a complete business. Cost of production is one of the most important levers to understand in any given business for this reason.

It is also key not to just understand cost of production as a day-to-day number or a number in relation to a unit of goods sold, but also to understand the cash flow required to support ongoing cost of production.

Deliverable Margin

The concept of deliverable margin is key to really understanding how and where you spend, as well as unfortunately, where you lose money in your business.

Deliverable margin is of particular interest to any business that does multiple different things. Whether you make a number of products or offer a variety of services that all draw on shared resources, it can quickly become hard to understand which products or clients are contributing or detracting from your overall margin.

The concept of deliverable margin is essentially based around the idea of asking what your *real* margin is after you account for all of the resources and costs that are needed for that specific transaction to take place.

A friend of mine runs a premium Mediterranean ingredients business in West London. The business is well established and successful. When COVID-19 came along they saw what many established brands saw, an increase in online sales. This was novel for them, as previously they had primarily acted as a B2B (business to business) orientated business, selling olive oil and a variety of other products to restaurants and retailers.

Selling products directly to end consumers means that you are able to achieve the full RRP (excluding discounts) rather than giving away margin to offer a wholesale price. In the B2B scenario, the client either needs the margin to make the product viable to resell or to use as an ingredient to make another product, in which case the margin covers the cost of making meals and offering experiences.

With all of this in mind, they were somewhat surprised when the management accounts for the trading period hit their desks. They were making much higher margins on e-commerce, but making a loss. This new shift to online sales didn't seem to be providing any real bottom line profit.

As would be the case for most businesses built around an ingredient, the focus is naturally more oriented towards wholesale (see *The Ingredient Versus the Finished Drink*). The business did not therefore have much experience with e-commerce. Every product and sales channel has its associated costs. In this case the true cost of making, marketing, selling and fulfilling these items was surprisingly high. The e-commerce was a channel that existed previously in the business, but was so small that its true operational costs were hidden from view. In addition, during the growth period it wasn't only the sales that scaled up, but also the associated costs of selling in that way.

The margin may have been high, but the ticket price per transaction was considerably lower than a wholesale order. Each of the e-commerce orders required individual management and processing. They required someone to pick, pack and fulfil the order. The aftercare required and the website work to merchandise existing and new products week to week are all expensive relative to the ticket value attributed to the products.

In e-commerce shipping is a substantial factor. The shipping on a large wholesale order of high value will likely be a low percentage of the cost. However, on an individual customer order with a value of £15, a business will immediately be hurt if it chooses to suck up £3+ on shipping.

You may ask, "how is this any different to simply knowing your net profit?" A good question. If you had a singular product business that only sold via one channel, net profit would be the same as deliverable margin and vice versa. In most businesses however, the challenge comes in figuring out exactly where contributions and subtractions to the net margin are located across different sales and clients.

In essence, the only way to get to the bottom of this is to do a laborious and detailed sales assessment. This is a common requirement for businesses in the coffee sector, although maybe less so for an individual coffee shop. All of this having been said, the granular detail of all costs throughout a business are not the priority or focus for most boutique businesses, and this means they can catch you out.

At farm level this same effect can be produced by different coffee qualities and lot sizes. Whilst an exotic cultivar or an experimental micro-lot may well have the potential to sell for a higher price per lb of coffee, that does not mean that it is delivering good profit for the producer.

Every time I raise this dynamic with producers and exporters, they share the sentiment that just because something is a high value premium coffee, doesn't mean it's highly profitable. The work and resources that can go into producing these lots and managing their sale and transit can really start to add-up.

Taking an example from my own experience, the limited release, super-premium lots we launch from our roastery do not pay anyone's salary. Hopefully, they contribute in a few ways to the wider success of the business, but when all is said and done, when you fully isolate and analyse the sales, they appear to make a slight loss.

The limited releases require a lot of work. We make and commission unique artwork and communications. We profile the roasts as we would do for any other coffee, however the quantity is so limited and small that all of the front-loaded work with a team and infrastructure that is built to produce a bigger volume is hard to pay back (see the section on *The Sweet Spot* later in the book for a continuation of this theme).

There are valuable reasons to create and release products of this sort as part of your business and brand, even if they are not profitable. I expect this discussion would come as a surprise to the customer who paid £40 for 150g of coffee, just as it did to my friend at his olive oil company. In fact, the starkest point he made in discussing this realisation, was that his lowest gross margin products were ultimately more profitable. This is mostly due to scale. The lower margin product cannot hit profitability unless a certain volume of sales are achieved, and likewise, the higher margin product is less efficient, and its true cost and margin are often missed.

The lesson with deliverable margin is that you need to have the ability to understand contribution and resources relative to your sales. This is particularly relevant to a lean net profit industry, such as coffee. It can be helpful to apply perhaps could be more valuable to understand per customer.

Starting a Business in Coffee - Barrier to Entry
Essentially, the term "barrier to entry" just means, "how difficult is it to get going?" What are the things that will stand in your way when you start to bring a new business to life, or take an existing business into a new market, or introduce a new product line.

This concept is relevant in all business, but I think it is a particularly pertinent topic within coffee, as different parts of the industry show a very varied barrier.

A low barrier to entry will allow a lot of people to start easily and become a part of the industry. In coffee, the lowest barrier to entry you will find is likely a form of an online reselling business. This allows you to buy someone else's coffee product and resell it via an online platform.

In order to start a website reselling other roasters' coffee, you need to buy a small amount of inventory up-front, at wholesale prices. This allows you to offer the coffee online, through a simple website. Your customers pay you directly, and you pop down to the post office to ship their parcels once you have received the money. This is super easy and almost anyone could start this business tomorrow. It is just one step beyond selling your own second-hand furniture on Facebook Marketplace.

A coffee shop requires significantly more commitment. A rental deal and fit out cost of some kind (hugely variable) along with all the requisite equipment, and potentially staff, etc. However, the barrier to entry here is still reasonably surmountable. Of course, a flashy £500k fit out is not a low barrier, but a scrappy approach to design, combined with some inventive resource and help, and you can get a shop going quite easily. You could argue that this is all part of the early independent third wave coffee shop aesthetic - low budget but authentic fit outs. This is not as prevalent these days for a number of reasons.

For most other coffee businesses, the barrier to entry is higher. In theory, growing some coffee plants on a small parcel of land and selling the cherry to a local mill, is a relatively low barrier to entry depending on access to land in the specific country. Arabica seeds are not overly expensive but will need time to grow and produce fruit. Low barriers to entry in most markets yield lower value. To pursue a higher profit return in farming access to more land is needed which will be a barrier to entry/growth.

Whilst at the start of this section I stated, in the most basic sense, that the barrier to entry references just the hurdles to getting any business started, I think it's perhaps more valuable to include the impediments to having a fully-functioning, sustainable business in the space.

It was a surprise to me to learn that Robusta has a higher set up cost than Arabica. This is because the crop setup for Robusta makes use of clones instead of seeds. The other big barrier to entry in all agriculture is sophisticated equipment. There are many examples in Brazil that show how clever systems can be used to not only pick coffee, but perhaps more impressively, to sort coffee cherries once picked, and then to continue this process all the way through wet and dry milling, to the finished bagged product. The cost of advanced farming equipment is extremely high, and without a big enough farming operation it wouldn't be justifiable.

In coffee roasting, in its most simplified form, the barrier to entry may be lower than cafés. You can rent a unit without footfall, and expect a reduced rent in return. The operation can be run by a single person, typically an owner/operator in the early days. Fit out can be very basic. However, this lack of footfall presents its own challenges. It can be hard to pick up meaningful customer numbers. The equipment isn't cheap, but there are more and more small entry-level roasting machines that are the same price, or cheaper, than a premium espresso machine. This setup won't get you very far - with success you will max out your capacity very quickly. However, with some growing momentum it will become easier to both justify and borrow the money required to move to the next scale.

Your initial setup also needs to compete with other players. Roasting is less location driven, which creates a competitive disadvantage. When a product can be bought from many different locations and shipped with couriers, you have a lot more immediate competition. A roastery with a shop will benefit from their physical engagement with customers, and shops only have to compete with other similar businesses that are local to them. Roasters and pretty much all other businesses in coffee compete on a larger market scale, against increased competition.

Typically, growing coffee has a high financial barrier to starting. Unless you are buying existing land that is planted with coffee shrubs, there will be 4 or more years between planting and having a harvest that you can sell. The break-even on this business model is longer. However, commercial coffee is what can be called a liquid market, with a low barrier to entry. When the market has demand, you can find a buyer for cherry or parchment coffee easily. The commercial market (and the big players within it) need access to coffee. In order to keep the potential for supply as open and de-risked as possible. They make sure it is easy for coffee to be bought and sold. In specialty boutique coffee it is not as easy to access the market which is a barrier to finding success in this segment.

I think it would be fair to say that at the finished product end of the market, this dynamic is flipped. It is easier for a small, boutique coffee brand to start selling a serviceable amount of coffee through the specialty coffee community than it is to enter into meaningful competition with big, commercial coffee brands.

There is a large value add at the wet milling stage of coffee processing. This leaves open the possibility of starting a wet mill in order to buy, process and sell-on other peoples' cherries. This might be a way to support the planting and scaling of a larger farm, just as a hotel or restaurant can support a vineyard in its early years, or distillers gin bottling can produce revenue, whilst their whisky is maturing.

The barriers to exporting and importing green coffee are significant. Access to finance is the biggest challenge, as this is what drives these businesses. It isn't access to capital, but rather access to competitively priced finance. Whilst a young business may be able to export some small volumes, with momentum the access to finance becomes more critical. There is a knowledge and experience element required to practise effectively in this part of the supply chain, which is its own barrier.

In the ways I have explained in this section, barrier to entry is actually a far more complex assessment than it may first appear. Ultimately, to really understand how easy it is to both enter and succeed in a business sector it will require an understanding not just of capital and cash flow requirements, but of many of the defining characteristics of that part of the industry.

Risk

All business has risk. Things can and do go wrong, sometimes in ways that could easily have been avoided. Most risks (as the term is used in business) are things outside of the company's control.

The likelihood of exposure to risk, combined with the severity of the risk, is usually termed a "risk profile." This varies significantly depending on the business. You can, for example, have two companies operating in the same area of an industry, but with highly different risk profiles due to a number of variables such as: the client base, size, profitability, and access to finance of each business.

One of the challenges in writing this book, and even in trying to learn about coffee as an industry, is how soon into the process you will be presented with a statement along the following lines: "I couldn't possibly say, this subject is too variable, and there isn't a singular answer." Whilst I appreciate that in the relatively young, specialty boutique coffee industry, there is not always enough context to support a given answer, this response is often driven by the desire for easy solutions and quick fixes, leading to things being overly simplified to the point of being mistruth.

Even considering all of the above, one can start to address some of these more challenging questions by creating a variety of profiles that are representative of what is commonly seen within the coffee industry. The goal of this exercise would be to make reasonable statements about how things work.

The farming of coffee undoubtedly incurs some of the highest risk profiling in coffee. The primary factor here is the variability, unpredictability and nature of, well, nature. Coffee is very much an agricultural product. It is the seed of a fruit and the challenges end up being similar to those of all agricultural farming. Annual production will vary due to many factors. There is an element of this that can be predicted and planned for, but there are also natural events and occurrences that can be catastrophic to coffee production such as: frost, long periods of heavy rainfall and coffee leaf rust outbreaks. Much like the searches done before the purchase of a new house, each specific plot of land will have different levels and types of associated risk. These could be significant, such as flooding or landslides.

Risk in business is as much driven by the competitive landscape and how sticky customers are. *The C Market*, which is a commodities market for coffee (see The C Market chapter later in the book) is a global example of a competitive landscape whereby each grower is at risk of a volatile price variation because the market is so large. Variation in supply around the world creates a price risk for coffee farmers. Other coffee businesses in the chain are more shielded from the volatility, though the risk affects them also. With fluctuating prices comes the risk of losing customers to competitors who can hit a better price, or who offer a differentiated product and service.

A lot of new, small business owners are themselves a big risk. If they get unwell or anything untoward happens to them, their business is likely to fall apart, as they are yet to reach a structural point where they can step away from the business.

There is not a business that has no risk, and many ambitious business models have a decent "risk appetite". Even so, the risk profile in a business and industry should feed into a medium and long term strategy. Risk is also something that changes as a business changes, grows and evolves. One of the biggest challenges in considering and implementing change in a business is that it typically creates risk. Keeping things the same is a way to avoid embarking on that risk filled journey, though there are inherent risks in remaining stationary in a changing business landscape.

It quickly becomes evident that good risk judgement is vital within a business of any kind, and the same is true in coffee.

The Impact of Scale

Scale can be a matter of perspective, especially in boutique independent business. What can appear to be large in one context will be viewed as miniscule within another frame of reference. It would be fair to say that, on the whole, specialty boutique business operates on a smaller scale, typified by independent businesses and the opportunity for human connection. At a larger scale you can't really call something boutique anymore.

One inference of the term scale is magnitude. This is what is meant when a person says, "that works at scale." But, scale as a concept simply relates to the size or extent of a thing - minuscule to enormous.

A simple example would be the roasting drum size in a boutique roastery. Much like the example I chose in the *Cost of Production* chapter, all else being equal, a boutique roaster who utilises a 5kg roaster compared to one who utilises a 25kg roaster has a dramatically different roasting scale.

A 25kg roaster is not huge by industry standards, but it's a damn site bigger than 5kg. This dramatically affects the cost of production per kg of roasted coffee in two ways. Firstly, the labour to run the roaster is time-based. If you can achieve five times the yield in the same timeframe, this produces a huge difference in labour cost per unit. Secondly, there is the total quantity that can be produced.

There are only so many hours in a day. Even if you roast from sunup to sun down on a 5kg roaster, you can't match an output easily obtained via the 25kg machine. Of course, the 25kg likely needs a larger space, but where volume is required, there's no match. There are plenty of other aspects that might contribute to the cost of production for a roastery, but the roaster size is an easy factor to comprehend.

There is a widely held assumption that very large commercial companies can hit economies of scale that allow them to obtain lower production costs. This is true. There are a number of competitive advantages that can only be achieved at scale.

It must also be respectedthat the scale brings potential complexity, risk and inefficiencies. There are often constraints that make larger scale less desirable.

Smaller, boutique scale business itself has an internal gradient. This means that within specialty boutique coffee there is a wide variety of production costs, based on all of the different variables that feed into the cost of producing a kg of roasted coffee. This could be staff pay, or the variety, size and frequency of your product releases. It costs a lot more to profile, package and launch different coffees every month than it does to stick to a consistent, core range. This cost isn't just incurred in the preparation of the coffee, there are many steps including: sourcing, product development, copywriting and merchandising.

The margin and pricing for the roastery's part in the journey is often quite commoditised. Specialty coffee typically has a higher price per gram of coffee, whether green, roasted or brewed. However, the typical value put on boutique roasting is quite consistent regarding the pricing and margin applied by a specialty roaster to a bag of coffee. The roasteries in this space who have achieved a bigger scale, have the ability to hit a better per unit efficiency in their production, or at least they should be able to.

As a business grows in size and complexity it also has additional costs. New processes, departments and systems have to be put in place. This can and often will add cost. The growing amount of product sold requires the support of a larger business entity. This is Josh Dick's Lobster analogy at work.

This means that even though scale has benefits, it presents a significant number of hurdles, such as decisions to hire more staff or implement new equipment. Smaller and lower net profit businesses will be challenged to find the available cash to reinvest in growing the business. The smaller the business, the harder it is to access finance. I mean this in the terms of debt rather than equity, which we will cover later in the book. If boutique businesses are unable to access finance, then the growth and reinvestment is limited to purely what is available within the business's own means.

In coffee farming, a fixed plot of land presents a different perspective on scale. In this case scale has more to do with maximising the yield and quality within the limitations of the farm, unless the operator can buy or utilise more land. A fascinating dilemma around optimal scale can occur in coffee farming. When I spoke with Alejandro Cadena R. of Caravela, he speculated that in Colombia an ideal farm size is around 30 hectares. As growing coffee on a very small scale doesn't make sense financially, it is natural to ask "why wouldn't you just want a larger farm?" Alejandro explained that the limiting factor becomes the labour required to pick the coffee. In most countries Arabica is still hand harvested, and the bigger the farm, the bigger the challenge of finding and managing seasonal labour during harvest. The bigger the labour force, the harder it is to maintain quality.

I noticed this pattern, when getting paid to prune vines in New Zealand. Although there is the capacity to increase volume, there is the possibility that quality will suffer, reducing the value of the crop. The highly impressive post-picking technologies seen in Brazil may help to solve this quality issue in time. However, the equipment is extremely expensive and the investment is hard to justify unless you have an enormous farm. In this instance the "benefits" of scale are clearly not simple.

Brand awareness is sometimes overlooked in conversations around scale. With a certain scale comes a tipping point, providing a company the benefit of wider brand exposure. Growing confidence in the brand, simply by virtue of its success, can feel like a snowball rolling downhill.

Boutique brands also walk the tightrope of boutique perception, which can be key to their success. You see this in fields other than coffee, the perception of what the brand will change if it increases in scale, especially if its original image represented something rebellious and small. The customer cohort who remark loudly about this, however, may not be the core customer the brand is actually looking for.

The very concept of scale and growth in specialty coffee is a conflicted one. Whilst there is much talk of accessibility, it often seems that if a brand manages to access more customers (via scale) it is not viewed positively.

Of course, in terms of scale, specialty will ultimately be limited. It is the boutique, pointy end of the market. There are therefore limits to the possible scale of the space. At some point boutique is no longer boutique. Where that point is for each company is a blurry line, and a matter of perspective.

However, the "specialty aesthetic," which we discuss later in the book, has the potential and the likelihood to scale much further than the market for high scoring coffee itself. This idea of market potential also clearly influences the ability for multiple businesses in the space to all scale and keep growing. If, for example, companies find themselves exploring lower grades of coffee and lower prices to keep their growth and scale increasing, this presents an interesting question around whether they are scaling specialty, or rather diversifying into high commercial grade coffee to maintain their growth.

Access to Finance - An Industry Built on Borrowed Money

The coffee industry is reliant on the ability to access finance and debt. Agricultural crops all showcase the same delayed revenue model, which begins with a farmer investing in the potential of future crops. This isn't just an upfront investment to start the business, but a yearly one, in terms of resource and monetary investment for each upcoming harvest.

Mills and exporters each finance and invest in coffee for a period of time between harvest and sale, before passing this along to the next buyer in the cycle. Importers do the same, they shoulder a long lending period by offering financing and terms on the coffee over an agreed drawdown period. During this period the client, typically a roaster or coffee brand, will work though the allocated coffee bit by bit over several months, only triggering the requirement for payment when the coffee is released from the warehouse.

All the way through this supply chain there is a reliance on the ability to access finance to support cash flow.

A coffee roaster needs to commit to at least some coffee, whether this is traded directly or not. The coffee needs to make its way from a port in the origin country (unless it's consumed internally of course) and spend months at sea. As the roaster is unlikely to use the whole quantity of coffee in one go, the coffee then makes its way into storage. Typically, a roaster secures enough coffee from the harvest to last them a minimum of six months, and likely closer to a full year.

There are few businesses that could moderate their gross and lean net margins whilst buying an ingredient up-front that will take the whole year to sell. This is why coffee roasting businesses rely on green coffee businesses to finance coffee for them.

I was having lunch in London with David Papparelli from M-cultivo, a company who specialise in providing access to funding for business at origin, for farmers and exporters.

After discussing the fact that nearly all roasters, even very large ones, utilise the access to the finance that green coffee companies offer, he acknowledged that the whole emergence of any given coffee industry, and what it can achieve in a country, will be down to the strength (or weakness) of that coffee community's access to finance. This is particularly true in the case of boutique and specialty coffee, as the players are smaller and the likelihood of having access to significant finance at workable rates will be slim. That access is achieved through green coffee companies.

Whether it is at a trading and importing level, or an exporting level in the country of origin, any business that manages and moves coffee as a raw ingredient from the farm or dry mill might find themselves reflecting, "I think we are becoming a bank." And it's true, essentially anyone who sits between depositors and borrowers is behaving as a bank.

Access to finance is required for the growing of coffee to support the time frames every year between harvests. There are a variety of inputs and costs that occur every year before the harvest is complete and the coffee sold. These can vary throughout the year (and between years), from fertilisers and agronomy costs to the sharp increase in labour costs around the time of harvest. These business activities need funding. The most common form of funding is the same throughout the coffee chain - debt with interest.

Large green traders typically set up offices in Switzerland. Andrew Bowman of Gemstock, a Macro fund based in Switzerland, pointed out to me that people often think that Switzerland is simply a good place to do business for tax reasons (which it is), but there is more to it. The Swiss economy is stable and strong. The stability and success of the Swiss economy results in a strong currency and a low inflation economy relative to other countries at almost any moment in time. This means that access to capital in Switzerland is very competitive, creating a clear advantage. As green coffee trading is driven by finance and a very low net margin, it makes sense that most of the world's green coffee touches Switzerland in some way.

This is quite a contrast to the subtropical economies where coffee is typically grown. Each country has a varying risk profile in which to do business. The profile is connected to the typical cost of and access to finance in that place. Switzerland has a low risk profile. Global money isn't moving through the higher-risk economies at the same rate it moves through the lower-risk ones. The higher the risk profile, the tougher the access to capital and the higher the cost of finance.

I spoke with Jonny of Agri Evolve in Uganda, who expressed to me that while a lot of education has been done to positively impact coffee farming in East-Africa that the real barrier remains to be access to finance.

There are many cases in which back-to-back financing of commercial coffee can be used to fund specialty coffee exporting. David Pappareli explained to me the story of a Guatemalan coffee producer and exporter that he works closely with. The producer was planning to export 15 containers of high-quality coffee - expensive coffees.

He has access to the market and a captive audience for the coffee, but still struggles to finance the export. His workaround solution is to agree a contract for 75 containers of commercial coffee with Cafcom (a large-scale exporter). The finance for the 75 containers that are yet to be delivered is used to fund the export of the 15 containers of boutique coffee. Once this coffee is shipped, he can then arrange the commercial coffee, and deliver to Cafcom, and the back-to-back financing circle comes to an end, until next time.

There are many examples of industrious and entrepreneurial approaches to managing such ongoing financial challenges. The primary focus of many coffee businesses from week-to-week is managing finance and debt.

Finding alternative sources of finance is a huge challenge for boutique, green coffee importers. In many cases, the boutique importers are financed by large green coffee trading houses. They are happy to lend against coffee, which, as we have discussed, is what they do.

Roasters and cafés benefit dramatically from the financing that has occurred further up the coffee chain. These businesses don't have anywhere near the same concerns about financing. The finance journey of coffee in a café is short, ending when the coffee is ground, brewed and served to a customer who exchanges cash for the drink. Although, to add a slight degree of complexity, the journey only truly ends once the café and the roastery pay their outstanding balances on the coffee.

There are companies addressing the supply chain without the need to access finance. For example, stable, profitable roasteries that have saved up their net profit for multiple years will be able to pay for more and more of their coffee at the point of export.

There are examples of importers (such as Cafe Imports) who pre-finance the producing partners they work with. In Cafe Imports case, the finance isn't sought via Switzerland, instead they bank financing against the company's own cash reserve. When the coffee market goes up this can present a challenge as they are required to borrow more money, as they have the same cash position as when the prices of coffee are lower.

In this chapter I have described the financing needs as they apply to the growing and movement of green coffee. There are, of course, multiple other business activities across the industry that require financing. Access to financing at any moment in time will have a significant impact on the way a company or trader will choose to do business.

Ownership, Investment and Valuation

Behind every business is some form of ownership structure. It could be a family business that's passed down through generations or a sole operator slinging shots as a freelancer. Many boutique businesses also happen to be collaborations or partnerships of some kind. The owners could be a couple, or they could be two business partners who bring different approaches and skills to the table.

An equally common dynamic is one not only of partnership but of investment. Some individuals will bring creativity to the table, or operational experience and expertise, whilst others will either bring the money or the money and a financial background. Of course, this is not an exhaustive list of founder or ownership models.

The distribution of ownership has a big impact on the way a company is run and how it unfolds over time. It is not only the vision and direction that needs to be thought about, but also how ownership can drive strategy and company behaviour, as key stakeholders seek to realise the value in their ownership.

Ownership typically is divided up at key points in a company's journey. A company's inception means establishing an ownership structure. If it is just one person establishing the business and funding it themselves or through loans then it is quite straight forward. They own it 100% and they may start as a sole trader or set up as a limited company depending on various factors.

If there is more than one founder, there will be a distribution of ownership that is agreed amongst these founders. There is no blueprint here, but rather a negotiation to a point where all the stakeholders feel the distribution of ownership is fair and reflective of what each party is bringing to the table. If this can't be agreed the burgeoning business falls flat before it even starts, and the stakeholders each move on to other things.

As time passes and the business moves forward a number of scenarios can occur that result in an evolving and changing structure of ownership. Commonly these changes occur around funding needs. If the business needs more funding it creates a review of the ownership distribution. It could be that a new individual or business entity buys into the business, receiving equity in return for their investment. It may also be that an existing stakeholder increases the percentage of the business they own by putting in more money, with the other shareholders being diluted down in the process. Alternatively, owners can buy other owners out. In this case the business doesn't see any of the money as funding. The money simply buys a stake in the business from someone who is already in it.

One of the major challenges of ownership is releasing that value. An obvious way for small boutique ownership to play out is in the form of dividends. Simply put, the owners can share the profit in a ratio that matches their ownership stake. This only applies if there's profit to go around. In many cases though even if there is profit, a certain amount needs to be kept in the business for cash flow and also as contingency.

If the business is growing, the money needs to support growing cash flow needs, as well as potential capital expenditure such as new equipment. If the owners are working in the business and taking a salary that is sustainable for them then the question of ownership value can be explored over a longer period of time. Likewise, if an investor has the cash and the inclination to play a long game they can go many years without seeing any return on their investment.

It can also be common for key team members to be incentivised with shares that vest or an options agreement. Although this may feel like a good impetus on the surface, if there is no way for the team member to realise the value easily, it isn't always a great deal for them. Options that are lost when they leave also seem like a raw deal. For me, bonus structures and shared success work as a stronger incentive in most cases. These do rely on the business being profitable enough to offer these options.

A "liquidity" event or an "exit" are references to an event that allows existing shareholders to release some of the value tied up in their shares. Effectively it means that there is a new round of investment and there is the option for some of the existing investors to be bought out. In the case of a full sale, the whole company is bought and all the shareholders will receive their share of the sale value. Alternatively a company of reasonable size could "list" on one of the stock markets, creating the opportunity for the shareholders to cash out their equity if they wish. For specialty businesses that are more ambitious, these different scenarios are vital in determining their investment strategy and their ability to raise money and fund their growth plan.

Ultimately a business is worth what someone is willing to pay for it. However instead of plucking a number out of thin air, there are also benchmarks of what one would expect to be a realistic valuation for a certain business. Each business is unique but the previous valuation and sale of other businesses in a market can provide precedent. The saying goes, revenue is vanity and profit is sanity. This holds true in the long run, but in the short run businesses are able to achieve high valuations or sell stakes at high valuations if they show great potential or growth even without profits. There could be a number of reasons that you can push for a higher valuation for your business. There could be a portfolio battle between companies where your company is in a space that other companies are keen to expand their interest in, or it could be that you are selling a business in a strategic location(/s) that has value to another brand.

It is much easier to argue a high valuation for an idea at its inception than it is for a real business that is up and running. A new idea for a company or a new direction for a business represents a purely speculative conversation. Sales projections will be theoretical. However when you have a business that's real and alive, it has real sales and real costs and real profit.

With all of this in mind, what are the typical valuations for companies in specialty coffee? Assuming the business is not carrying a lot of debt, which would lower the valuation, as it would need to be accounted for, each of the typical industries in coffee have some benchmarks at the time of writing. These benchmarks are based on SME businesses in the space, and not large highly successful brands.

Cafés and coffee shops - Hospitality: an achievable result for an independent operator would be **4 x EBITDA** (see net profit) and **6 x EBITDA** for a multi-site/chain operator. If the business was able to hit 15% EBITDA (net profit) then this would be **0.6 and 0.9 x revenue**.

Roasteries - Food manufacturing/brand: coffee roasteries are essentially food manufacturing brands. An achievable result in the specialty roasting sector would be **6 x EBITDA** and with a strong brand and market position **8 x EBITDA**. With a 10% net profit this would be **0.6 and 0.8 x revenue** respectively.

Green exporting and importing - Financial and logistics: green companies are primarily in the business of moving raw materials. This means the valuations likely sit in the logistics sphere. Yes, a key aspect of what they do is financing, but they are mostly leveraging this from another banking source. It is hard to find good multiple valuations in the space but I think we could say **4 x EBITDA** would be likely, which at a lean net profit is a pretty low valuation relative to revenue at **0.2 x revenue**.

Coffee Farming - Agriculture: farming and agriculture is different in that most commonly the valuation conversation is twofold. It is not only about the business being run on the land but the market value for the land itself. In many cases the farming operation could be valued on a **4 - 6 x EBITDA** multiple, which at a 25% net profit would be **1 to 1.5 x Revenue**. However, in many cases the land is also owned by the farm business. If the land is large or has specific strategic value within the industry or for other use then the valuation could be much higher, say **3 x the revenue** of the farming business operating on the land. Agritourism as part of farming will also change these industry numbers.

Business Category	EBITDA Multiple	Revenue Multiple
Cafés and coffee shops 15% EBITDA	4 - 6 x EBITDA	0.6 - 0.9 x Revenue
Roasteries - Food manufacturing/brand 10% EBITDA	6 - 8 x EBITDA	0.6 - 0.8 x Revenue
Green exporting and importing - Financial and logistics 5% EBITDA	4 x EBITDA	0.2 x Revenue
Coffee Farming - Agriculture 25% EBITDA	4 - 6 x EBITDA excluding additional land value	1 - 1.5 x Revenue excluding additional land value

Typically valuations are higher either at the beginning of a business's life or once it has achieved high growth and sales. If you look at publicly traded coffee brands, the multiples are much higher, but this is because they have achieved huge market success. There are some very high profile boutique coffee brands that have far surpassed these multiples, however they appear to be unicorns (see: *Unicorns aren't the Norm*).

Due to the growth and interest seen recently in the specialty coffee space, there are many valuations in the industry that are closer to the big tech valuations than more equivalent food, manufacturing and hospitality industries. However, even if these businesses were able to raise money at these valuations on crowd platforms, or from individuals and through venture capital networks, the ability to mature a business and exit at these valuations has so far been rare.

The goal, I think, for most businesses would be to work towards these valuations as a proxy for what good looks like, and if a business is able to hit a high EBITDA, or create a unique brand value, it will be able to surpass the numbers.

This whole mindset is based around a grow and sell mentality. Another long established approach to business would be to build something over time that is profitable and sustainable and not loss making, and to take dividends. The greater success in this strategy comes from achieving some form of profitable scale, and provides the opportunity to the owner to have a lifelong business, or something to pass onto their children.

As we have also explored previously, for many passionate operators who are looking to have a business in an industry they enjoy, the goal is simply to have a sustainable business that allows them and their team to strive day to day to build and nurture something they find valuable and rewarding. In this instance valuation is not a key focus.

Compliance

Compliance and regulation is a typical part of any business, particularly in the food sector. Requirements in this regard are very much as you would expect, incorporating basic health and safety working standards, and food safety guideline adherence. These are most often either enforced by local authorities or encouraged through liability and the resulting insurance requirements.

Generally, the enforcement of compliance by authorities is more significant for larger companies, however, a basic level of compliance is important and valuable to all businesses. As the business grows the requirement becomes more significant. This is due both to the growing need to provide structure in order to maintain the business's standards, and to an increased client requirement for said compliance.

Later in the book we look at certification programmes and audits, whereby businesses in the supply chain are looking to comply with a set of standards laid out by a membership body.

Compliance is not always something implemented by a third party body, government or private. A common compliance concept is also built into commercial relationships in the supply chain. A buyer may require several criteria to be achieved as part of the supply agreement. This could be to do with quality and foreign bodies present in the coffee, or various proofs of process that have been agreed between parties.

One could argue that all internal processes are a form of compliance. Effectively, the ideas of quality, professionalism and service; ethics that structure a coffee business; are a form of adherence and compliance to a set of rules. Complex processes and onerous compliance isn't everyone's bag, and undoubtedly it can be taken too far, thereby reducing creativity and flexibility within a business and hindering positive results. Specialty coffee is typified by a passionate, creative environment that doesn't feel as stuffy or commercial as a large corporate structure might. Meeting the minimum required food safety and food labelling standards is of course, a necessity, but the exact level of compliance required beyond can be surprisingly variable.

All of this can mean that the idea of compliance as a cultural aspect of doing business in specialty coffee is not particularly significant. Roasters in particular can seem very relaxed environments that feel more like a social hangout than a production space. I can see the benefits of a relaxed creative culture, but have also witnessed the drawbacks produced by a lack of rigour and compliance.

There came a point at Colonna roastery when we wanted to achieve certain compliance certifications. This meant cultural change, changed behaviour, and perhaps what was most interesting to me, was the way this process highlighted a lack of compliance thinking within the business. For example, how do you prove that the coffee in the bag is what you claim? The person who packs the coffee might say, "because I put that coffee in that bag", which is a fair point, but how do you prove that? How can you take this thought process further, and provide a full traceability report for a bag of coffee that shows checks and measures built around proof, not anecdote.

Thinking this way has to become a habit, and it requires different stakeholders to audit one another within a business. I think that there are multiple benefits to building a compliance minded culture in a business, so long as this is all proportionate and reasonable with relation to the product and the company's value proposition.

There is a general lack of "compliance thinking" in specialty boutique coffee. The absence of a necessity to prove things shows up throughout the coffee industry, especially in relation to claims made about the coffee product and its supply chain. I think it would do many coffee companies, and the industry as a whole, good to ask more probing questions of how you can prove you are doing what you say, and to what standard it is being done.

Customer Acquisition

What is the real cost of winning a new customer? This particular question and wording is very much associated with e-commerce, but is a basic concept at play in nearly all businesses. The true cost of acquisition is difficult to fully single out with a specific sum or calculation. Anything that your brand has done from inception, or needs to continue to do to keep winning new customers, can be deemed as a cost of acquisition.

The rent on a coffee shop or retail space for example. On the one hand, it is a fixed cost that allows you to trade, but on the other, the amount of rent you pay is usually relative to the commercial value of the property, which correlates to more prominent locations with higher footfall. This means that your rent is a customer acquisition cost, at least to an extent. You can equally choose a less "valuable" location and put more money or time into marketing the business, to attract customers to you. In this way rent is a marketing cost as well.

The most obvious cost of acquisition can be broadly summarised as any kind of advertising spend. This can be an online ad or a physical stand at a trade or customer event. The challenge in all cases is gauging the actual return on these spends.

You can see why the internet draws more and more advertising spend as the effect can be tracked and the sales attributed (to some extent). The ability to track online clicks and utilise cookies to follow customers' online browsing means you can better judge the success of marketing campaigns and target cohorts of customers who are more likely to want to buy what you have to sell. It is not an exact science however, and lots of attribution will be claimed by each platform, not always in correlation to the sales that they have converted for you. For example, if a customer who already buys from you is targeted on Facebook with one of your ads, and they subsequently stop by your website to purchase some coffee, Facebook may claim that they are responsible for your sale, but this is not true.

The issues with attribution online, means that the only way to ascertain if an advertising strategy has worked, is to spend sufficient money on advertising that it cannot simply be "converting" existing customers. You will often hear e-commerce ad specialists state that you cannot really test whether an ad spend approach works without both scaling it, and taking time to let it play out. Clearly, this is costly. There is a notion that online ad spend is a golden bullet and that if it isn't working, the company or the agency simply haven't cracked the special code, but I don't think that this is true. A brand's proposition and connection with customers has more complexity than this philosophy allows.

More importantly, and as we will cover later in some depth, I think that coffee, and in particular specialty boutique coffee, has a classic word of mouth branding space. From a customer acquisition point of view this can make things challenging and unclear, but this can also be seen as a positive. It is a more traditional business proposition in the sense that you have to build a brand organically, assembling a tribe of customers, and creating a reputation for your business and what it does.

Building an authentic brand often costs more, and in an expertise or specialist part of a field, it's harder to fake it, although not impossible. Authenticity in this sense refers less to the product and more to the intention and ethos of the business' founders and the eventual aspiration that the business holds. The experimentation that is part of what defines specialty coffee is costly in time and resource. If these activities are what attracts customers to you, you can argue that they are an essential part of the acquisition cost. Research and development also fall into this category. Anything a business engages in, in order to build a customer base, is a cost of acquisition.

This can be tangled up in the need for a business to spend and develop to keep its existing customer base. As well as acting to engage customers with new products, discounts for long term customers (or indeed a discount to win a new customer) is a direct cost that can have some benefit. These costs need to be considered strategically, but also recognised simply for what they are. With a new marketing initiative, the budget is not isolated, rather an added cost to be factored against the business' base cost-benefit analysis of acquiring new customers through marketing.

One of the things I love about specialty boutique coffee is how businesses throughout the supply chain grow and succeed with more authentic, word of mouth, brand-spreading, which often is achieved without exorbitant budgets. This is a defining strength of this space.

Lifetime Value and Loyalty - Customer Range
This is another common e-commerce term, mostly used when trying to understand a "subscriber business." It may be the case that a business spends so much money on advertising and free giveaways, that in order to win new customers, the first transaction between business and customer is not profitable.

Some following orders may also not be profitable, but at some point the money spent on winning the customer needs to be paid back, and that particular customer needs to become profitable for the business. In many online subscription businesses, this notion is linked closely to a predicted time frame at which point the customer will be more likely to stop using the subscription. This can be referred to as "churn." This is a key metric, especially for a business of this type. At its core, this is an analysis of the relationship between the customer and the business, with the goal of obtaining a wider perspective on the relationship.

A simple way of understanding lifetime value is to see it as the average value of your average customer whilst they are shopping with you. Of course, a business will hopefully have customers who will be with them for many years, but nonetheless, some will leave after one order. As a business ages it is interesting to see how this dynamic shifts, you would hope that the average customer duration will increase. For e-commerce businesses these metrics are key to the strategy. If their acquisition cost is high and the lifetime value isn't high enough, or the churn isn't low enough, the whole marketing strategy will be considered unsustainable.

I may have phrased these specific KPIs (key performance indicators) in modern e-commerce language, but they are reflective of age-old business concepts, and they play out in coffee businesses in a variety of ways.

In a coffee shop a classic loyalty scheme is a reversal of the typical e-commerce approach. Instead of an upfront discount or freebie, the incentive is later in the customer journey, for example, after they have ordered 10 drinks.

I have never really understood these loyalty schemes in the context of specialty boutique coffee. I don't think that a 10-drink discount is why customers typically choose these establishments, and when every shop has a version of the same, there is no real point of difference being offered. It has become a sort of business hygiene factor, by which I mean to say, it is now a basic part of the coffee shop model rather than a customer reward. There are other ways to reward your loyal customers, and in reality I feel that coffee shops who are delivering consistently great coffee and service build their own loyalty, and that consistency of quality and experience is a more valuable attribute.

The coffee subscription model implemented by Pret A Manger is perhaps more interesting. Pret charges a set fee per month for unlimited coffee. Their strategy is to win the grab-and-go food customer. The same reasoning has led to the very low price of McDonald's coffee, even though they offer a reasonable quality of coffee product.

In both of these models (and many more) coffee is offered at a lower profitability, or even a loss, as leverage to convert a customer from another food competitor. Pret's focus is on cosmopolitan areas where customers are time poor, their underlying theory is that their customer needs to buy coffee and food at the same location, and as such, they make buying decisions about food and coffee in tandem.

I don't have access to the exact numbers of how customers use this service at Pret. It is possible that most customers are not collecting more coffee than the value of their £20 a month fee, which would make this policy a little bit like a gym membership, wherein many never visit the gym, but continue to pay the monthly fee. Alternatively, if customers are getting a lot of coffee for their £20, (on average) then this is a loss making exercise that supports the overall ticket price and bolsters customer numbers. The rumblings I have heard suggest that this has been a very positive initiative for the company. The parent company JAB holdings has implemented the policy in other food and drink brands in their portfolio.

There are additional benefits to having paid-up subscribers as part of a company. Subscribers are valued differently to transactional customers, and as such, this impacts a company's valuation.

Building relationships and loyalty with customers is a key practice for all businesses that handle the coffee bean on its journey. Focusing on a one-off sale of coffee is never a workable model in this industry. Coffee is a consumable product, priced in an affordable way, which means that, in order to trade in coffee successfully, you will need repeat custom. This is true for even the highest value coffees.

There is a lot of attraction to doing business in the specialty boutique coffee space, as the product itself is interesting and engaging. Once you are operating in the space, there are a lot of cool ideas, collaborations and interesting side projects that you and your business can be involved in, but if you aren't selling a volume of coffee every day (be that cups or beans, green or roasted) then you likely don't have a coffee business that works.

Cafés and retailers have a large volume and spread of customers, which also acts to spread the risk across the volumes required for success. If you need a lot of individual customers to make a workable business, this means that you can lose one without it dramatically challenging your business. Equally, gaining a new client doesn't require a huge investment on either side of the transaction. In a broader sense, there are a lot of customers in this space - the consuming end of the coffee industry represents the most individual customers per gram of coffee.

For a business managing the bean on its journey, lifetime value considerations are somewhat different. Most companies who deal in a form of wholesale business or raw ingredient supply will have a spread of customers, from larger clients, only a few of whom may be required to make up a substantial proportion of their business through to their smallest clients. It is typical for there to be a higher volume of the smaller clients; this is often described as "the tail."

Customer and Supplier Alignment

Naturally, larger customers can represent great business. There are, however, plenty of caveats here. They are only good for a company if they are paying a sustainable price for the product. In addition, these customers are risky, as they can withdraw at any time, and leave a gaping hole behind when they do.

This second limitation is particularly important, as a business must build its infrastructure and team around its current level of business. When done correctly, this means it will have an operating expenditure that matches its revenue. Practically speaking, most businesses need to have a bit more wiggle room than this, and as such they have the resources (or capacity) to make a slightly higher volume than their current output. For this reason, losing a big customer can be catastrophic.

Some specialty boutique operators actively reject larger clients that would represent, for example, more than 10% of their revenue. This avoids the position of risk created by one client being too influential. A successful company must however stomach some degree of risk-reward in its sales dynamic, something which exists in all industries. A big client can be wonderful, and the relationship can be positive for both businesses involved.

As discussed in the scale chapter, "big" is relative to a company's size, and this can change over time. Whilst large customers offer some drawbacks, most businesses will also have customers that are problematic for being too small. Whilst of course, a business is grateful to and for all of its clients, the relationship needs to be quid pro quo. A guest in a coffee shop who buys one coffee and uses the cafe as an (almost free) office for the day, does not offer a quid pro quo exchange. The same could be said for a roastery client who purchases a small collection of retail bags at wholesale price.

Whilst no business wants to have this kind of conversation with a potential client, these matters of scale are an inherent business truth, and each individual business, based on its current size, will have a sweet spot. A business will have customers that would be too big for it to service competently and at the right price, and likewise, it will have customers that are too small in scale to be a good match.

When beginning a new project, I was once given the following business advice - do not seek to work with partners who are at the opposite end of the business scale to your own. This has no relationship to whether they are good at what they do. It is simply because, if your business is very small, then you will be at the back end of a much larger company's "tail". Your business won't move the dial for them.

This is an alignment issue. Every business needs to focus on its bread and butter, anything else would be bad business. This should not be interpreted as appreciation (or not) of someone's business or snobbery around business size. It is actually about efficiencies and deliverable margin.

A great example at the large scale end is Nespresso. For them to initiate the marketing and internal resources to bring a new coffee into a pod, and then to market, is a substantial and expensive operation. For this reason it wouldn't be worth them considering a coffee for their range unless it is at least a container's worth of volume, and even this would be small. Small volume produces all sorts of problems. They would have to decide which channels would receive the coffee, as they wouldn't have enough to disseminate across their global customer base.

This is an extreme example, but as is often the case, there are takeaways that still apply to boutique scale business. For example, this same metric explains why a roaster would have minimum and maximum order quantities for a client who wished to collaborate on a non-core product line.

The notion of ideal client size is also crucial at a farming level. A roaster seeking to buy a few bags of a boutique coffee directly may not be very appealing to a producer at all (see my example of a Guatemalan coffee producer's struggle to ship their higher grade coffee in the chapter on *Access to Market*). For many farmers of specialty coffee, this won't move the dial. In this case it is likely much better that those couple of bags are consolidated with multiple other coffees destined to be sold to a spread of clients. All of this trade can then be handled by one intermediary - a green coffee exporter or importer.

The producer, the green company and the roaster all likely have similar goals. They are looking for an ideal customer mix. A spread of customer sizes can work, as long as the transactions made by smaller customers are streamlined, ideally ordering stock products through light touch ordering journeys, such as an automated, online ordering portal. Likewise you would be wary of committing all of your crop to one client, which leaves you at exposed risk if anything were to happen to that client.

I think it is essential for each business to put itself in the shoes of its suppliers, and try to understand how its requirements impact on the businesses it works with. Ask yourself the question, "what's in it for them?"

The Ingredient Versus the Finished Drink
The highest monetary value per gram of coffee, (for any given coffee) is generated when the coffee is brewed and served. This is particularly true in café and restaurant environments in which the coffee is consumed on-site.

All businesses before that point in the chain of production, are essentially making or working with an ingredient. At each point further along the chain some value is added, and potential value may be lost.

I often find myself in discussions around the nature and opportunities that specialty grade coffee has in a retail setting, more specifically in UK supermarkets and e-commerce businesses.

A straight to consumer sales channel requires more work than a bulk sale, (see *Deliverable Margin*) which means that most coffee businesses will struggle to make ends meet if they are only selling the coffee ingredient to end consumers. A bag of coffee will take much longer to consume than a single cup of coffee. This may sound ridiculously obvious, but it is a factor that is often overlooked. A standard 250g bag of coffee will be used to make somewhere between 15 and 20 cups of coffee, depending on the drink recipe.

Selling 15-20 cans of a finished drink, generates a lot more revenue for the drink producer than can be made by selling the customer the requisite ingredients to prepare 15-20 of those drinks themself. This means that for a company to generate revenue with an ingredient, they need to greatly surpass the sales volume required to achieve the same revenue if they were only selling a finished product made from that ingredient. In the coffee industry, as you move back through the supply chain from the finished drink towards the producer of the coffee, this necessity for volume and bulk sales increases.

Of course, selling the drink itself has associated costs, especially if the environment in which it is done is costly to run. In a café or restaurant, you are selling a seat in the space, and the service of the barista, as well as a beverage.

These mechanisms have made RTD (ready to drink) formats appealing for many businesses, as RTD beverages create the greatest revenue from a given ingredient in a retail setting.

This format is appealing for another reason; a pre-made drink has all of the quality control, and brewing done before the point of sale. In this format the whole drink is a guaranteed and consistent product, in a similar way to a bottle of wine or a can of beer. A downside is that each ready to drink can contains a lot of water, which makes them heavy and costly to ship.

There are alternative formats to the ready to drink option that create value in a similar way. Often these do a lot of the brewing in advance, but leave a few simple steps for the consumer to finish at home. Coffee capsules and instant coffee are the most pervasive examples of this model. These formats manage to bridge the gap between ingredient and beverage both for the drinker, and in terms of value at point of sale.

In a capsule the grinding and portioning of the coffee has been done, and the matching hardware will heat and dispense the water. In essence this is a push button system for brewing coffee from grounds stored under nitrogen, that creates a freshly brewed cup of coffee for the end user. Perfecting instant coffee is a much tougher job, as the technique involves brewing and then dehydrating the coffee. The coffee's volatile compounds are released during this process, capping the beverage's potential quality. For the home or office user however, instant coffee remains the most achievable and convenient option for making a hot brewed coffee.

The journey of the coffee bean in its transformation from an ingredient to a finished drink, is key to understanding the business of coffee, and the value created by a coffee company relative to each gram of coffee made.

The Sweet Spot - Volume and Price

Every business is aiming for their own sweet spot. The goal sounds straightforward - maximise volume at the best price for a given product and quality. Less straightforward is determining that exact sweet spot for any given business. It is different for each company, though in nearly all cases the bullseye is not around the company's highest or lowest priced coffee.

I once had a difficult conversation with a boutique chocolate maker regarding the appetite for higher-priced specialty chocolate. His company had made a delicious bean-to bar hot chocolate that had a good balance of quality and approachable flavour. When the price list came through, we politely declined to stock the product. Our café wasn't (and still isn't) a chocolate-focused business, and the cost of the bar was six times what we were paying for our hot chocolate at the time.

Granted, his was a superior product, but the price didn't work in the context of our store. This was quickly followed with a retort from the chap, along the following lines - "oh, so you are willing to pay a premium for coffee, but you won't for chocolate?" I could see his

his perception, that what he thought specialty coffee roasters and shops were paying for coffee was off the mark in comparison with his chocolate, and I can see how this happens. Roasters and shops in boutique coffee often draw people's attention to their interesting, special, high-priced coffee products. These coffees are very interesting, they taste highly specific and complex, and can have a special story behind them as well.

The thing is though, these coffees do not make up much of the volume that underpins the business of a typical third wave café or roaster. Nor does it represent the typical production of a farmer growing specialty coffee. Your average specialty grade coffee that makes its way into a house blend, and for that matter, the daily filter, is not six times the price of commercial coffee.

There are exceptions. A farm like Esmeralda in Panama, or a small, premium coffee company that sticks to modest sales of highly-priced coffees. If you zoom out though, these are anomalies in the specialty movement that is gaining momentum around the world.

Specialty coffee affords an opportunity for many businesses in the supply chain to differentiate and provide a USP. This allows the business to be competitive and find an audience, as well as to shield it from some of commodity coffee's pricing fluctuations.

If a business is in pursuit of pure volume and scale, it will require the movement of lower-priced products to achieve market size. In doing this, the business will be in competition with much larger players, starting at a competitive disadvantage. At the other end, the market narrows as price increases, as consumer appetite and ability to purchase these coffees diminishes.

Many large companies are acutely aware of the marketplace, (and their place within it) and will have processes in place to keep an eye on price elasticity relative to the market at that time.

Back when I was 19 years old I got a job in a petrol station to help me save for a Seven Stop Ticket to travel the world. I would do shifts in the rural countryside location and at the motorway station, and I noticed the prices were higher for a litre of fuel in the latter location. Yes, there are different circumstances and cost of production, but clearly the motorway prices are consistently more expensive due to the captive market. The sweet spot price for a given location is calculated by the company, in this case utilising the active audience to charge higher prices, whilst keeping an eye on the competition so that motorists do not drive to the next station run by a competitor.

Stress test pricing is easiest to do on e-commerce stores. You can change the pricing online whenever you want, and watch to see how conversion is affected. Do people still keep buying? Although, if you are working with loyal, regular, returning customers, you shouldn't change prices on their core products on a daily basis. This is a real issue in a café. It is not easy to play with prices, or at least it feels like you can't, as there is a direct feedback loop with regulars who notice and question the price increases. Since card transactions have become the predominant form of payment, price changes are less readily recognised. The tap of the card is quite different to the customer making sure they have the right change in their pocket to hand over for that coffee each day.

Price is much easier to test with a new or special release coffee online. One can explore differently priced tiers of products and see how they convert. The same can be done on a physical retail shelf. This kind of testing is less effective when using drink menus, because the fast food ordering behaviour of most cafés leads to the core offerings selling the most - so simply sticking a higher-priced coffee on the menu doesn't show the true overlap between appetite and price. This can be an issue more generally when selling premium priced coffees, they test the opportunity to upsell, but they don't test the elasticity of pricing for core products.

I have the feeling that in indie businesses, most pricing on bestsellers, the core drinks, is done on a combination of feel and looking around at other similar operators. In the case of high-quality operators who deliver an exceptional service and product, I think that their price ceiling may be higher than they might think. They are after all selling an experience as well as a beverage.

With regards to new product lines, it can be tough to gauge whether there is an opportunity to increase the sweet spot of value or not. A coffee farmer may see huge demand for a one-off experimental lot. Is the demand based on the newness of the project? Or will the demand be sustained year on year? If they are able to increase the production, would there come a point at which supply outstrips demand, leaving them with high-priced coffee that they can't sell. Otherwise, maybe the whole farm should move everything to a higher-priced cultivar and process.

Lowering prices to increase the sweet spot is no easier. If you have a premium price product, reducing the price by 10% may not be sufficient to convert customers who are seeking lower priced products. In this case you may just be selling the same product to the same customers for less money.

You can't talk about any of this without mentioning the context of brand and reputation. It is easy to talk about specialty coffee as a fixed and shared product that all companies are dealing with similarly. However, your company's brand and identity and the relationships it has built, will directly impact the possible sweet spot in conjunction with the quality of the coffee itself.

This assessment of where the sweet spot is does not always have to be about growing - it can be utilised to shrink a business positively, in order to end up with more profit. For example, a company may start charging shipping on online orders when previously they didn't. We did this at our roastery. We did lose customers, but this did not outweigh the benefits of covering the cost of shipping. This made our e-commerce channel profitable where it wasn't before. We improved our sweet spot, even if it meant losing some trade.

Alternatively, an example could be a large volume account, whereby the true deliverable margin, when all is said and done, does not hit a profitable sweet spot. Top line growth can be reduced to increase bottom line profit.

These sweet spots of value are unique to each company and tend to represent a moving target relative to the company's position and the marketplace it is in. The market is an evolving, moving beast and the sweet spots change not only because the competitor landscape evolves, but also because consumer/client behaviour is subject to change.

A key tenet of business is to know what it is you are trying to build, and what the company's values are. With the goal clearly identified, the question of the sweet spot can be answered in relation to your product and intentions. In specialty boutique coffee, this will include quality, service and experience. The two aspects must be viewed together, how can you stay true to your mission and maximise the sweet spot? Otherwise your business can be chasing ideas of sweet spot around without direction, and harming its identity in the process.

Customer Relations

The relationship between business and customer is often oversimplified, by being reduced down to simple, transactional concepts. A common motto "the customer is always right," a pet peeve of many in hospitality, further compounds this notion. In different cultures this proverb varies slightly, from "the customer is king," to, at its most extreme, "the customer is god".

This notion was novel when it was started. At a time of misrepresentation, the idea empowered the customer to address the imbalance in fairness. Taken to its extreme though, this is obviously illogical. A simple addition to this phrase would make it more accurate for me: "the customer is always right, just so long as they are your target customer".

When two parties enter into an exchange where there are misaligned expectations, neither party ends up benefiting. The free market means that, for most businesses, there is no need to engage in this kind of transaction. Exceptions include public service businesses, who take on the unenviable task of trying to please everyone, and likewise, situations can arise in which customer in the supply chain is someone that you "have" to sell to - this can occur in certain "in-country" systems - then a business will be left with no choice but to "please" this customer.

Customer relationship management is often divided into before and after the sale. Engaging with the customer before the transaction is made up of sales and service. Once the sale is complete it is followed by a form of aftercare, whereby the company can support the customer regarding any needs that may arise surrounding the purchase that they have made.

Whilst these processes are key in all businesses, the relationship between business and customer is especially important in specialty coffee, throughout every part of the industry. The place of customer service at the retail end of the journey is easy to comprehend, however, every business in coffee is both a customer and a seller. Every business must purchase ingredients and services as part of the process of making their product.

In most businesses, the way to maximise customer relations (and to make your business a success) will be driven by the "why." If a business can identify the product and experience that it is trying to offer, it can work more effectively towards optimising their customer-facing offering. This whole customer proposition is an interplay between products, platforms, systems and people.

Let's start with the product. A specific product, such as specialty coffee, requires a specific customer. The business has to establish, and find a way to communicate with, their customer. Specialty boutique coffee businesses often put a lot of work into this consideration, as the business has put a huge amount of thought into creating a product in which they perceive value.

The element of taste is in play, which means that the more interesting the product, the more likely the business is to receive negative customer feedback - the customer will tell you that this isn't what they wanted. When the product divides the crowd in this way, it creates a very interesting dynamic for the operator. It is worth remembering here that the world's most revered restaurants don't have the best ratings on Tripadvisor. Establishments that make something that everyone understands to a standard that doesn't stray from an established norm are more likely and able to reach the top spots.

The specialist business is playing with a subversion of expectations. This can delight people, but it can also piss them off. You will only know if you have got it right when you can build a business with a tribe of customers that jive with what you're doing. I have always been interested in how to approach this challenge in our coffee shop. In this environment you can see the dynamic clearly at play, and I have chosen to focus on communicating transparently about what we were trying to achieve. My measure of success in this scenario wasn't for everyone to love what we were doing, but rather to understand it, allowing them to opt in or out in future.

Despite how this may sound, I do believe that you need to have time for all customers, even if they are distinctly not your customer. An operator may correctly outline the limits of the highly specialist approach, and they would be justified in doing so. The marketplace is not able to support every business that chooses to focus on a niche, and as I have mentioned before now, if a farmer simply grew super unusual coffee for a niche client who was into that, they may find their sales falling short of a sustainable point.

Each business is contemplating the specialist products that it thinks should be presented to customers for their consideration. Customer behaviour and feedback plays into this equation, but doesn't define it. The leaders of the product offering must decide what to offer and what not to offer.

Secondly, the platform and systems that the business operates on must be customer-centric. Whether it is an offer list, a shop environment, an aftercare system, or one of any other manner of systems and environments through which a business operates, the customer experience is defined by this point of contact. How the system a business chooses, or builds for themselves, delivers on their product or experience is referred to as "the user journey". The essential point here is quite simple, the systems you build will allow you to actually deliver on the product that you market.

Finally, there are people. I have left them until last, but in more of these businesses, they are the most important factor. The point at which customers connect with people in your business usually creates the biggest impact. We are humans after all, and we naturally focus on interactions with one another.

Human connections are especially pertinent in specialty boutique coffee, in which many are drawn to the scene in order to engage with coffee not just as a beverage, but also a passion and a basis for human connection. For this reason, it is not surprising that

93

the small, owner-operated business model often connects well with specialty customers. This is especially the case when the owners, who are naturally passionate about their own business, are able to do a lot of the customer interaction.

This type and scale of company will face a challenge in the case of expansion or diversification as they will need to build a team and culture that can deliver customer service of the same type and quality. Clearly, you cannot scale that passionate, owner/operator service, but you can seek to create something that utilises some of the same DNA.

All of this actually forms a big part of a brand. A customer's idea of a business's identity only fully forms when they have experienced a full customer journey. You may choose to create a strongly branded product, with a visual aesthetic or certain attributes or functions, but the tone of voice that flows through a customer's interaction with the business and its people will contribute hugely to how they will perceive the brand. This dynamic is the most powerful when the experience of customer interaction is part of what you are buying, but it remains to be true to an extent in any businesses.

Customer Research

What do your customers think of your product and your company? More importantly, how do they actually engage with your company?

All businesses have some kind of feedback loop. In smaller companies it is not usually an overly formal arrangement. Regardless of how you receive feedback, having your finger on the pulse is key to making the most of what you are doing.

It may seem simple: observe what people want and make it for them. Somehow it often isn't quite that easy, particularly in a specialist space. Specialist companies are often engaged in pushing things forward, and sharing a vision or an idea, which means that their product is not simply a reaction to what is in demand.

More and more boutique brands are honest about the fact that their coffee offering is driven solely by what they like - they represent the coffee that they enjoy, and are excited to roast it in the way they think is best. There is a subtext to this; they aren't trying to please everyone. They know that there are other ways to do things, which for some would be preferable, but they are doing their own thing. This very much projects a "you do you and we'll do us" vibe. This can be a powerful marketing approach if you can make it resonate with people.

In this scenario, customer feedback may seem superfluous. You just do what you think is best, and see what people think. However, all businesses are (or should be) interested in how they are interacting with the world. This remains true, even if you, as the business, are happy to assess and discard the feedback when it's not aligned with your goals. The customer and the business are not always a good fit.

Often the feedback loop isn't simple. Rather than simply asking if everyone is happy with your service, a business needs to engage the right customer, in the right way, to assess their experience of the brand's vision. This approach is built on the knowledge that there is no business that pleases all customers. Broader businesses will aim to please the widest possible audience, whilst more specified businesses will be interested in a fairly narrow portion of a market. Increasingly, specialty boutique coffee pops up across this spectrum, as the question around how broad its appeal can be is continuing to be explored.

I believe that the complex place in the market inhabited by specialty boutique coffee is a strength, but it also creates challenges and conundrums for businesses. Many businesses throughout the supply chain show a diversified offering whereby they target different customers across their range of products. A producer might target both experimental, small lot customers whilst also producing larger lots of washed coffee. In the same way a café operator with a broadly appealing house blend may also offer a fun and different guest coffee, or a menu of coffees kept in the freezer.

One question I find productive to ponder on is; if you ask the customers what they thought your business was "about," would it match the vision of the founders?

At the beginning, a vision-based business is driven by sheer will, and a clear belief in the project. This vision is important at the beginning of a business's life, as it gives the company an identity. However, as the business looks to refine and evolve what they have built, or to branch out into new areas, market research becomes increasingly useful.

The fabrication of feedback techniques is actually surprisingly complex, and they can often provide false data. I used to go to the gym with a psychologist whose work focused on the flawed nature of the majority of focus group product development procedures.

His point was surprisingly simple. Just because people say they will do something, this doesn't mean that they will. The very nature of eliciting feedback creates an abnormal environment. When asking someone what they think of something, they are being put on the spot to "have a thought" and give "useful feedback". This dynamic, in which you are framing a situation for the subject, creates a cascade of varying motives around the feedback. The subject is under social pressure, their brain is racing, "what should I say?" They think, "what is the right answer?"

In addition, if we assume that the subject's feedback is honest and unaffected, in truth, a person won't necessarily know if they would prefer something done differently. If this previously abstract situation were to be acted out they may find themselves thinking, "actually I preferred it before". Many examples of this sort can be given, but the point is, it's messy.

Larger businesses are becoming more and more sophisticated in approaching these questions and developing or changing products and services in accordance with feedback. For most small businesses this is all just done on feel and intuition.

Just as we have seen that e-commerce can provide useful metrics for *Customer Acquisition* and stress testing price to find *The Sweet Spot*, in customer research too, e-commerce has unique benefits. When monitoring online activity, you aren't asking someone to tell you what they would like or how they would behave, you are following what they actually do. Do they *actually* click, do they actually convert? And so on.

The boutique end of the market is framed by the fact that most consumers do not self-identify as coffee experts. Trust in a brand or a person is key to success where the customer is buying a specialist product, and building that via a feedback loop is more important than trying to please every customer the company interacts with.

The majority of specialty boutique brands are performing this process in a very earnest way, based around a mixture of filtering feedback relative to mission, and keeping an eye on what is gaining momentum and interest across the community.

The momentum dynamic can be misleading, just because something is getting hype or has become a talking point, this doesn't mean that it will convert into good business. In coffee production we see continued chatter around experimental coffee processes and cultivars as they gain a lot of attention across the industry. This causes the demand for these products to appear high, but increased supply would quickly outstrip actual demand.

All businesses experience a constant feedback loop with their customers. Very few industries are (or can afford to be) static in this regard. A business that is able to navigate these observations with good judgement, whether through analytical systems or gut feel, will have an advantage in their continued pursuit of success.

Teams, Roles and Structures

In the early days of a start-up or independent business, the team will likely be small. It may even be just founders, friends and family. As the business either grows or becomes established over time, it is usually necessary to build a team with a more sustainable structure.

Founders and owners can work really long hours and be on top of their business, but keeping this up over time is not sustainable, and if the business grows in any considerable proportion the job will simply not be possible. It is also very important to note that a whole team, successfully working towards achieving a goal, will always produce greater results than an individual can. For founders and entrepreneurs this is often a lesson that needs to be learnt. A person who has taken on this role can be very good at getting a business going, and more likely than not, can do a lot of the jobs themselves. However, they will need to transition to thinking about building a business culture and a team that are all working towards the same goal.

Part Two. Operating a Business

American economist Larry E. Greiner developed the "How Companies Grow" theory which charts the evolution and revolution of a growing company. The theory states that as an organisation grows, it will encounter a period of revolution or crisis, whereby there is major upheaval of the management structure that's in place. In other words, as a company ages and grows over time, it will need to be run differently.

Stages of Organisational Growth

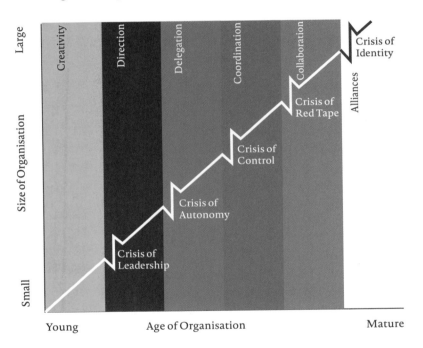

In the beginning, (stage 1) creative founders pursue a vision and the team is small, allowing frequent and easily achievable communication in a casual manner. This creativity and problem solving will get a company off the ground, but these very activities can start to become a problem. As the team grows, casual, informal behaviour doesn't get the job done, things start to go wrong, and there is a crisis of leadership.

At this point, (stage 2) a leader is needed to install structure and business practices for the growing team that isn't a small core team member. During this phase a more formal structure is put in place and it works well until the point that this directional leadership doesn't allow for the autonomy that more experienced team members would need to utilise, to take initiative and continue the business's development. Most of the responsibility at this phase is with the managers at the top of the hierarchy. The crisis of autonomy brings on the next phase, (stage 3) which is demarcated by delegation, individuals are given more responsibility and autonomy. This allows the business to diversify and utilise different roles and departments more successfully.

The crisis that can hit this phase is a loss of direction and control across the company. It is at this point that stage 4 comes into being, whereby the company seeks to take back a form of directive control. This phase of coordination will be process and structure driven, with a lot of detail and constant review culture in place to make sure the systems are coordinating the different autonomous roles and teams across the business.

This approach can yield good results until the ever-larger company starts to struggle with the limitations of formal, rigid systems. At this point there is a red tape crisis which brings about stage 5. This is based on a matrix of teams and managers that work together collaboratively. The focus becomes behavioural management styles and social control, in which self-discipline replaces formal control. The result is a mixture of spontaneous decision making and problem solving that sits in a wider matrix culture of cross team cooperation and review.

I find these phases really valuable to think about, but I don't think in reality they tessellate so neatly, occurring sequentially one after the other. A multitude of these behaviours can be present in a company at one time, requiring resolution simultaneously.

There are different ways of structuring a business, this is clear. Some teams are like a sports team, with everyone in the thick of it together. One of my previous employees described our roastery production floor like a ship, describing the team members running different stations, but working cohesively to get to the desired destination each week. Other companies can be more department based or even very disparate, with a collection of nearly autonomous personnel. You can also have different cultures in play at the same time, across different parts of the business, where parts of the team work together daily, and other members are more autonomous or disconnected.

Business owners in most fields will say that their biggest challenge is people. For all businesses, and especially SMEs (small to medium enterprise - an organisation with less than 250 employees) building a strong successful team is key to the business's overall success. I have realised more and more that as a business grows, the focus of founders and leaders should be as much on team and culture as any other aspect.

This is a real challenge for independent and boutique operators. Unless they have previous experience building and running a larger team in another role, it will be a learning process that is ongoing and in many cases a process of trial and error. For many there will be a need to bring in someone to help them build and shape their organisation. This can be challenging, not only behaviourally, as founders are used to being in control, and the team have settled into their style of working, but also because bringing in that experience and expertise costs money.

As I have stated previously, specialty coffee is not the sole domain of boutique and independent business. Larger, more structured businesses produce, move, buy and present specialty coffee also.

Being small and specialist can have competitive strengths, but with all the businesses in the coffee sector staring down the barrel of lean, net profit, there is no wiggle room for building loose and creative teams. Instead, team structures have to be based around efficiency, effectiveness and clear deliverables.

This actually means that for all the focus on quality and exploration in coffee, building and running a team requires a clear business mindset. There are areas within boutique businesses that ask their employees to think less about business and more about engaging the community, such as brand ambassadors, trainers and coffee competition competitors. Getting the balance right, allowing passion, learning and engagement to sit alongside solid business fundamentals is not an easy task.

The exact structure will, as Greiner's model outlines, be influenced by the size of the business at any one time. For smaller businesses, this typically means spreading tasks across multiple roles. On this scale, a business doesn't have the revenue or requisite demand to build highly specific roles that focus on perfecting one specific task.

There is a constant battle in business to optimise each model along the journey. The small business needs to work hard to try and compete and deliver when teams are stretched across a variety of tasks, but this also means that the team moves fast, and when working well, is very robust. Larger teams benefit from expertise and specialism in specific areas, but can struggle to create speed and efficiency across teams and departments, and always present a danger of becoming clunky and uneconomical.

The importance of working on a team and structure cannot be overstated, after all it is the lifeblood of every business, and can easily be neglected. For most, this process will never be complete, it is something a business will need to be prepared to nurture and adapt regularly over time.

People and Progression in the Coffee Profession

Boutique coffee is a melting pot of different people from different backgrounds and skill sets brought together by a passion for this subsection of the world of coffee. A lot of those working with specialty coffee will have first been exposed, and learnt about it by already having been in the industry in some way. This "on the job" learning mirrors apprenticeship style programmes in a few ways.

There has been a marked increase in educational programmes throughout specialty coffee. However, whilst a career in coffee may be supplemented by these structures, it is not typically front-loaded with further education or a degree in the way a traditional career path might be.

A lot of people with degrees end up in coffee, not as a result of the academic training, but rather due to a learned interest in coffee. The experience of working in coffee, especially specialty boutique coffee, is an exploration of the industry, an education taught through navigating a variety of jobs.

Curious individuals are bitten by the coffee bug and start to pursue different roles in coffee to learn more about the subject. There are (of course) very few jobs in coffee that solely involve learning more about coffee. Some roles are more knowledge driven, such as, a quality control role throughout the supply chain, a head of coffee role, or a barista or roaster training role. However, even in these cases there are quite a few professional skills and duties that not only are important, but are the primary goal of the job.

A job at a green coffee importer will help a person gain more exposure and knowledge of tasting, how coffee is traded and how different coffee origins function on a practical level. Without question, every person I know who has worked for a green coffee importer has become more open minded and contextually aware when it comes to the subject of great coffee and the ways in which the industry functions (for better or for worse).

Exposure and first hand experience is a valuable education. In order to obtain these privileges, the person also most likely had to become some form of a sales person, as this makes up the majority of key roles in the green importing business. They could take on an account management role, or they could be a buyer who spends a lot of their time managing contracts and supply relationships with a specific portfolio of products in mind. They are unlikely to be simply buying the coffees they find the tastiest. In both of these cases, the person must learn business skills in addition to coffee skills.

There is a difference between professional development and coffee development. Whilst there are roles in which the two can evolve and grow side by side, there are also multiple roles in coffee that have nothing to do with the coffee itself. When discussing coffee industry roles with people, I often suggest that they ask themselves the question, would I want to do this role if the product wasn't coffee?

What if you were packing flapjacks and not coffee beans, or serving plates at a restaurant and not coffee in a café. This thought process only becomes more necessary as roles develop to become more in-depth with more responsibility.

It is very easy to get into coffee and pursue progression, only to end up a victim of the Peter Principle. The Peter Principle refers to the concept that a promotion-based culture causes individuals to be promoted to a point at which they are not competent at their role. They then don't progress further as they no longer excel in th e role. This is not beneficial for the person or the business, likely the customer too.

The same question about where your strengths really lie is key, not just for employees but for founders, entrepreneurs and business owners. A friend of mine got his first job at 14-years-old and his dad said to him, "think about how your job helps the business succeed and be profitable, and you will do just fine". A simple but powerful piece of advice.

Career development in specialty coffee typically cannot be highly-structured. This is a double-edged sword. On the one hand, individuals can move around the industry, trying their hand at various roles, and picking up a diverse range of experiences and skills through their work. There are certain fluid and explorative character types that this can work for very well. This loose and transitory framework can however be very frustrating for those looking to embark on a more structured work path and journey.

This less structured journey is typical of start-ups and small businesses. Not only does the business require people to wear many hats, but it also lacks the size and structure to train and develop roles. It needs team members who are self-motivated and can develop a lot of the skills through problem solving. Larger companies will typically provide better training and progression.

It may sound contrary, but in order to develop some of the professional skills required to thrive in the industry, a stint outside of specialty coffee can be the best route. This can allow a person to come back into a specialty company with valuable capabilities and the ability to progress their career by moving out of the core coffee roles, of which there are fairly few. Within pure coffee roles, the choice to move across the coffee sector between boutique companies and larger commercial operations can also provide valuable perspective, experience and training.

There is a growing body of teaching structures and programmes relating to the knowledge of coffee itself, the study of the bean, not of the business. These have made it much easier for people new to the industry to learn quickly about coffee, at least in theory. Much coffee knowledge is tied to tasting the coffee, and in this way, the apprenticeship aspect of learning about coffee remains vital. This skill can only be learned through time and exposure.

As should be clear from the information laid out in this section, one of the main challenges people interested in the specialty coffee sector will encounter in their careers will be finding roles that allow for career development and are focused on coffee of specialty quality. For the most part these roles only occur in businesses that grow beyond small founder-operated businesses. For this reason, those who have dedicated time to learning about the coffee industry and the businesses that it is built upon, may then take the plunge, and start their own thing.

The distinction between employee and owner mindsets is well-trodden ground. Ownership is typically seen as something for the autonomous individual who relishes taking on responsibility and forging their own path, whilst employee roles typically favour team players. This is clearly a significant over-simplification, people are not at all this binary, and decisions about which path to pursue are rarely clear cut. For those choosing to work in this unusual industry, not only does every day entail learning about coffee, but also exploring how to evolve their own careers.

Expertise and Talent

There is a definite value placed on expertise in the coffee industry, and naturally, the idea of knowledge is considered particularly precious in the specialty arena, where quality is prized.

For this reason, a well-known and successful coffee producer may be found consulting on other farms, or even in other regions and countries on matters of agronomy and processing, and there are storied examples in which, just like David Beckham's legs, the tongue of a large coffee company's quality control taster is insured for a hefty sum.

As we noted in the last chapter, non-coffee expertise is also crucial to all coffee businesses. This is often a key lesson that needs to be learnt by small boutique operators, who require a change of mindset to think about their business as a business, and to correctly value the different expertise needed in all parts of the operation. Of course, small boutique coffee companies put a focus on coffee knowledge and expertise, but in time most also learn to holistically build a good business.

This may turn out to be a contentious thing to say, but specialty coffee does appear to lack expertise relative to its goals. This is not just in terms of professional skills and expertise, but in terms of coffee expertise as well.

If you think about it, the combination of a low barrier to entry, and swathes of small independent businesses joining the fray, was always likely to lead to a good number of inexperienced workers joining the coffee industry, and as per the previous chapter, there is a lot of on the job learning that happens. This applies to coffee skills and knowledge, and business practice.

This effect varies depending on the market and its maturity. The number of people who have moved through the industry at a time or place, and the current level of competition for roles that require knowledge and expertise will impact the pool of applicants you might expect to see for a given job.

In the early phases of specialty movements, companies find themselves needing to prioritise in-house training, due to a lack of experience and expertise. In the UK I have noticed a considerable development in the knowledge and expertise of baristas in the marketplace. Brexit didn't help, but the standard remains higher than it has ever been. The barista workforce in the UK is the most populated, and as you move through the supply chain to more disparate roles, the sharing and pooling of knowledge is less natural.

If a business wishes to be driven by quality, they need to make sure their teams and structure are built with this as a priority. In the world of specialty coffee, product knowledge is key. Each of the businesses in the coffee supply chain requires expertise and knowledge around how that business works with coffee, and also a contextual understanding of how the other businesses in the supply chain work.

Building businesses around baristas and coffee geeks is fraught with problems. It can often mean that coffee development is prioritised over professional development. It is laudable to create a coffee business with a team who share passion for coffee and are all turning up at work daily with a love for the bean, but the primary responsibility of most roles in coffee businesses are separate from coffee. In almost all roles a person is required who couples passion and knowledge of coffee with professionalism and enthusiasm to do a great job in the entirety of the role they fulfil.

Friction occurs throughout many specialty boutique coffee businesses. A person can begin on the path of coffee as a means to work with an interesting ingredient, but also because it can seem like a field that is very un-businessy. It is a field which is made up of businesses, yes, but many don't appear on the surface to behave like "normal" businesses. This has led more than a few coffee businesses to reach a point of frustration, when their coffee knowledgeable team members don't "get" the business aspect of the company.

A company may then explore the idea of building a team around "non-coffee" people, which can have benefits and bring a diversity of approach and experience to the business. It is clear to me however, that a company built around a passion for coffee needs to nurture excitement around quality coffee driven experiences. So, really the business is trying to figure out how it can encourage and combine both coffee and professional expertise.

An avid coffee-lover is likely to make decisions about where to work based on a lot more than salary and responsibility. Their choices are also driven by considerations of the kind of company they want to work for, how they want to work with coffee and who they want to work with. Some companies have people queuing up to work with them, as they offer an environment with a focus on coffee education and experience. Perhaps they also have a brand that appeals to the applicant's identity. Another business may really struggle to fill similar roles, and perhaps more importantly, to retain good talent in those roles.

Finding a balance between attracting and keeping coffee talent whilst being business-focused, is a balance that is not easily achieved. Larger, less trendy coffee companies can benefit from staff who are on a journey, choosing to pass through the business as they seek to build experience. Of course, the staff need to stay long enough to contribute to the business, and not just learn and leave. I see the movement of staff across the industry, between small and large companies, as positive for the industry as a whole, and a very natural pattern.

Individuals that have expertise and experience often come to their new role with a "view" and a preference. Key roles drive the quality and nature of the coffee offering within a business, which is clearly commercially impactful. The choice of coffee, in style, flavour or quality, at a green importer, roastery or café feeds directly into the commercial success of the business - this is effectively product development. In another role, an individual may take the lead in achieving product consistency, which can have significant commercial ramifications.

It is nearly impossible to run a specialist business of any kind if you as the leader or owner are not working on developing your own expertise in the field. Without a solid understanding of the topic, you are not able to review the expertise and success of important roles in your company.

As markets mature, more experience and expertise will naturally be available. The many different coffee competitions, combined with the community's knowledge-sharing culture, and some great educational materials have created a culture of development and expertise. However, any specialist business should still expect to create environments, teams and feedback loops that promote expertise. It should also be noted that at all levels, the expertise itself will also be characterised by an ability to review and learn as the industry changes, both in terms of new learning and understanding, and in terms of new flavour trends.

Marketing - Access to Market

In *Part Five* of the book I focus much more on marketing as a part of branding. In this section of the book, it is simply important to understand how the ability to access your market and engage with clients is a key component of any business. It may well be one of the most important.

Just because you make a thing, that doesn't mean that people will buy it. I know that this sounds very obvious, but it is a thought process that is often lost when working within the coffee supply chain.

A coffee shop has perhaps the most straightforward opportunity to sell a product to a customer base (unless it is based in a remote location). The physical premises provided by a store location typically creates immediate access to the market, although converting those customers to sale is a different task.

At the other end of the market, it is easier for coffee growers to access commercial sales avenues than specialty boutique sales. In the UK the specialty coffee scene has done a good job of creating the business opportunity for small and independent businesses to open and get going. Conversely, to start competing in the UK's commercial coffee products field is hard. Gaining access to a supermarket listing or winning commercial coffee driven accounts is a tough task.

From a farming perspective, the opposite has been true. Huge, global coffee companies need a supply of coffee, so it is in their interest to build or support supply chains in which it is easy for coffee to be sold (to them). Commercial coffee represents the industry's largest market, so it makes sense that access to this market is better developed. The challenge is more likely to be finding a way to compete on price. Access to the market isn't necessarily desirable if the price isn't right.

Contrarily, I do not think that the specialty movement has shown the ability to solve price mechanics in coffee or create alternative supply chains. What it can claim is simply to have grown the access to market for premium specialty coffee, through the promotion of these coffees. This is achieved collectively by all individual businesses waving the banner for quality coffee and putting this type of coffee in front of their customers.

As these businesses have managed to find an audience and more similar businesses open up, we have seen a growing opportunity for producers and farms to develop recognised brands and reputations. This effect takes place in the boutique end of the market, whereby higher prices are paid for higher quality coffee.

There is not a dynamic presently that would encourage a higher price to be paid for lower cost coffee. Specialty coffee is not improving coffee's baseline price except in situations where coffee quality or USP merits this. This is normal in all markets.

Examples can be given in which great coffee is being farmed that didn't previously have good access to the market. Farms with resources can market their coffees, farms and collaborative projects at international trade shows. Where the farm does not have this scope, this access to the market is often provided by an importing partner. This is a quid pro quo association - the importer will represent the coffee to a variety of clients and grow recognition of the coffee's quality and the producer's narrative, improving price or sales for importer and farm simultaneously. This is effectively a marketing relationship.

I have spoken with importers who have expressed annoyance that through this process they have helped to grow an exporter or producer's brand in the UK, who have then moved on to work with a different importing company. This is a natural process, distribution and brand representation partnerships are always up for review and change.

As an example, if you have a company that imports coffee equipment into the UK from another country, and you build a decent business, it is still very possible that on the renewal date of the contract, the two businesses may part ways. For each business there must be an ongoing process of reviewing what's best for itself. Of course, I can see how this would be frustrating for the importer, and bad for their business.

Recently there has been a trend of origin-based, smaller-scale exporters opening importing offices in key markets. Whilst this business initiative requires various resources and beneficial positioning to undertake, these offices can work extremely well, as the human connection is such a powerful part of specialty coffee business.

There are also a growing number of initiatives in specialty coffee, predominantly coordinated by exporters and importers, but in some cases by individual roasting companies, that seek to offer access to market for coffee producers and farmers in more disadvantaged positions.

Government policy in a country that produces a lot of coffee can benefit a farm's access to market via countrywide initiatives. There is also a form of soft power that is carried by the perception of a coffee producing country by coffee drinkers and buyers around the world. This directly affects both demand and access to market. Colombia is often cited as excelling in this regard.

With the advent of social media and other online connections, the distance between coffee growing and coffee drinking has become smaller, which can create easier access to the market for many businesses along the coffee chain. In the boutique coffee sector, Instagram messages are a legitimate communication channel for farmers and exporters to connect directly with roasters and buyers.

Direct dialogue may offer an open conversation between grower and roaster, and there are more and more services that offer open book financing and logistics, but if the amounts are small, and the coffee doesn't fill a container, it can be challenging to make this kind of trade effective. For this reason, in nearly all cases there will still be need for the finance and logistics of an importing partner.

It is impossible to stress enough how crucial access to market is for the life of any business. Identifying and developing access to market strategies that actually work, provides one of the greatest opportunities for any business to improve or grow.

Research and Development

Any innovation that has been brought to life, represents a process of research and development. R&D does not always have to be about new innovation, per se, it may also be about the necessary product development required to launch something new, and it can follow an existing process of development and creation.

It is interesting to draw a line between true R&D and the simple repetition of a process. In most specialty boutique businesses a reasonable amount of R&D occurs, but the business considers very little distinction or separation between this and other production activities. In a business of this scale there normally isn't an R&D department or budget to speak of.

There is a reasonable amount of R&D at farm level, in both commercial and specialty coffee settings. A farm will benefit from analysing the agronomy of the land and testing and measuring key indicators, allowing changes to inputs in order to maximise the quality and yield.

At a farm with a more specialty driven approach, you would expect to see smaller projects alongside the main crops. It would not be uncommon to see an "exotic garden," which is a space dedicated to planting and trialling different coffee cultivars and varieties. In larger, sophisticated operations, producers embark on a process of quality mapping, whereby they are able to assess the potential quality of each block of planted land. Based on the raw potential, the land can be separated and processed, designating a final product type, with knowledge of what that plot of land is able to create.

Similarly, the exploration of coffee processing is an R&D department in itself, even if not rigidly defined as such. Farmers or mills will implement small batch trials of processing techniques before they attempt to roll out the approach on larger lots and at scale. Depending upon the result, a given process could remain as a more niche, small lot process.

Specialty coffee is just as much about exploration and experimentation as it is about pure quality. For this reason, you will see this type of experimental R&D throughout this segment of the coffee industry. From small batch trialling of a new roast approach before rolling out to production in a roastery, to implementing a new brewing technique on the bar in a café, that was tested and developed by the team before it made its way onto the menu. It is a pet peeve of mine that this R&D process doesn't always happen, which leads to the customer getting a product that is still in development, and that the baristas themselves don't actually think is ready to serve.

This flexibility to experiment is a strength of boutique business, but once again, the lack of scale can also act as a limitation. The extent of R&D that can be undertaken is inherently limited due to the cost in both money and resources. Bearing in mind that the net profit of a specialty coffee business is relatively lean, there is not a lot of room in the budget for pure exploration and experimentation. In many small businesses the weight of this task gets picked up by a few individuals who go above and beyond. They may take the opportunity to further their curiosity for coffee, typically out of hours or on top of other prescribed tasks, by exploring processes and different approaches.

Consumer product businesses will have a considerable focus on R&D. Most businesses, if they don't have a "product pipeline," will die. This is to say, unless you have a consumable, repeat purchase product, you will need to continue to generate new products for people to buy.

The price of these new goods, and the margin they achieve, needs to allow for ongoing development of fresh products. Effectively, the model has to allow for ongoing reinvestment from the profit of existing and future products. This applies to coffee equipment companies and the like.

One of the nice things about working with the coffee bean itself is that there is an inherent inbuilt product pipeline, more so for roasters and cafés, who can try new coffees all of the time. The work involved in bringing a new coffee to market is nothing in comparison with a physical product, which could take years and huge investment, to get to the point of manufacture.

For a farmer, new product development can be more onerous if it requires new coffee plants. Essentially, this requires patience and risk. The sensible way to trial a new coffee variety is on a small scale, however this will mean waiting three-to-four years before the initial cherries can be sampled. If the trial is a success, then the cultivar is planted somewhere on the farm, and the stopwatch starts again for another three-to-four years. There is a further risk that the small garden trial is not fully indicative of the results that will be achieved by planting elsewhere on the farm.

A lot of the upfront work on new and existing cultivars is taken up by national research organisations, such as Cenicafé, Anacafé and IAC, as well as NGOs such as WCR, (World Coffee Research) who attempt to find suitable conditions for cultivars, allowing them to issue planting recommendations.

A lot of R&D and science in coffee is driven by a single evaluation metric; how does it taste? Another emphasis is on yield, which makes complete sense. Any improvements in the plants themselves, the agronomy, the pruning, and or the processing and milling, that can make more of the potential coffee being harvested (or the percentage of that coffee) reach a higher quality, the better. Even single digit percentage improvements are a big deal in lean industries.

One of the green traders I work with has a research and development team whose sole focus is weather. The majority of the large trading houses have these teams. Being able to accurately predict weather patterns is key to understanding the predicted production of a given origin. Getting this data ahead of time is an advantage, for example, if a company could foresee the frost that hit Brazil in 2021, they could model the reduced harvest numbers and the resulting price increase to some degree. This in turn can mean that they manage their contracts and hedged position better. I suspect it unlikely that anyone could have predicted or even been able to mitigate fully against the impact of this event, but it would have been a significant benefit.

In all cases, R&D from a business perspective should be focused around the *Value Add*, which in turn means that the impact from the investment is the largest relative to that particular business's potential. In the next part of the book I will look at the concept of innovation in coffee, which is interwoven with the R&D process. However, as this chapter has explored, R&D is not just about flashy new technologies and big new innovations, but also the management and development of a business.

Adversaries or Partners?

Are you in collaboration or competition with your suppliers and clients? A lot of back-to-back business interactions can actually inhabit both of these positions at the same time.

Adversarial relationship in business refers to a situation in which businesses are looking to win against the other business in a given interaction. In a partnership, the businesses are aiming for a quid pro quo, allowing both sides to succeed.

In the adversarial scenario, one company aims to achieve a better deal in the situation by leaving the other actor with a smaller share of a transaction's potential value. At its most extreme an adversarial supply relationship in coffee can be particularly harmful to certain businesses when they are tied into working with that company who is driving the adversarial behaviour. In an open market it means not doing business with those partners, but if a business has no choice to sell through an auction system or a certain exporter due to blocking behaviour, there can be a monopolistic dynamic which leaves them at the mercy of aggressive adversarial behaviour.

There are situations in which an adversarial relationship is a motivating factor for a business to pursue forms of vertical integration, as a way to bypass the conflict. "If we do this ourselves we can avoid this adversarial relationship."

Partnership relationships have the opposite characteristic, as they can allow for two or more parties working in the same direction to achieve mutually beneficial outcomes.

In the Harvard Business review David Frydlinger, Oliver Hart and Kate Vitasek describe the negative behaviours in an adversarial supplier relationship using the term, "shading." Whilst there is similarity here to the discussion in the the *Customer and Supplier Alignment*, in this case the alignment of two businesses does not work due to the assessment that one party has not acted fairly and the outcome isn't what was expected. The aggrieved party reacts to this situation by becoming less collaborative or proactive in meeting the other party's needs.

In the article, which is intended to advise on how to prevent such adversarial relationships arising, the authors go on to outline that companies should avoid the short term lure of opportunistic situations, as they will suffer long term consequences in the quality of the business relationships. They explain that a "formal relations contract" is an effective antidote to this problem. The document puts the quality of the relationship front and centre, and acknowledges that a contract is never fully complete. There is also an inclusion of joint objectives and relationship management processes. In the article they cite a variety of examples, mainly around the pandemic, and the need to work together to properly manage uncertainty for both parties.

Whilst I haven't seen these contracts in play in coffee, I have noticed a variety of methods that mimic this. The most common example is transparent, open book relationships that share the costs associated with a product or service, via a rolling or periodic review around product and pricing. The idea of using this model is that both parties gain insight into a balance that can work for both sides. It does however mean disclosing your business's workings, which is something that not everyone is comfortable with.

An opposite example, looking to address the same concerns, might be a rolling tender process, whereby the client gets several companies to regularly pitch for the business, encouraging an adversarial supply dynamic in which the different companies fight for the contract, so to speak. This dynamic breeds the potential for what we explore in the next chapter - a race to the bottom.

Race to the Bottom

A relatively free market, without strict pricing regulations, will result in a natural state of competition. In this scenario, as long as there are enough competitors, the lowest competitive price will be reached for a given product or service, or for products that appear comparable. This last point is key, it is very possible that products can appear similar that actually aren't in reality.

A race to the bottom refers to a situation in which aggressive competition can result in the lowering of quality and standards, something that follows on from unsustainable pricing. Rational economic decisions are exchanged for strategies with the singular intention of winning the sale. Most often, in this race, everyone loses out. The customer ends up with lower quality products over time, and businesses end up in unviable situations with regards to the sales that they have committed to.

The specialty coffee space has become increasingly mature and competitive around the world. Different countries are at different points in this journey, from those with a young, burgeoning specialty movement, to those with a more developed and mature business landscape, with more competition and saturation. It would be fair to argue that no country appears to have reached a "fully mature" or saturated landscape. When this might happen, or what it will mean are questions that industries like ours should ask but, ultimately this is a "wait and see" situation.

In the UK I have seen a change in the specialty roasting scene as things have become more competitive. Costs have all increased for roasters, but the prices per kilo that are offered to win wholesale accounts, have constantly decreased. A few things are at play here. The businesses that started earlier, have grown and achieved valuable economies of scale. They have sought to grow their businesses by winning new customers, and this has exposed them to a more competitively priced market. This could be characterised as the process of finding the most competitive price, rather than a race to the bottom.

The other players contributing to these lower prices are the new entrants. These could be small independent businesses looking to get a foot in the door, and win enough customers to get things off the ground, or it can be funded entrants who have a fast growth strategy.

In the case of the funded entrants, their goal is to onboard new clients and grow a presence in order to achieve a kind of tipping point. They will use low prices as a carrot, dangled with the intention of breaking an existing relationship and winning a new tender. In this case there is some semblance of a strategy, albeit one built on shaky foundations, as their prices will need to add up at some point down the road.

Putting off the idea of doing sustainable, profitable business has some significant drawbacks. If the business later finds that it can't keep the client when charging a viable price, then there are few options, and naturally temptation will creep towards lower product quality in order to achieve profitability without price increases.

Talking to green importers who work with a great spread of roasters I have heard it suggested that a lot of smaller businesses don't really know their numbers and that they engage in blind pricing. This is not supposed to be a derisive remark, so much as a reality check.

Small, passion-driven, independent businesses typically operate small teams in which detailed, financial analysis is less common. A lot of pricing in this sphere is done based on comparison. "What do they charge? We will charge a similar amount or slightly less." Customers will likely contribute to this, as they will be keen to point out to a roastery the prices that they have been offered by other roasters for a particular spot, such as their house coffee. It may only be later as the effect of the pricing trickles through the business, that it becomes clear that the coffee wasn't priced correctly.

If you add all of these factors together, then you might notice a race to the bottom that most specialty boutique coffee people didn't realise they were part of, because this is not knowingly their objective.

Coffee shops are much less likely to contribute to this phenomenon. If anything, cafés are likely to find themselves in a status quo pricing dynamic, where they are reluctant to move pricing in any direction to save themselves from customer feedback.

Specialty coffee's cupping protocols mean that it is unlikely that lower quality coffee will be passed off for coffee worth a higher price as it makes its way through the supply stream. However, once the coffee gets to a roaster or coffee brand, the race to the bottom is more likely to play out. A roaster or café is unlikely to have regular scoring to assess if their product is hitting a certain value. This provides a stark comparison to a producer being offered significantly different prices depending on a cup score they get. The roaster or café is able to lower quality in the cup as a result of a race to the bottom without it being as easily identified.

Later in the book there is a chapter titled, *Semiotics, Specialty as an Aesthetic*, in which I delve into the expectation that has been set for what a specialty coffee business does or should look like. In a race to the bottom, when talking about coffee brands, the competition is often an adversarial supply situation, in which a client is looking to find a supplier with the correct aesthetic, that signifies "specialty" or quality. This can be more important to them than trying to get hold of a specific quality coffee product at a lower price. These lines can easily get blurred as the buyer needs to have good expertise and knowledge of coffee if they wish to assess what they are really getting for that low, tendered price.

Killing Things That Don't Work

This is crucial in business. The severity of not addressing the need to discontinue the elements of a business that aren't working, will depend on the precise situation, but at its most critical, ignoring this lesson will quickly drag a business under.

Younger and growing businesses tend to explore and try a lot of things out, throwing ideas at a wall to see what sticks. This is a costly strategy if not much sticks, but it's also essential to explore new avenues if a business wishes to identify opportunity.

Before you know it, you can have a lot of products, initiatives and channels that are live. Some will need to be chalked up as ideas that you tried but didn't work out. The reason for this is not just the raw product cost, you also must consider the opportunity cost expended, as your team directs resources and energy into areas of your business that aren't giving much back.

When considering what should be cut, you can look beyond sales initiatives and new products, and include internal processes and procedures. This is really about asking the question of whether you are doing something simply because you have always done it that way in the past. Does it actually work? Is it contributing to the business?

I often come across the concept of "positive failure" in conversation around work culture. This is this idea that it is a positive thing to fail, and that it is necessary. This is true, but more importantly, you must be able to recognise when something needs to fail, before it becomes a burden to the business. This has parallels with the sunken cost fallacy.

One of the best examples that I have heard on this subject was on the WorkLife podcast by Adam Grant. In exploring this topic, he gave the example of a team member in Google X being tasked to explore a hydrogen energy business. The team member built a proposition and concept and then pitched it, and was given the go ahead to utilise a budget to spend a year fleshing out the assumptions and beginning to realise a model.

After one year she came back, and when given the opportunity to present the work she had done, she made the recommendation that the project be shut down. It was her assessment that in taking the project forward and identifying real world costs and risks, that it did not make sense to pursue the project further. This employee was given the largest bonus that year for shutting down her own project.

Clearly, this is not easy to do. Your project is your baby, you are responsible for it and it is very difficult to stay objective. Your success can appear to be tied directly to the project role. To different extents, this is true for all roles and tasks in a business, and this creates a bias, making it hard to see things clearly.

The setup and economics of Google X is of course not relatable for any of us running boutique scale businesses. Big and deep-pocketed companies with a strategy to explore new ambitious projects that may never see the light of day are not really comparable to boutique businesses.

In a similar vein, watching the Dyson electric car project get shut down after hundreds of millions of pounds of investment was quite amazing to observe, but it was not relatable.

Nonetheless, there are clear lessons for us all here. The ability to imagine the business you are in as not the one you are in, is very valuable - to ask those difficult probing questions that an outsider would ask.

Viability questions are particularly challenging to answer if a project or product is new or different. If the project doesn't seem successful on the surface one can ask questions such as "maybe it just hasn't had enough time?" Or "maybe we just need to find a different way to give it a chance to succeed?" Yes, we have all heard stories where an individual or business belligerently kept slogging on, and eventually the business or idea worked, but there's a fine line between a genius idea that just hasn't hit its stride, and a failure.

These ideas are particularly relevant in any field where people are exploring new areas of value, or growing something that exists to be a bigger, more successful version of itself. We all fail, try new things, and make mistakes. The key is to avoid making the same mistake twice, but also to manage the inherent risk involved with explorative business ideas, so that the failure doesn't destroy the whole operation.

On the radical end of the spectrum, there are times when the whole operation just needs to be shut down. I was speaking to a friend recently who has a business that they started several years ago. It had a strong start but slowed down, and now is trundling along. It has accrued debt that it is not able to repay, and their new business that is doing well is propping the older business up.

The question naturally arose as to why they are keeping the struggling business alive. There are of course lots of reasons, these are not easy decisions. They don't want to let the customers or partners down who like and have supported the product. One of their biggest concerns is their team and the loss of their jobs. As is the case for my friend, for founders or owners this becomes a very personal decision, as the business is part of their identity.

The decision is naturally linked also to what other opportunities exist around you. If a business is losing a lot of money the decision is somewhat easier, it will get made for you when you run out of access to debt and are unable to pay the existing debt or running costs of the business. The scenario in which the business can stumble along and does provide some value is more challenging. If things aren't likely to change in this business, then it will have a limited life.

Re-thinking things, consolidating, re-focusing and quitting things that aren't working, are all a natural and integral part of a good business approach.

Prioritisation and Resource Management

This topic is woven through many of the chapters in this part of the book, but also deserves its own chapter. All start-ups and small businesses are likely to contend with stretched resources. There will be a small team who are working across a profusion of tasks.

Tasks that do not have their own department or manager can often be the very fundamentals of running a business, for example a café operator may manage their accounts themselves alongside other tasks. Even as businesses get bigger, they still will struggle to cover all bases.

The chapters on *Deliverable Margin* and *Killing Things That Don't Work* directly reflect on the need to prioritise in business. An ability to be able to prioritise is really fundamental in running a business that is profitable and makes money in any field. Perhaps, with the complexity in coffee this becomes even more important.

Unfortunately, prioritisation is often reactive. When ambition to achieve many things outstrips the ability to actualise those goals, then day-to-day it becomes clear that the goals cannot be achieved and tactical decisions are made to prioritise certain activities above others.

In an organisation, a stakeholder will typically prioritise tasks and activities that relate to them achieving success in their role or project. Over time this can take its toll culturally, creating the feeling that the team is falling short of its objectives on a regular basis. It will also not just be a feeling. In this situation there is likely to be actual failure to achieve meaningful results with clients.

In an overstretched business, it is hard to continually get the prioritisation right, sometimes more than one project needs to be finished and it's not easy to pick which client to let down. This creates an impossible situation from the point of view of business rationalisation and in terms of meeting client expectations.

When a business is constantly spinning too many plates it will create a number of problems that are further reaching than each department making mistakes, resulting in the delay of longer term strategic goals or values being achieved. Longer term projects are always in danger of being shunted down the road if fires need to be put out every day. Sustainability ambitions and wider, company improvement goals are often the first to fall victim to this phenomenon.

Of course, all of this having been said, it is also true that if you are not ambitious, and only ever aim to achieve goals that sit well within your business capabilities, and create a buffer of resources, your company is over-resourced and likely lacks efficiency. In the specialty boutique coffee industry this will very likely mean that you are not profitable.

This is a tough balance to get right. A rigorous and objective rationalisation of resources is necessary in most businesses throughout the coffee industry in order to be both sustainably profitable and to achieve the company's vision.

Unicorns Aren't the Norm - Winner Bias

Winner bias refers to the distorted point of view that comes with winning. When you win, everything that preceded the event makes sense - it was after all, the journey that led to the win. This doesn't actually mean that this can work again, or that it will work in a different context or at a different time. Sometimes the win is pure luck. Right time, right place. And importantly the winner is also normally only one entity in a given scenario, where there were also many non-winners.

On the *How I Built This* podcast, the guests are always an example of a fabulous success story. The best stories often start with individuals or teams who aren't doing very well, and at some point their fortunes completely turn around. Often they are doubling down and their friends and family are worried for them. They are struggling for funding, or losing money. You get the picture. These are against the odds, underdog stories.

At the end of each episode Guy Raz, the host, asks each guest the following question: "How much of your success do you attribute to luck, or just hard work?" Most guests explain that they see it as a mix of the two. There is the argument that hard work creates luck, and there is truth to this. However, we are listening to these stories because they are unusual. They are not the norm. That's what makes them fascinating.

Often these stories are innovation or pioneer based. There are only a few opportunities to be the pivotal business in a specific industry. These unicorn businesses definitely have things to teach us all, but it is worth noting that they are also limited in the lessons that they can provide.

Studying highly successful but anomalous businesses can be dangerous. It can mean viewing a space through the lens of winner bias. Looking at one-off data points and pursuing opportunities that require everything to align in a way that may only happen once in a generation. These businesses come with a much higher risk appetite, and it is easy to forget that many businesses tried to be the same unicorn, but you don't hear about them, because they failed.

This is quite different to studying and understanding replicable business ideas and ways of generating value. By this I mean businesses of a scale and type of which there can be many. Specialty boutique coffee is particularly interesting in this regard. In this boutique space the word community is used often. Specialty coffee does represent a community of businesses, and among them there are huge success stories. But for most of those who are starting out or taking part in the business of coffee, the stories of normal businesses in the space are perhaps more useful to study and understand.

It is also worth noting that outside the unicorn businesses there is segmentation of businesses to be observed in terms of scale and success. The dynamic of the business landscape is not simply normal or unicorn (with nothing between). Perhaps, what we really should look at outside of the unicorn, is what does a "good business" in the industry look like.

"True" Profit

There are a number of reasons why a net profit number can be misleading. Sometimes this can be purposeful, but more often than not, the number simply lacks context, and does not provide a fair comparison. Comparing apples to oranges as opposed apples to apples.

I will explain. In the case of small, owner operated businesses, the founders or owners often don't take a direct salary, or alternatively, take only a small salary (for tax reasons) and then draw down the rest of their earnings as dividends. In this case the salary is not an accurate representation of the job being done. If instead, an owner, who has created a profitable business decides to take the majority of the profit out of the business as salary, the business will show as less profitable, but when benchmarked appropriately, this question of salary should not have an impact.

Of course, in these instances the numbers are true, but these kinds of specifics are why the term EBITDA is used in the world of mergers and acquisition, as it can provide a like for like comparison. EBITDA stands for earnings before interest, tax, depreciation and amortisation. In simple terms, the number is supposed to give an indication of underlying pre-tax profit excluding non-typical expenses.

The use of this term is mostly to do with taking exceptional costs out of the numbers. An exceptional cost refers to a one off cost, something that won't be ongoing. This could be an investment in a new piece of equipment or infrastructure, or it could be some consultancy or marketing that won't continue. Different costs can clearly make a given year very low in profitability for a business, but that doesn't necessarily mean that the business has lost a portion of gross profit or suffered soaring operational costs, rather that it has invested in the business that year. This idea can also be stretched to maximise the visible profitability.

When a company is trying to sell or raise investment, it needs to show its best possible profitability scenario in order to obtain the best sale price/valuation. Likewise, the buyer is looking to understand the underlying mechanics of the business. This will often be a discussion point between the two parties as they go back and forth negotiating the businesses value.

Multi-site coffee shop operations are a good example of the challenges of identifying true profit. In most cases this kind of business requires a head office, the salaries of which contribute to the overall business, but rightly don't sit in any individual coffee shop. A reasonable approach would be to allocate a portion of these head office costs to each café site as an additional cost that hits the bottom line. If they are excluded, but the shop needs the head office to function, then the net profit number per shop is misleading, and is displayed as a higher number than the reality warrants.

Sometimes within a business it's hard to truly identify the net profit per product or client as all parts of the business share resources and cost cannot be simply allocated.

Suffice it to say, seeking to understand true net profit is essential in running your own business, and also in benchmarking against other businesses, if you are trying to understand what the goals should be for a good business in the space.

Part Three. Market Forces

Introduction to Part Three

In *Part Two* my intention was to examine the building blocks and key levers of running a business. I pointed out that nearly all businesses in the market share a similar conception of business foundations. Whilst this may be true, there is a wider landscape concurrently at play, which shapes us all in a multitude of ways. The scope of coffee as a global industry is quite staggering.

A coffee shop operator who is concerned about the local competitors who have just opened down the road, or whether the visitor numbers in their shop will drop with bad weather that's on its way, has coffee sitting in its hopper that was grown and transported by businesses that are worried about the impact that coffee grown in other countries around the world may have on the price of their own crop, and how their government might react to this.

The seed to cup journey for coffee is truly global and this means that it is impossible to really think about the business of coffee without considering the different macro factors and market forces at play.

In this part of the book I will therefore endeavour to look at wider market forces that influence and ripple across the coffee industry.

Macroeconomics

Whilst microeconomics, which are single factors and individual decisions, are more the domain of part two of the book, this short chapter is about macroeconomics, which refers to very large dynamics at play including the economy in action within a nation, and the wider context of how the world's economies all fit together in a global economy.

Macroeconomics are notoriously hard to predict. People build theoretical "models" which, much like predicting the weather, are hard to get fully right. Macro models are complex, and require you to build a predictive model based on a multitude of assumptions that all combine and layer on top of each other. Unfortunately, when one of these assumptions is proven incorrect by, for example, an unforeseen policy change or unpredicted global event, then the whole model becomes wrong by extension.

The C Market is itself an index for the macroeconomic value of coffee around the globe at any one moment in time, and traders and analysts spend a lot of time trying to predict the future outcomes of the market. For the most part, these conversations are typified by speculative and cautious thought processes that try to understand how harvest yields, policy and commercial behaviour will impact price. Even the most experienced traders will tend to caveat their predictions with, "but we can't really know for sure."

Suffice to say we are all at the whim of these macro winds. Many, many parts of this part of this book including quite a few other chapters, could instead be in this chapter. As macroeconomic waves ripple around the coffee world, I am often reminded of the industry's global and interconnected nature.

Innovation

Innovation is a buzzword across all businesses, and for good reason. Innovation has the potential to drive a business's success, and even to disrupt and change a whole marketplace.

There are five levels of innovation that were put forward in the 20th century by Genrich Altshuller, a Soviet Engineer, inventor and writer. His theory spawned a scale called TRIZ, which is based around the theory of inventive problem solving. The scale can be used to understand innovation. I was introduced to this theory by Luke Atwood, a designer who leads on multiple design projects and was formerly a lead designer at Dyson in the UK.

The scale of innovation ranges from a minor industry improvement through to fundamental scientific discoveries that underpin a whole new area of discovery and innovation. Level one on the scale, a standard solution, would be a simple tweak of an existing idea that produces a quantitative improvement, making something slightly faster or bigger etc.

Level two, a change of system, can be explained as a qualitative improvement, and represents the coming together of different functions to create a new product made up of existing functions already seen in that field.

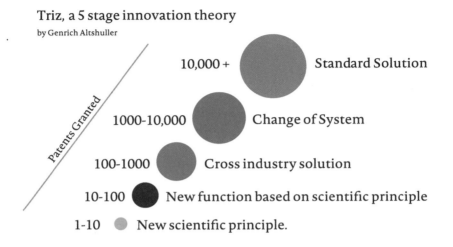

Triz, a 5 stage innovation theory
by Genrich Altshuller

Patents Granted

10,000 +   Standard Solution

1000-10,000   Change of System

100-1000   Cross industry solution

10-100   New function based on scientific principle

1-10   New scientific principle.

Level 3, a solution across industries, represents a cross-industry innovation, whereby a unique function is implemented into a field where it has never been seen before. For this to occur in the coffee industry it would involve applying a technology or approach from another industry successfully into a coffee process.

Level 4 uses a scientific principle to create a radical new function that has never been seen before anywhere and level 5 would be a scientific discovery of the kind of foundation principle that level 4, a solution across sciences, is based on, the kind of innovation that wins a Nobel Prize.

It is tempting to state that the more innovative an idea is the bigger the impact it can have. However, if the invention is too fundamental and novel it may also be ahead of its time, or simply not adoptable in the present moment. This means that even though the idea is excellent and has high value potential, it may not have the market readiness needed to take off. All big innovations rely on customer behaviour to change to some degree, or other structural changes to occur in a market place, before they have the opportunity to be adopted. There are of course more sinister reasons a new innovation may not make it to market. Perhaps it is perceived as a threat to an existing industry in some way.

The idea behind any innovation in business is to identify an area of value. This could be a problem that needs resolving, or simply a facet that hasn't been fully explored by customers yet. This second approach is a classic "they don't know they want it yet" approach.

Innovation based around new "physical things" such as devices, machines and products, is the most apparent from a consumer perspective, however, innovation in business can also be an approach to branding and communication or customer experience and engagement. There are no real confines within which an innovation has to occur.

The ability to innovate successfully in a marketplace can be extremely beneficial. It can drive disruption for a new company or keep an existing company ahead of their competitors. The reason that the innovation chapter has found its way into the market forces section of the book is that an innovation is likely to affect everyone in the marketplace, and not just the company that developed it.

For an innovative idea to be successful it needs to correctly identify value. This is often the result of the curious questioning mind, asking why things are done the way they are, and how they can be made better. Can they be done differently? Perhaps just as importantly, should they be done differently? Novelty for the sake of novelty, is not valuable innovation. Focusing innovation on an area of impact is key.

A lot of innovation comes from a genuine place of experience. "What would I like to see? What is missing that would make my job better? What would be of value for me?" Sometimes this approach works wonderfully. Many other people may have been thinking and feeling the same way. It is equally possible that this assessment can be too personal, and these innovations do not end up resonating with a wide group of people. The ability to see which innovation will benefit a broad swathe of people, or even a whole industry, is a valuable skill.

It is easy to take all of the innovations that have come before you for granted. We are all walking on the shoulders of giants in this regard. With the constant march of progress, it is natural, especially in the inventor's mind, to focus on what can be done differently moving forward.

The mainly internet-based communication platforms that have made the coffee supply chain smaller, leverage communications innovations. This has helped to catalyse the developing understanding of coffee as a culinary product with all the factors that impact quality. This is, in many ways, open source innovation, as the coffee community shares ideas, discovery and understanding about coffee. It has never been easier to learn a lot about coffee.

Of course, a lot of innovation is not open source. The ability to follow an innovative concept along the road of discovery is fueled by money, and therefore is typically privately pursued by a company looking to drive a competitive advantage. This means that although there are small innovations to be had by boutique coffee companies, larger innovations are often undertaken by more substantial companies with sufficient resources. Boutique coffee can explore the opportunity to apply these innovations once they are in the market, rather than attempting to build platforms and formats from scratch.

There is another genre of innovation occurring all of the time in which individuals and small groups create IP (intellectual property) and then seek to licence it to bigger coffee companies or companies that service the coffee market. More often than not, these are inventors or teams who have been part of larger companies. This is not to say no technological innovation is happening in, or for, small coffee companies, but rather that it is less of a hotbed for significant innovation. The innovative thinking in specialty boutique coffee may well be bleeding edge, but the resource to realise these ideas is less readily available.

There is an inherent cultural challenge presented by the combination of innovation and manufacturing. In coffee, many of the businesses who handle the bean, have cultures and systems based around making something repeatedly, day in, day out, year in, year out. The behaviour and approach required to create something new and innovative from scratch is very different to that required to make the same thing over and over with efficiency. The innovative environment is explorative and creative, whilst the manufacturing environment is rigid and controlled. This is one of the main reasons that companies seek to separate R&D behaviour from production behaviour. In boutique businesses the two are required to sit together in an uneasy compromise.

In the ecosystem surrounding apps and e-commerce platforms such as Shopify, the process of innovation can be mutually beneficial. When platforms create and launch new products, this is in the hope that they will be adopted by the community of specialty coffee businesses and customers, allowing both the online companies and coffee companies to gain. A similar journey is undertaken by equipment companies. When they produce a new or updated piece of equipment to be used in the coffee world, they have a potential market of many tens of thousands of customers, maybe even millions.

It is worth noting that the coffee market also represents many businesses who are not attempting to innovate. Many boutique businesses in coffee are operations looking to create an individual version of a business or product that already exists.

There has to be a strong commercial incentive to support and drive technological innovation, something that often gets overlooked. There are many examples in coffee in which the existing technology could be better, but the available improvements would not equate to enough commercial value to support the funds required for R&D. This reality counters the dreams and ideation of what could be possible.

Some of the innovations that we will see in coffee's future will be in areas that we are well aware can be improved, whilst others will be in aspects that we are yet to recognise. In each case they will be successful through the value that they can create. There will be plenty of innovations that won't come to pass, even though they would be good solutions and this suggests that the current technology or approach hits a commercial sweet spot, even if it appears suboptimal.

I have seen some really interesting innovations in development that absolutely make coffee taste better, but just cost too much at the moment. The area of super high-end coffee can support some of these ideas, but the size of this market is small, which limits the commercial opportunity, as will be the case for any innovation aimed at that minority.

A final note regarding innovation and commercial success in coffee is this: just because the innovation works, and creates results, this doesn't mean people will adopt it. Persuading the coffee community to understand and recognise the value of what you have created will always be just as important as creating something good.

Innovation done right has immense commercial value, and is therefore tied to the world of idea protection. The next chapter looks at the nature of intellectual property in coffee.

Intellectual Property

"Intellectual property is something that you create using your mind - for example, a story, an invention, an artistic work or a symbol."
- Gov.uk.

Intellectual property is a pretty tricky topic. I don't intend to delve into the philosophical debate here of what constitutes a unique idea and at what point inspiration veers into the realm of idea snatching and plagiarism, and that's before we even start thinking about the emergence of AI. Instead, I wanted to look at the way intellectual property is enforced (and when it is not) and how it influences business in the world of coffee.

The general premise is as follows: I create something unique and quickly officiate the fact I have come up with this idea or concept by filing for IP. This can be in the form of a patent, which is used in the case of more complex concepts/ideas, or in the form of a trademark, copyright or trade secret.

To achieve this formalised recognition there is a lengthy process, effectively asking you to prove that this idea is novel and unique to you, that is, that no one before you has already created something the same or sufficiently close to your idea. Doing this isn't a small task, the wording that describes the idea is crucial to the potential success of the patent.

Once this process is complete, the commercial value of this IP can be recognised in various ways. The obvious one is it allows you to fight against other companies copying and commercialising your idea. Well, at least, that's how it is supposed to go. Another use is the licensing of your idea to someone else, so they can make it, whilst you retain an advantageous position as the creator. This can be achieved using a commercial agreement such as a royalty or upfront fee to buy the rights to the idea, among other mutually beneficial agreements.

A more Machiavellian approach to IP, one utilised by large corporations, is to register and create IP for the purpose of blocking competitors and other businesses from pursuing an avenue or an idea that could compete in your space. In this scenario you make or buy IP to keep an idea away from the market place entirely. Using trade secrets is a way to protect IP, whilst also not disclosing the idea to the marketplace, meanwhile patents may afford protection, but they also allow the market and your competitors to see a detailed outline of your idea.

How does protected IP flow through specialty coffee? I would argue that on the whole it doesn't really. It is at least, not overly common in the journey of the bean.

Fundamentally this is similar to wine - unless you need to defend the trademark of your brand or something else that is specific to your reputation as a coffee producing business, then in a market reliant on telling authentic stories of provenance and craft, as well as focusing on well established ideas and products, there is little room for patents.

However, even in the case where there is a right to enforce a kind of IP, the reality of enforcing it can be sobering. A lot of IP just simply isn't worth the paper it is written on, and although you may feel safer for having something filed, it is only at the point that you come to try and enforce or defend it, that you will know if it is truly robust and valuable. This is a game of language, and one wrong word can render your patent worthless. The risk you run when enforcing IP is that you will incur significant legal costs without the certainty of winning.

Nonetheless, even though it is not an area defined by IP in the way that biotech and pharmaceuticals are, there are examples throughout the coffee world. IP is most commonly filed in the technology arena of the coffee industry. These IPs can range from an integrated espresso machine scale, to a new way to brew coffee in a centrifuge, and so on.

Industrial processes and format platforms are commonly accompanied by filed IP, such as the Nespresso compatible pod systems, or a specific instant coffee technique. More often than not these practices and innovations are part of larger commercial coffee businesses, however Cometeer's newly developed (at the time of writing in 2023) frozen coffee concentrates, are a good example of a start-up in the space focusing heavily on an IP driven product format. In this case the IP is based around multiple aspects of the preparation of the product. This is an atypical project for the specialty sector, as the funding is high for a first generation boutique product.

An intriguing place where IP has begun to show up is at the coffee farm. This is usually filed in regards to coffee processing techniques. In Colombia, highly experimental processing trends are at their peak, and the line between the influence of process and the addition of flavours is becoming quite blurred. The idea of a transparent, authentic, provenance-driven approach to the raw ingredient is a big part of what makes specialty coffee what it is, making this an interesting, and potentially controversial area where IP is being sought and implemented.

Highly specific processes that kill all local bacteria with ozone, and introduce specific, manufactured bacteria cultures to manipulate and create highly specific flavours, are now being utilised. This requires millions of dollars of investment to instigate and the process is being treated as protectable IP. In the context, this makes a lot of sense, and is no different to the "secret sauce" approach taken historically by many food and drink products.

While, as in the former case, there is clearly protective behaviour to keep competitive advantages secret, the coffee industry also has good examples of open source approaches. In the case of a lot of coffee gear and hand brewing tools, whereby the market is represented by small companies, creating or iterating on an idea quickly, a company's success is often built upon being the first mover in the market, or producing a better version of a similar idea, rather than protective IP. Certain product types have also been in the market a long time, and without a revolutionary approach to the product concept, no IP would be grantable. A company may see an opportunity for a product gap within the market that can resonate in coffee and sell well, without warranting or needing the support of IP.

In many ways the focus on transparency and craft makes specialty boutique coffee quite anti-IP. Instead it is often community-based, and the sharing of ideas and approaches is encouraged. This logic makes more sense for things that can be easily replicated and achieved by small independent businesses around the world, but as soon as an idea or product is ambitious in execution, and the investment required becomes significant, the person/business needs to be able to get back their investment, which is most easily achieved through the opportunity to exclusively commercialise their idea.

A counter to this is that when IP is less achievable, an idea can naturally iterate in the marketplace, and can benefit from increased visibility and market competition. This is a debate that can go back and forth.

It feels to me that although there is creativity and entrepreneurship abounding throughout the coffee space, it is on the whole a marketplace without huge amounts of IP. The boutique space builds businesses instead through relationships, explorative product approaches and branding.

Technology
Functional Technology in Coffee's Journey
All industries in the world, without exception, are influenced in some way by technology. Some industries have been transformed or even eradicated by technological advancements. Coffee has also been transformed by different technologies, however many parts of the industry are also still quite analogue and remain relatively unchanged. By this I mean that, even though technology has influenced and changed coffee a lot throughout the industry, the business remains to be very much based around an agricultural ingredient, its preparation and its consumption.

This is not to say that technology isn't instrumental in the industry. Brazil is the most mechanised producing origin when it comes to the utilisation of technology to farm and harvest the coffee.

However, other origins may begin to gain some ground, and in 2018 a handheld, selective harvester was launched in Colombia. The Brudden DSC-18 harvester has vibrating tongs strong enough to take off red cherries, whilst leaving unripe green cherries to continue their maturation. This has been shown to reduce labour costs dramatically and can help in mountainous growing regions. The price is not too prohibitive either, showing a good sweet spot of innovation.

The reason why Brazil is able to support fully-mechanised harvest is its ability to grow coffee at reasonable altitudes, on relatively flat land. This allows for harvesting to be done by tractors with batons that shake the cherries from the bush. This technique can be calibrated but it still inevitably results in a lot of cherries being harvested at various stages of ripeness. This means that you need to time the passes in the year to make sure you are making the most of the harvest.

More technology is used in the several stages following harvest to help sort the cherries and to compensate for the variability of cherry ripeness. Then following processing, the coffee can be further sorted utilising screen size, LED sorters and oscillating tables, among other technologies. Whilst spending some time in Brazil I was quite amazed to see first-hand how effective this is. My travelling companions and I all had the fun opportunity to hand pick and process our own lots. It was eye opening to find that after meticulous picking and sorting (albeit by us amateurs) that the coffee still had problems picked up by the technology.

Throughout the seed to cup journey, specialty boutique coffee companies often express a negative association with certain technologies and automation, preferring a more manual approach. This is understandable and is linked to the coffee that is most often produced using said methods. I would suggest, however, that an automated or highly technological system is usually not as disadvantageous as it may seem based upon the results that you may have tasted. You have simply tasted a utilisation of the technology that, whether by design or poor use, resulted in a lower quality product.

The same dynamic can be readily observed in the case of a batch brewed coffee versus a hand poured coffee. The batch brewer is often utilised in an environment and operated in a way that does not seek to maximise the possible quality of product that the equipment is able to make.

Back at the farm, mechanical dryers can often be used to dry things quickly and speed up efficiency, meaning that the coffee quality is lower, because the drying temperature was too great. This does not mean that the dryer couldn't yield good results if used at cooler temperatures. It can be argued that the consistency of a mechanical drier ought to outperform traditional coffee drying beds, which show big ranges in heat throughout the day and night.

There are, of course, lower quality pieces of technology in every field that produce poor results consistently. However, as you can see, to properly judge the use of a technology in a coffee's journey, requires quite a nuanced assessment of inputs and utilisation.

Limitations and Mistrust of Technology in Boutique Business
From a business perspective, existing and new technologies are of paramount consideration to all in the coffee industry, however boutique coffee businesses often appear very reluctant to mechanise something that is currently done by hand, simply due to the aesthetic that this creates. When caught in conversation on this subject I always counter with the question: "so your business identity is defined by putting beans into a bag by hand?"

The answer is never an immediate "yes," but maybe this is an important factor in the identity of some businesses (whether or not it should be). A lot of the specialty boutique industry's branding and identity is concerned with fitting a certain business aesthetic. This can come to define these businesses even more than their reported values at times. In this regard, I perceive a lack of confidence in many specialty boutique businesses when evaluating and pursuing the best solution for their business and ethics. This can result instead in an attempt to keep pace with the other businesses that are part of the same "scene."

There are of course other barriers to implementing new technologies and automation in any business. The primary hurdle is likely to be cost. Upfront, capital expenditure is often prohibitive, especially for businesses operating on a boutique scale, and the payback is usually slow. In some scenarios, when a business hits a bottleneck or capacity issue, technology can be a solution to unlocking this, leading directly to increased revenue and efficient payback from the investment in equipment. Even in these cases, the lean net profit of coffee means that implementation of new technologies is rarely easy.

There are also genuine concerns around complexity. Whilst some automated processes are simply plug and play, others can require a business to develop a deeper, engineering understanding to run the equipment.

Using technology for verification is an interesting thought process that is currently being explored, though at the moment the costs are prohibitive. Complex and expensive auditing systems are currently in place to ascertain a coffee farm's level of shade cover (with 40% being the currently targeted metric, considered to help biodiversity on farms). Multiple smallholders in certain countries are already achieving this number, potentially without recognition - technology could start to fill gaps such as these.

Nestle has been looking into satellite usage for mapping coffee farm environments. Cloud cover can make this challenging, and whilst drones could fill aid in the process, suitable technology currently isn't cheap. The danger with some of these interesting technologies is that they continue to be initiatives that can only be undertaken by large, highly-resourced operations, whereas affordable technologies have the potential to create a more widespread impact.

There are also limits and compromises to the extent of what technology can currently, competently offer in place of a well trained and experienced human operator. A lot of the supply chain currently relies on humans tasting coffee. When it comes to complex systems such as this, a trained, experienced human can make a nuanced analysis of multiple factors just through flavour.

Artificial intelligence systems could be used as a technological aid by coffee professionals in a number of businesses. The roastery environment shows the most obvious applications. A roaster will still want to dictate the taste of the coffee being produced, however, data-driven help based upon the variables and running of roasting equipment could prove game changing. At the moment, roasters have to build libraries of data, allowing them to cross reference their previous roasting approaches to certain coffees at certain times. If there was a system that could aid the operator in making the most of their own experience, this would surely be valuable.

Several years ago, certain companies' marketing narratives began to predict the demise of the barista, and the emergence of machine-made coffee, precipitating an existential barista crisis. The argument being made was that, as fully automated systems improved, they would begin to make the role of barista redundant. I pushed back against this at the time, not because I was worried about the potential result of these events or because I thought that this shouldn't be the case, but rather because it just didn't seem likely to me.

Firstly, even though some automated equipment such as Eversys can brew brilliant coffee, any such system will tie the operator into an integrated system. A deconstructed manual brew set up allows the explorative boutique café to swap things around as the coffee community discovers ever new techniques. The café has the freedom to change the grinder, or play around with distribution techniques, start freezing their beans and so on. Whilst there is automation in some parts of their process, keeping the espresso and filter coffee preparation equipment modular suits these businesses.

Secondly, for the baristas, value is found in making something by hand. They have to pay attention to the preparation rather than simply pushing a button. This leads to more engagement in the job role which leads to commercial value in a number of ways. Engaged, passionate staff who take pride in what they do, and are happy to discuss it with customers, will create a very different environment to employees who action push button solutions.

Thirdly, customers are also engaged by the obvious craft and theatre of coffee preparation. This can be taken too far, and theatre for the sake of it, can produce issues. But as we explore later in the chapter on branding, customers are looking for visual and behavioural cues to associate with quality coffee. This mimics other current trends, such as the resurgence in vinyl. Consumers have begun to consider how to balance their increasingly digitised life by adding in areas of analogue engagement. Coffee appears to be an arena that can offer a rewarding analogue experience for those customers who are looking for it. There is also a lot of value to be found in the novelty offered by specialty coffee, which shows itself most at the consumer end of the coffee technology marketplace.

With all of this in mind, I suspect that automation will continue to grow and excel in environments that are not barista led, like an office or an airport lounge, or a less boutique or coffee-focused café. The technology we will continue to see at the pointy end of the specialist coffee spectrum is much more likely to retain tool and device led manual processes that continue to support the game mechanics of coffee preparation.

Despite the perception of specialty boutique coffee as an industry built on manual process, I hope it is now clear to see how technological developments have and will continue to have a significant impact on this area. The coffee lover in me is most excited by technologies that can make coffee taste better at any point throughout the supply chain, technologies that rethink or refine what we already do. The business side of me is excited and curious as to how technology will impact the industry, hopefully making it easier to build businesses around great coffee.

Weather, Terroir and Agriculture

Weather impacts all business, especially when it is extreme or comes unexpectedly. Whilst there is a real discussion to be had regarding the costs of temperature controlling a commercial environment, such as a café or a roastery, the real critical impact of weather in our industry is seen at the agricultural level.

As would be the case with any food crop, the impact of weather patterns on the process of growing coffee is consequential and can result in disaster. At the time of writing this book we have recently seen a surge in coffee prices following a major frost event in Brazil that has been estimated to have reduced the country's annual output by 20%. This is enormous, not just for Brazil, but for the wider coffee industry, as Brazil is the largest producer of coffee, accounting for roughly 40% of global supply. This has created a ripple effect across the industry. Likewise, continuous heavy rains in Colombia have dramatically reduced harvest, in some cases by up to 50%.

The discussion surrounding these events will vary depending upon who you are talking to. Some traders will reference the historical frosts that have hit Brazil, and point out that we have had a relatively stable decade of coffee supply. This new event can be better understood as part of an ongoing cycle. On the other side of the debate, you will hear the interpretation that this frost is only the beginning of a growing series of worrying climatic events, all a result of climate change.

These views are, in some senses, both correct. There have been comparable weather events in the past that have had a similar impact, however, the frequency of these events is highly likely to increase due to climate change.

Climate change is, of course, having more of an impact than just an increase in freak weather events, as it also causes a change in the steady underlying norms of an environment.

The ideal geography for growing a given crop is linked not just to soil and altitude but also to the specific climate, the amount of rainfall, the amount of sun, cloud cover and wind. Since the advent of human agriculture these factors have been tested, and crops grown in more suitable environments.

It is well documented that the Arabica species of coffee is not the hardiest of shrubs, and that environments that are too hot or too cold will be detrimental to this plant, affecting the coffee cherries and seeds it produces. Modern farming techniques can bridge the gap and help create a better growing environment, but dramatic changes in temperature and climate are not as easily addressed.

An ongoing underlying change to an environment's foundations moves the conversation away from weather and towards ecology. The microbial activity and organisms that live in a particular place will change relative to the climatic conditions in that specific location. We will touch again on climate change in the sustainability chapter, but it is clear that the change in climate is a critical concern in coffee, as it is for the wider world and countless other industries. As is the case in English wine, there will also be some opportunities for businesses to exploit, such as an improvement in growing conditions for specific crops and styles of food product. For me, these positive examples are far outweighed by the negative forecasts ahead of us for the climate.

Agronomy, ecology and weather are all inextricably linked. Agronomy refers to human crop production and soil management. When visiting larger farm operations in Central and South America it is common to meet a resident agronomist, who will be involved in analysing and reviewing these factors so that they can be managed on the farm. In many cases this role is undertaken in the capacity of an outside consultant. This person can review and advise multiple operators, helping to achieve better results on their land, just as might be seen on a vineyard or another crop-based business. Smaller businesses don't support a full-time role in this area, but are still keen to benefit from and implement this knowledge.

As explored briefly in the IP chapter, certain practices at the farm level can be considered intellectual property. These would be practices that have an impact on the growing and harvesting of the coffee that have become unique to that operator. Agronomy is mostly separate to coffee processing, though if a farm uses ozone to kill local bacteria, or conversely manipulate microbial and yeast activity from the environment in order to make use of them in fermentation processing techniques, there can be some crossover.

Essentially, there are many questions that are still not fully and scientifically answered when it comes to creating specific flavours in coffee, and these include the ways that this relates to the coffee's natural environment.

Interestingly, the idea of a unique piece of land that creates a unique flavour profile, is a very strong business proposition. Whether it is in regards to agronomy, climate, processing, or another of the multiple factors influencing the farming of the coffee bean, the ongoing question of how to create the most value with coffee, means that these key factors all need to be understood in a commercial sense, as well as part of an investigation of the concept of terroir.

As a coffee producer the constraints and possibilities of a given piece of land are an intrinsic limitation to the business that you run. This has some crossover with the nature of shop ownership. In these businesses, the owner must make the most of their parcel of space, before considering whether they ought to open a second parcel of space or change location entirely. The businesses between the farm and the shop are able to have quite a different mentality as they are generally more scalable and less tied to a location. Each set up still has constraints, but the ability to evolve and scale the size of the intermediary businesses is quite different.

When viewing a business through the lens of limited capacity and size, all thought processes are different. For example, the decision to become a certified business (such as B corp or Rainforest Alliance) will only make sense if the certification in question can benefit the business either through the process of implementation or in future sales. If the business cannot generate increased volume, the investment in becoming certified, might just be an added cost.

Whilst it is clear that there are limitations produced by working on a fixed plot of land, there are also some business benefits to explore. If a coffee farm is able to create coffee with a reputation tied to a specific place or terroir, it can be possible to develop provenance into a brand. This is hard to replicate by competitors who do not own land nearby, and when it works, it is likely the best commercial approach to maximising the value of the operation.

This thought process can be rolled out to the industry as a whole. Being able to develop a brand, leads to the most value realisation. Alternatives revolve around supplying a service or ingredient that may be seen as easily replaceable. This highlights a strength of specialty coffee. This is not just the undertaking of boutique producers, but can historically be seen in the identity of whole countries, and how they are viewed as coffee producing nations.

Just as physical location is a strength for those in the position to benefit from it, it can prove a massive handicap for those who are not. Wine offers a very good comparison in this regard. The recognition of the value of specific regions is a major part of how the wine marketplace works. Those who are not in the "best regions" usually cannot command the best prices for their wine. In wine, definitions around provenance are often now controlled by legal mechanisms, such as AOC (appellation d'origine contrôlée) in France. The benefit of these controlled zones is that quality and price can be regulated, and the market can't be flooded with new products under the same name. This is interesting from a quality point as the AOC encourages the producers within it to work collaboratively, they are essentially operating a collective brand. At the same time, movements in wines, such as the new world movement, have provided a way to explore alternative markets outside of those that had become increasingly strict and narrow.

Ongoing variables outside of a farmer's control are a further weakness of being tied to land. There is not much that an individual can do over time as climates change, government regulation and trading practices are adjusted, trends and preferences change and the reputation of areas and farms fluctuate. As is the case in most of the conversation that surrounds the evaluation of coffee farming business, there is a lot of context required to understand individual scenarios. Saying this though, it can't be denied that weather and ecology directly influence, and to some degree determine, the business opportunity in coffee.

Recent developments in the processing techniques that dominate coffee's cup profile have begun to suggest an ability to create flavour profiles that are less location specific. Where coffee's flavour is produced by microbial activity, this can be replicated in a variety of locations, unlocking flavour profiles with perceived higher value in locations where previously this was not considered possible.

It is my belief however, that any scalable solution allowing flavour to be repeated at many locations will not hold value. The scarcity of a specific profile directly feeds into its potential value in the marketplace.

This approach could help create mid-level, commercial products that fill a gap for fruity flavour profiles, especially if the market of traditionally processed Arabica experiences a supply problem in the future due to both economic and climate change forces (see: *Is There a Coming Divergence?*).

A unique flavour profile, (that people go mad about) tied to a specific cultivar and terroir, ultimately will always occupy the position of highest value. This does not mean that there isn't value to be leveraged through getting more coffees to showcase a given attribute, and moving forward, processing techniques are proving to be a very powerful way to dictate cup profile.

Sudden Change - A Pandemic

Covid changed things. Most of us have never lived through so much rapid change; a global pandemic that resulted in a cascade of societal and economic change that took place over a remarkably short period of time.

Businesses are alive, they are part of our day-to-day lives, and big changes in public behaviour can directly impact whole market places. Suddenly, entire areas of business were shut down, whilst others saw dizzying explosive growth. If you made cycling products, you likely had crazy sales, and spent the ensuing months trying to source stock to keep up with demand. If you organised events, you saw your whole industry abruptly strangled.

Coffee was a mixed bag. Looking at it through the macro lens, it was one of the more fortunate industries to be in, whilst a pandemic took hold. On a business to business level, there was a wide mixture of experiences.

On the one hand, coffee shops suffered a similar fate to event businesses, as crippling restrictions were put in place. Throughout the period, specific rules required shops to transition between opening up for takeaway only, closing completely and managing socially distanced environments. The exact government support varied from country to country.

Whilst hospitality operators were living by their wits, adapting to the ever-changing public restrictions, there were other coffee businesses that revelled in the opportunity presented by such a shake up.

Many café customers found themselves at home, with time,

wondering how they could replicate the boutique coffee they used to pick up from their favourite coffee shop. Quickly, they contacted their most coffee-knowledgeable friends to seek advice on what brewing and grinding equipment they should buy.

Equipment manufacturers stocked out of their products and well-known roasters saw several hundred percent growth in their e-commerce stores. Youtube videos on how to brew like baristas were watched in huge numbers. These customers had gone from buying coffee from baristas to having the time and inclination to learn coffee for themselves. At the same time sourdough bread making was seeing a similar phenomenon take place.

The move to online sales for at home consumption happened across the market, not just for the newly self-trained baristas. Catering and office supply companies had seen their customers disappear. The shift to working at home meant that homes had become the primary consumption point for coffee, whatever the format, from carefully crafted to convenient. It wasn't just e-commerce coffee sales, but also grocery sales that saw this uptick.

For most roasters, this meant that they saw one channel shrink and another expand, like some kind of seesaw.

With uncertainty afoot, businesses rapidly sought to explore the diversification of products and sales avenues to adapt to the quickly changing trading environment. Diversification became the business buzzword du jour.

People would compliment me on my diverse business interests in coffee, as if I had seen COVID-19 coming, but I had not. The truth was that before Coronavirus I was somewhat lamenting the range and complexity of my businesses, and struggling to see the range as a positive. I had begun increasingly to admire highly-focused businesses that did less, and did it well. I was concerned about opportunity cost and lack of focus in the model that I had been creating. This was a stark reminder for me that the perfect model in one environment can be quite the opposite in another.

Restrictions have subsided, and the drastic effects of COVID-19 have softened. Hospitality is, for the most part, back on its feet, and boutique roasters have mostly reverted back to wholesale. They have also typically kept an uplift in their online sales.

It is an interesting thought that consumers are always becoming more knowledgeable about coffee, and one of the pandemic's effects was to trigger a much speedier engagement, catalysing what was already in motion. There is now an increased understanding of coffee as a culinary product, which is a legacy of the event.

The global car market provides a good example of how global supply chains that have been optimised for efficiency and profit cannot handle unforeseen disruption. The supply chain in this industry effectively bases everything around just-in-time manufacturing, whereby there is not a surplus of stock or contingency of parts throughout the industry. Holding stock costs money, hurts cashflow and can create risk. Making things as close to when they are needed as possible reduces this, and in industries that seem stable and constant, this approach is sensible.

When Coronavirus hit, large US car rental firms sold a bunch of their vehicles to release cash, as the economy had been shut down. However, with the international borders all but closed, a lot of Americans started to travel domestically, increasing demand for hire cars. This surge caused rental companies to begin buying cars both new and second hand. Car companies couldn't meet demand, as they had slowed production amid the uncertainty, causing record delays on new cars, and soaring prices in the second hand car market. This type of industry needs to keep moving at a steady rate, and cannot deal with stops and starts, and disruptions.

A similar phenomenon occurred within the global shipping and logistics industry, which, unlike cars, directly affects coffee, as this is the means of transport used to move green coffee around the world. The industry saw an immediate drop in trade at the start of the crisis, due to factories closing down, followed by a surge in demand, for all of the reasons I have mentioned above. This stop-start set in motion a series of shortages, delays and high prices that will continue to affect the shipping market for years to come.

COVID-19, as an event, hopefully will not repeat itself anytime soon. In fact, the pandemic was quickly followed by other macroeconomic and geopolitical events that have quickly overshadowed it. Ask a coffee company what they think about the impact of Coronavirus and they will likely need some time to think back, as their mind space is currently dominated by rising costs and inflation that squeeze their business from all angles. A lot of this inflation can be traced back to the government monetary policy around the world of furlough schemes, grants and similar contingencies, which have created a phenomenon that economies will continue to be affected by for many years yet.

I wanted to include COVID-19 in this book as an example of how major global events can quickly change the way our industry works. It created an exaggerated example of how all businesses are an evolving moving entity at all times. Adaptability is key in all business, and perhaps all of us who have lived through a pandemic, will continue to have the idea in the back of our mind that we need to be able to pivot and change what we are doing when the need arises. Even though our industry can feel like a slow moving tanker that has been on a steady course for a long time, it may also hit an iceberg.

The C-market, Differentials and Currency Value

I think it's fair to say that the C Market is confusing, and often misunderstood in problematic ways.

One such misunderstanding surrounds the relationship between the C Market at specialty grade coffee. In the past I have often heard it said that specialty coffee is not impacted by the C Market price.

Price increases that rippled through the whole industry in 2022 as a result of a severe frost in Brazil showed that this was clearly not true. Although higher scoring, higher priced coffee can be buffered from some price fluctuations, price trends still break through, and in the case of recent price spikes, they have burst through.

The only coffees that manage to be so far removed from the C Market that they appear to behave as a separate market are super premium coffees, sold at auction (that represent a minuscule amount of the world's coffee production). In most cases the price of the C Market, combined with a differential, (something I will talk about later in this chapter) provides the reference point for Arabica coffee of all grades.

To understand the relevance of the C Market in specialty boutique coffee, we need to begin with a more solid understanding of what the C market is (and what it isn't). Most simply, the C Market can be viewed as an index for Arabica coffee as a globally produced food crop. It is a market that represents the rough average value for coffee globally at any one time. It is a reactive market. It is not a controlling body.

The C Market is devised based on coffee stocks that are certified by ICE (Intercontinental Exchange). These are "tenderable grades" of coffee unrelated to certifications such as Fairtrade and RFA (RainForest Alliance). These provide a price benchmark for the trade of Arabica coffees of a certain quality. Coffee perceived to be above that quality achieves a premium price, and coffee below that quality will be traded for less.

The price on the C Market represents the average value for coffee per pound (of weight) in the currency of US dollars. It has been well documented that this price can mean extremely different things in different countries and for different producers and growers, and there is a knock on effect for all buyers and customers downstream.

The price is most directly affected by the mechanics of supply and demand, in just the same way as it would for any crop. If you are buying oranges, the "global" price goes up and down in reaction to events across the market, such as yield at origin, growing or emerging origins and demand in all of the countries that consume the product, in the case of coffee, this is no different.

The factor of "differential" is often overlooked. The C Price is the price traded for a given quality of Arabica coffee across all countries. For a given coffee, this price is always combined with something called a "differential." Whilst this is referenced far less often than the C Market, it is just as influential.

Differential is independent not just per country but also, per grade of coffee in each country, acting at each point as an adjustment to the C Price. Just like the C Price, this differential will vary over time, although it is typically not as volatile. When buying coffee, the differential shows up as a plus or minus number against the C Price.

Lower quality coffee will show a minus differential, and in the case of nearly all specialty coffee, the differential will be a positive number.

This means that when a coffee roaster or shop references the C Price in their marketing material, usually in order to state that they paid a higher price, it can be quite misleading. If the current differential in Colombia was $0.40 per pound of coffee, for example, then the actual market price for a reasonable grade (not super premium) might be $0.88 above the C Price per kg of green coffee. In effect, the C Price, plus the differential, equals the "actual" C Price in that country. A company who pays this price has not contributed more to a coffee producer, they have merely paid the going rate for their choice of coffee.

This infographic from Cafe imports demonstrates the c price with an additional specialty differential per origin. It then demonstrates the average premium that they pay on top of both of these.

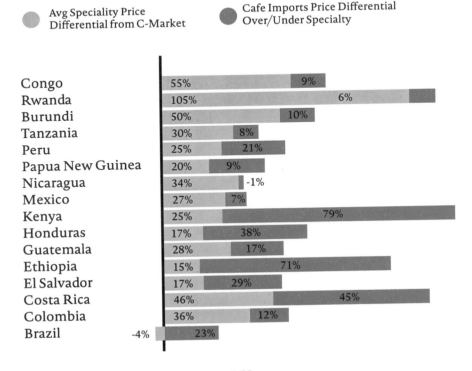

Avg Speciality Price Differential from C-Market

Cafe Imports Price Differential Over/Under Specialty

Country	Avg Speciality Price Differential from C-Market	Cafe Imports Price Differential Over/Under Specialty
Congo	55%	9%
Rwanda	105%	6%
Burundi	50%	10%
Tanzania	30%	8%
Peru	25%	21%
Papua New Guinea	20%	9%
Nicaragua	34%	-1%
Mexico	27%	7%
Kenya	25%	79%
Honduras	17%	38%
Guatemala	28%	17%
Ethiopia	15%	71%
El Salvador	17%	29%
Costa Rica	46%	45%
Colombia	36%	12%
Brazil	-4%	23%

Coffee C Market previous 5 years

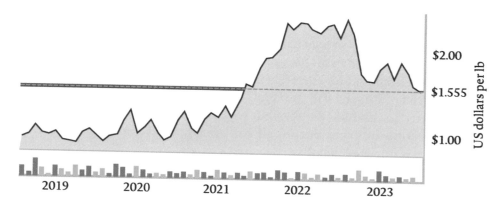

Brazil is the world's largest producer of Arabica, which means that the country has the most substantial impact on the C Price, and that the C Price will likely have the lowest differential attached in Brazil for specialty coffee.

Once you get your head around it, the concept of differential is really interesting. In effect, it shows a measure of flavour and provenance power in coffee. The differential provides an active demonstration of the higher value of some coffee origins. Whilst cost of production, which is typically higher in all origins outside of Brazil, is one factor, this price difference also stems from a recognition that coffees do not all taste the same. If they did, then the C Market would dictate that you should buy all coffee from Brazil. Alongside good business reasons, such as spreading risk, the fact that this does not happen, shows the real value that the industry places on flavour and characteristics of typical profiles in different countries.

Perhaps in a specialty coffee setting, in which a lot of value is placed on provenance, flavour and scarcity, this sounds obvious, but in the context of coffee's commodity pricing mechanism, the recognition of flavour and variation is more surprising. At the specialty grade end of the spectrum, coffees regularly demand prices that are far above the C plus differential price, though often only for rare and unique profiles or exotic flavours and processes.

Unlike C Price, differentials can often be baked into contracts.

It can be in an importer's interest to agree a contract with a producer or exporter with a fixed differential on top of C Price. The C Price is locked in at the point that the contract is "closed." Fixing the differential is a way to lock in the other part of the equation.

So, now we have an idea of how the C Market, combined with the differential, creates the price for a coffee. The other big factor that is required to understand the "real" price that is paid for coffee, is the local currency and its relationship with the US dollar. This is crucial, not just for producers, but for all coffee importing countries whose currency is not the US dollar.

In 2021 the C Price started to go up to highs not seen for many years, which affected all coffee trading. For us, in the UK, another thing happened in late 2022, which was that the British pound fell dramatically in value against the US dollar. The cost of anything traded in the US dollar was going up. If a coffee contract was agreed in dollars and converted into GBP in September 2022, and then again at the same dollar price in April 2023, the coffee's actual cost would have been 15% more in GBP in September than in April.

In Brazil the same dynamic is at play in the currency ratio between the Brazilian Real and the US dollar. The dollar price of the C Market may go up, but if the Brazilian Real starts trading higher against the dollar, then Brazilian producers will hold back from selling as they aren't getting as much for the coffee. Likewise, if the Colombian Peso is weaker against the dollar, then the price can be good even if the dollar price of the C is not particularly high. Of course you can't discuss currency in a given country without also understanding inflation in that country. Essentially this refers to the internal value of the currency, which can be just as important as how it stacks up against the US dollar at any moment in time.

Those in a position to hold a hedged FX position can look to mitigate the exposure to these changing variables. For many though, it's like a ship in a stormy sea, you simply have to ride and react.

Most of the activity on the C Market revolves around something called "futures". A futures contract is a contract for goods at an agreed price, that will be delivered in the future. In other words, coffee is being purchased before it has been produced. Futures contracts can be traded by anyone, which means that actors who have no interest in buying coffee can still trade the stock, potentially increasing volatility and distorting the market. This has an impact on the marketplace, influencing the real coffee prices for those actually doing business in the physical product.

For many of the reasons that we have looked at in this chapter, it can be easy to think about the C Market as simply a volatile price tool that causes problems, but from a commercial market perspective it does have benefits. Primarily, it provides liquidity. The term liquidity references the ease with which an asset can be converted into cash. The market creates an exchange platform that means coffee can always be sold, even if the price is high. During the current price increases, a lot of coffee companies held off from buying, waiting out for a lower price. The C Market meant that there were still buyers, and the industry didn't grind to a halt in a price standoff.

Somewhat muddying the waters, the contracted prices can still be affected by the continued movement of the market. When the C Market price moves too far from the original, settled price, there is a real risk of default, at which point coffee will not be delivered against a contract without some renegotiation.

There is no doubt that the C Market represents both the pros and cons of globalisation. Whilst there is price variation in all supply chains, even in each domestic market, when you link all the world's domestic markets together in one global market, the competition increases, as does the potential for volatility. Liquidity and price discovery (whereby a price is benchmarked against supply and demand) are benefited.

Well positioned, extremely large corporations can impact the value balance of the market, whilst small companies simply ride the ups and downs as best they can. When you combine all of these factors with the impact of annually varying weather resulting in varied yields and qualities of production, you can see that the business challenge is significant.

As we have seen, higher-priced, boutique coffees can offer some protection from all of this volatility, but they are not immune. Commercial coffee operators have to run businesses that account for, and plan around, the varying prices, and utilise financial mechanisms to reduce risk.

In the times of the now defunct ICA (International Coffee Agreement) the market price remained high due to quota systems, but in the current, open market, the C Price is something all businesses in the supply chain must monitor as it has a significant impact on anyone working in the coffee sector.

Government Policy

Wherever you are in the world, if you are working in the business of coffee, state policy will inform and influence the business in some way. Here in the UK, Brexit has dramatically impacted roasteries who had strong customer bases in Europe. Any tax or support policy around hospitality can have a big impact on cafés and restaurants, and those who sell to them. In the midst of COVID-19, each country was keenly awaiting state announcements surrounding how their government would handle the situation. Would they lockdown hard? Would they support businesses that were closed? And so on.

A government's economic policy in a given country will have significant ripple effects. Global markets will either respond negatively or positively to elections and changing monetary policies. This (combined with numerous other factors) will impact the strength of the local currency and cost of finance etc. Much like global macroeconomics, government policies diffuse around the world. Some economies are more shielded than others.

Most coffee producing countries have varying degrees of government intervention surrounding coffee, as it can form a key segment of their GDP. These policies will vary country to country. In Ethiopia, the policies around coffee pricing mean that the country does not price directly against the C in the same way other countries do.

In his article "March Forward, Dear Mother Ethiopia", Coffee industry consultant and buyer, Christopher Feran, chronicles in detail, changes that have affected the Ethiopian Coffee landscape, both in a historic context, and through his own observations based upon his regular visits to the country since 2014.

I urge you to read his nuanced, contextual coffee journalism.

Government intervention pops up regularly in the story of Ethiopian coffee, from the redistribution of land under government ownership, to the introduction of the ECX, (Ethiopian commodity exchange) which prioritised volume and consistency over traceability and separation of lots by provenance. Ethiopia can therefore be seen as a prime example of high government intervention in the coffee industry. These types of interventions directly impact the businesses in that origin, as well as the product that makes its way downstream through the supply chain.

Impact is not just derived from the governmental policies of the country in question, but also the foreign policy of other country's governments. This could be a tax placed on coffee, or it could also be funding driven, such as USAID's promotion of sustainable coffee farming in Peru. This is a strategic policy that is part of a strategy to reduce coca farming for cocaine production.

Perhaps the biggest ever political intervention on a global scale was the signing of the International Coffee Agreement. This was a formalised agreement that used quotas to control supply and demand with the intention of maintaining a stable, higher price for coffee. The agreement achieved just this for 27 years (and for a significant time before the agreement was formalised) before it was not successfully renewed and agreed upon by the ICO and the member nations in 1989.

The ICA was seen as the culmination of a process that started during World War Two. During the war, European markets were closed off and coffee prices were in decline. The United States feared that a declining price of such an economically important product would, especially in Brazil, create communist sympathies. An agreement was struck between the United States and Brazil whereby America would restrict its imports and Brazil would restrict its exports. This was effective in raising the price of coffee. Producers sought to maintain the pricing following the war, eventually bringing about the ICA, which was joined by many countries.

Of course, government policy affects everyone who is part of a global marketplace through the impact of macroeconomics and the interplay between nations. Different policies inevitably affect the constraints within which you can do business. When considering coffee as a business and assessing how a model could work, it is easy to fail to notice the changing landscape created by differing policies.

For example, the idea of vertically integrating a farm business by becoming an exporter makes sense. On paper the business can maximise its opportunity to turn a profit. However, exporting not only requires access to finance, but in different coffee producing countries it may involve a licence that is difficult to obtain. Likewise a farm may wish to build a dry mill, however this is not always so simple. In Kenya the dry mills are tied to government structures and licensing.

I have asked around the industry about whether there is a coffee-producing country with little to no government intervention, and there doesn't seem to be one. As the coffee industry forms a big part of many country's export economies, this is not a surprise. But it does mean that government policy will always be a key part of understanding the business of coffee, throughout the supply chain. This topic provides yet another example of why you cannot be overly generalistic when discussing the business of coffee around the world, and need to apply context to paint an accurate picture.

In coffee growing countries, crops can be utilised as an arbitrage mechanism for governments and other actors to access US dollars, in order to obtain leverage on the international market for importing goods. Where this is the case, coffee is not really treated as coffee, but as a way to access dollars. When this thought process is in play, it greatly changes how the crop is viewed by those stakeholders, as the coffee is no longer seen as a physical crop, grown for profit, but as a currency tool. This scenario creates a similar influence to the traders who use the futures market to make a profit from coffee as a stock, but who are not involved in any real way in the coffee industry (at least where it pertains to a consumable product).

In his book, "Grounds for Agreement: The Political Economy of the Coffee Commodity Chain," John M. Talbot uses the period of time in which the government intervention and collaboration behind the International Coffee agreement was present, to frame an argument for a return to political intervention as a way to address the lack of sustainability in the pricing of coffee as a volatile commodity market.

This feels right to me. From a capitalist globalised position, profitable and economically sustainable businesses in coffee have to be able to weather the supply and demand volatility of the market. Political trade intervention represents what feels like the only way to fully counterbalance such volatility, no matter how unlikely a return to the quota system of the past may seem at the moment.

Colonial and Imperial Legacy - Capitalism and Globalism

The history of coffee is not as ancient as many of the other psychostimulants with which it finds comparison, such as tea and cocoa. Although the early commercialisation of coffee took place in 16th century Yemen, as Gujarati traders sold the expensive seed as a luxury good, this small-scale, luxury market was not long lived.

Colonial powers started planting coffee in subtropical lands around the world. Slavery was used alongside colonial and imperial rule to commercialise the growing of coffee at scale, bringing the price down. This was clearly a form of colonial extractivism.

The legacy of colonialism can be seen throughout the world, and is easily spotted in countries that grow coffee, that were once colonies of foreign empires. There is a strong argument that the influence extends far further than is easily observable. It is one thing to document the history of the colonial empire around the world, quite another to look at the residual impacts that feed into the way things work today. I asked different stakeholders in coffee what they think the ongoing impact of colonialism in coffee is.

Whilst this discussion will, as much in coffee does, vary country to country, one of the most visible and obvious legacies can be seen in land ownership structures as well as socioeconomic opportunity. The way land was not only colonised but then re-distributed following the exit of colonial powers still informs the land ownership dynamics at play today. Beyond land distribution, socioeconomic positioning of different people in society informs the economic opportunities. This is seen in all global cultures, but can be stark in certain post colonial coffee regions in which land ownership remains to be in the hands of descendants of colonial settlers, whilst workers often are descendants of those once forced into slavery, as well as other natives of those places.

I am writing this book as a white, privileged European man. Whether through education or global networks, being born in a given country and into a given part of society impacts how the odds stack up for you in an area of doing business. Through access to education and networks comes access to finance, and business opportunities throughout the wider market providing key advantages in this (and any) industry. Speaking the English language, in which this book is currently written, also creates an advantage in accessing and maximising opportunity in key strong markets.

One wonders how today's market compares to the colonial trade system of coffee. As coffee is grown in so many countries, and is freely traded on the global C Market, you can argue that it is now an open free market in the same way as oranges or sugar cane. The industry is open to a global economy. Whilst this is true up to a point, and within considerations of different, potentially restrictive, government policies, the globalist, capitalist market place that is widely pervasive today is a legacy of colonialism. There remains an uneasy balance of power in global trading dynamics in terms of how suppliers and buyers are in a position to negotiate and manage their position.

Coffee was really not grown on much of a scale before it became part of colonising agricultural behaviour. Enormous coffee programmes imposed by imperial powers caused coffee growing to become embedded into the complexion of many countries. Even when colonial powers eventually left, the dependency on coffee has remained. Reliance on this business activity is entrenched for many individuals.

Multiple macroeconomic factors within each country play into how the country and its governments and people will look at and work with coffee moving forward. In most cases coffee continues to present an immediate and ongoing cash crop. Colonial imperial countries are still the main consumers of this crop - effectively the economics of exporting the coffee is a trade between the same countries.

The wider consuming market is inclined to achieve the lowest price. Whilst a country like Brazil may have invested in equipment to make the most of its topography, achieving economies of scale and a globally competitive price, in the majority of coffee producing countries, the price competes with cheap labour and a lack of viable economic alternatives. With all of this in mind, it is reasonable to conclude that the colonial power dynamics of trade, and the affiliated impact on price, are still at play today.

As well as these historic structures that remain in place, there are newer business behaviours and attitudes that link to this history. A lot of specialty coffee companies tell a story of helping coffee farmers and producers as part of their marketing, and it is true that there is good work happening, based on considerate thoughtful buying practices that seek to address some of the industry's in-built problems.

However, some actors approach the supply chain with a white saviour, post-colonial guilt, approach. Ironically, this is typified by a lack of respect and consideration for those working at the farming and processing end of the chain, whereby a coffee buyer may tell a coffee farmer the actions that they should be taking in order to resolve and address current challenges. Although, on the surface, this may be well meaning, if the buyer in this scenario does not have requisite expertise and experience, then the suggestions are unlikely to be helpful and can be damaging. On this note, even when coming from a person who does have a breadth of knowledge and expertise, unsolicited, interventionist ideas are not always welcome or useful. In all business, where the external advisor isn't at the coal face, they do not face the risk incurred by the ramifications of a suggested change.

This is a complex topic and one I personally have been trying to understand better. The globalisation that we are a part of is clearly a mixed bag. It can be argued that the idea of a free market works better in some markets than others, and there is evidence that it doesn't work optimally for all involved in the coffee industry. I realise the limitations of this chapter. In choosing to write a book that touches on multiple large and complex topics, inevitably some depth is lost. In this case, as with others throughout the book, I recommend looking at further reading and sources to continue to develop your own understanding.

Much of this chapter has been about coffee as an overarching industry. Specialty, as I have mentioned elsewhere in this book, is not a separate industry or an alternative supply chain, rather a higher-priced, premium version of the same product. Just as specialty is influenced by the C Market, it is influenced by globalism and coffee's historical legacy.

Addressing these challenges can seem overwhelming for a small company. There are limitations to what can realistically be achieved on a boutique scale. I think that acknowledging the mechanics at play is key, and that pursuing and practising respectful and considered trading approaches should be a primary goal for any specialty coffee business.

The term "ethical" is flung about a lot in the coffee space, and businesses often seem to have very little evidence to support the claim. The coffee may be a specialty scoring lot with a price tag that reflects its quality, but this doesn't denote ethical treatment (see *Greenwashing*). Whilst I don't think it is easy for boutique companies to meaningfully address these complexities, it is also up to each company to ask questions about the reality of what it is attaining and how this aligns with claims it is making on its packaging.

In the penultimate chapter of the book I look at this idea of a potential coming divergence in coffee. My suggestion will be that the market simply has to change due to underlying problems such as those discussed in this chapter. This is tied to an imbalance in the prices and risks associated with growing coffee, including specialty grade coffee. Even as economies develop, and opportunities arise in subtropical countries, the livelihood of coffee farming continues to, for many, be linked to empires of the past.

A Global Community

Specialty coffee is often described as a community. I think this is absolutely true. The community referenced by this turn of phrase is built on a common passion for coffee. Coffee is a product that connects people from different cultures around the globe, it is distinctly international.

There is a global community of people who either work in, or are passionate about, coffee and who connect with one another at trade shows, coffee competitions and online. The most obvious way that the global industry connects is through travelling. Boutique companies are usually keen to visit and better understand the origins they source from, and likewise producers and exporters who are able, often visit cities or regions where they have clients. Coffee shop and roaster culture also produces a number of "destination" brands that inspire or inform travel choices.

Specialty coffee customers typically identify as curious people in search of experience and quality. I did a lot of travelling before I got into coffee, and although it was challenging and interesting and valuable, and afforded all of the perspective and experience that travelling should, since joining the coffee community, travelling has taken on a new dimension of connectivity and enjoyment for me. The global network of coffee enthusiasts and passion driven businesses means that I can touch down somewhere in the world and connect with people and place around a shared interest in coffee.

It isn't just a human connection that this global community encourages, it also impacts the business of coffee. Community naturally creates a cross-pollination of ideas and perspectives on what coffee can be, and travel allows us the opportunity to see these ideas actualised through coffee business. In this way, the global coffee community encourages the spread of different ideas and approaches to coffee. Coffee shops and barista communities regularly share techniques, and equipment companies often tap into this viral community to share their inventions and developments. An ongoing domino effect has seen coffee storage and preparation trends spread around the world, and an often meteoric uptake of new cultivars and experimental processes. This is not to say the global coffee community shares all of the same tastes, and the success of certain ideas can still vary greatly from culture to culture.

Many specialty boutique coffee roastery brands find themselves shipping to a host of international destinations every month. In my roastery, the plan to focus on an international audience was borne from the unexpected global interest in the book that I co-authored with Christopher Hendon, *Water for Coffee*.

When working with premium products, it is common to see a smaller sales rate in any given market. This is not a problem, just as long as their small segment of interest is part of a large enough market to support the business. There is a history of premium brands choosing to be based in large cosmopolitan cities, where there is a high population density. This means that the large available audience provides a good amount of trade, even if it is a very small percentage of the population. It has long been the case that the most expensive coffees such as auction lot Gesha, have the most demand in Asia.

There are many different examples of how this global community functions and is evolving all of the time, as different countries and markets change in different ways. Anyone working in specialty boutique coffee will notice the global community having an influence on their business, in some cases more overtly, and in others, quite subtly.

Market Differences
Whilst we have explored how many themes and business influences spread around the globe, there are also clear differences between different markets. I am writing this book with an openly disclosed UK market bias, as this is the part of the industry that I predominantly work in. I do connect with and work on some business projects in other countries. I have also sought insight from a wide range of people and companies around the world whilst researching and writing this book.

Although the levers and themes of the coffee business run worldwide, there are differences in what works and why. There is a recognition that the business of coffee farming varies dramatically around the world. The downstream businesses can often be grouped together more collectively, but they too will vary country to country. This results in different tactical approaches to running each business. These differences range from the established business landscape, the competitors and saturation, through to the specific customer preferences for drink formats and flavour profiles.

Part Three. Market Forces

Throughout the supply chain we all use certain metrics to discuss volume. This could be the price of a pound of coffee, a carga of coffee, a container, a tonne or a kilo. Volume is often misleading if you don't understand the average price per unit of volume. A company that can achieve twice the price for the same unit of volume, only needs to sell half the amount to achieve the same revenue.

Take something as seemingly trivial as the typical espresso baskets in use in a market place. The typical espresso basket is directly linked to the dose of ground coffee used for each coffee made. This, in turn, impacts how many kilos of coffee a wholesale client would purchase to achieve their weekly in-shop drink numbers. This impacts the tonnage the roastery sells, and therefore the volume of green coffee they purchase. As you can see, a small difference can reach all the way back through the supply chain.

A simple Instagram survey that I conducted, supported my anecdotal experiences of a significant difference between the UK and Australian markets. Both café markets are heavily driven by espresso based drink menus in cafes. In Australia many operators use 20-22g baskets, and in the UK 16-18g is currently more common. For the sake of simplicity let's say that this represents 21g vs 17g of coffee used per double shot. The difference in volume of coffee used per double shot drink is close to 20%. This is clearly very significant, and will have an impact on the two markets, and the businesses within them.

The UK and Australia share an interesting similarity, they both have high instant coffee consumption. These countries have both had a relatively recent coffee revolution, although Australia's specialty movement predates the UK. The UK has seen a mass move away from a tea drinking culture to embracing coffee consumption, both on the high street and at home. This is in stark contrast to a market like the USA, in which filter coffee has percolated through the culture for many generations.

Volume of coffee drunk per capita in a given country will obviously play into the commercials and business in that marketplace. Growth and increased popularity of coffee in large markets where typical consumption was previously low, such as China, has caused companies worldwide to attempt to figure out how they can trade in the market.

Ideas surrounding emerging, growing and saturated markets are of course important, but, in this chapter I am more interested to touch on the fact that there are underlying market and cultural differences due to systemic variance in market behaviour, particularly in terms of customer engagement and consumer trends.

From a coffee flavour point of view, preferences are often debated with regards to factors such as fermentation and roast profile. There are clear consumer preferences regarding which flavour profiles are more desirable, and preferences for sweet, bitter and umami flavours differ around the world. This thought process could bring us back to the early chapter in which I questioned how the consensus around quality can vary from place to place.

These variances don't have to be exclusive to a given country either and often can be mapped out regionally. When speaking with Kyle Rampage, co-founder of Black and White coffee based in North Carolina, he pointed out to me how the demand for and success of cold brew varies significantly as you traverse the large country in which he lives. He noted much higher sales of cold brew in the north east than in the mid east. Though it may not be quite as marked, we do see regional variance in consumer habits in the UK as well.

As we have begun to do in this chapter, one can play a game of picking out differences throughout the industry in perpetuity. The influences that create these differences are multifaceted and complex and can start to bring in some of the levers and topics that we have discussed (and will continue to discuss) elsewhere in this book such as: government policies, trade relationships, economics differences, tradition and culture. The lesson for me is that to understand business in a given environment, you need to observe and understand these differences in your product and circumstance. A rule that applies to one aspect of coffee business, can be null and void in a different context.

Timing and Trends

Timing is key in all business. Almost all businesses are part of a market, shaped by a variety of trends and habits. These markets usually have other players operating within a similar space. And, as we explored in the last chapter, there are also global trends that travel through the specialty coffee community, and influence businesses and consumers in this area. These factors will all determine when a business might find success. Many big success stories, that we see held up as exciting case studies, have something in common: they got the timing just right.

I was once fortunate enough to head out to Silicon Valley and spend a week with Kevin Hartz, the founder of Eventbrite, now a publicly listed company. Kevin was an early investor in many well-known Silicon Valley success stories. At the time he and his team were looking at starting an online coffee pod business.

Getting an insight into Kevin's world was fascinating. He has hundreds of investments of varying sizes, and he spent a lot of his time at his home office in the early hours of the morning working on these. Thanks to my jetlag, I had the opportunity to ask him some questions at 5am, which he kindly answered. I noticed that his portfolio contained all sorts of weird and wonderful founder led businesses, and that they showed a higher ratio of failure than success. When discussing a particular business that hadn't worked, I asked Kevin "can you pinpoint why each business fails?".

Kevin explained that one could ponder if it was the limitations of a founder, or the team, or a strategic misfire, but that after twenty years of doing this, he wondered if more often than not it was simply timing. He has seen enough examples of concepts that failed at one point in time, but which then succeeded when launched by another business only a few years later, to support his thesis.

A friend of mine, Steven Dick, has a small group of coffee shops in Milton Keynes. He used to hold a commercial role at Virgin Active, where it was often recited "we don't want to be the first mover, we want to be a fast second." The inference here is that being the first mover is fraught with challenges, and the inevitably of getting many things wrong. Getting traction for a new concept also requires a good deal of heavy lifting. This all creates a lot of risk. Coming into the market second means that you can be quick enough to capitalise on the new opportunity in a space, whilst skipping a lot of the mistakes.

Trends in business move surprisingly quickly, and before you know it, a new market trend can move from being burgeoning, to growing and then to saturation. It is commonly noted that if you see a "new" trend being adopted all around you, you are probably too late to enter that market.

It would be fair to say that trend and novelty have an important role in the business of coffee, across the industry, in both commercial and specialty coffee, whether in the advent of cold brew, the emergence and adoption of the flat white, or the fruit bomb fermentation techniques of Colombian micro lots. From a business perspective, there is a huge incentive to be aware of trends as they happen. Large, established brands need to make sure they don't fall behind. They need to have a product pipeline that keeps them relevant and successful. In the case of a new business, awareness of trends in the market can allow them to start with impact and a unique brand position.

The boutique end of coffee is interesting in this regard. It seeks both authenticity and integrity, but its success also grew from the seed of being different and new. Some of the values at play in the space are exploration and scarcity, which creates a natural breeding ground for novelty and trend.

I did some work for a very large coffee company that was using an internet listening tool to try and identify the next consumer trend. They had noticed that their bestselling products and concepts were no longer coming from their product development team's ideation sessions but were organic trends that had emerged from the independent specialty space, later catching on in the wider coffee space. They wanted to speak to different people, to sense check the terms the computer chucked out, and to make sure that ad spend wasn't skewing their results.

There is a recognition that runs all the way from the most boutique spaces, to coffee's commercial giants, that trends are important in the coffee industry. Ours is an evolving marketplace, and the consumers' relationship with coffee is something that is changing and evolving over time. For the businesses that get the trend and the timing right, success will surely follow.

Part Four. Values

Introduction to Part Four

Specialty coffee is, on the whole, a space with many individuals and companies that share the intention to do something of both quality and integrity. Boutique specialty coffee has the potential to demonstrate the ability to run sustainable businesses, but this is also often confined and has its limitations.

In *Part Three* we looked at several market forces that impact the industry as a whole. These forces feed into coffee's commercial landscape and what it means to be a stakeholder in the industry. There is an inevitability in global economies and commodities. Countries that drive the model economically are the best placed to maximise on opportunities, whilst other countries, less desirably placed on the global competitive leaderboard, have less control over their part.

As we have explored in previous chapters in the book, multiple factors feed into how a business can be competitive in a given space, and there is an ongoing question of how to make coffee profitable and sustainable for all stakeholders.

I also use this section of the book to challenge and critique some of the claims that exist as part of value based branding and marketing in the space with topics such as transparency and greenwashing.

The values we see advocated through the business of specialty coffee are not just based around supply chain equitability. Coffee is a global community, and this circumstance highlights a variety of ethical and moral topics that all similar industries should consider. In this chapter I look at some of the key values-driven topics that either have been, or are increasingly becoming central to the consideration of how to do business in coffee. Values in coffee are at play both upstream and downstream in the supply chain.

What is Ethical Coffee?
Discussing ethics, morals and values in all businesses and all industries is important, however, it makes me very uncomfortable when I see coffee branded as ethical coffee. Ethics are at play everywhere. There are many moral questions across society on which there is no agreement. The same is true in coffee. There really

is no such thing as "ethical" coffee, as specific ethical constructs surrounding coffee are not agreed, and therefore you cannot claim your coffee is ethically compliant, as there is not a set of ethics agreed to comply to.

In most cases, the term is being used in reference to some form of equitable supply chain, or a support of more disadvantaged groups and individuals. It is a very valid point that many smallholder coffee producers around the world live below the poverty line and as we have looked at, scale is a major barrier to making it economically viable to farm coffee. This problem is not solved by a specialty coffee that has earned a typical premium if the available farmland is simply too small. In the coming chapters we will look at the ability to achieve claims made on pack, but the term ethical coffee is ultimately unachievable either way.

Each brand has made certain decisions about how it would like to source coffee because, let's be clear, that is nearly always the narrative non-producing country coffee brands are referencing with a pitch like "ethical" coffee. There are more and more brands in non producing countries focusing on what they are doing in their own business with culture, team and local community, however, in these cases the coffee is not described as ethical. The ethical narrative from many non-producing country brands has postcolonial and white saviour messaging and thought processes, the perspective we touched on in *Colonial and Imperial Legacy. Capitalism and Globalism*. There are clearly different challenges to growing coffee in different countries.

In some cases the challenges are more business-driven and in others they are definitely more moral. In the context of a certain supply chain in coffee, a more appropriate way to convey the choices the brand has made is simply to communicate them. If the company chooses to work with only smallholder farmers then they should say that, and make sure the statement is appropriate in relation to the supply chain the business actually uses. The reality in most cases though, as we look at in the *Greenwashing* chapter later in the book, is that many independent boutique businesses are using blanket terms as a catch-all approach to buying some specialty coffee, without considering the supply chain in any depth.

A major challenge in narratives around the coffee supply chain is how sweeping they are. Not only is coffee grown in a huge variety of subtropical countries, but there are vastly different setups and situations to consider. Specialty coffee often paints the coffee farmer as a stereotype. Whilst there are undoubtedly many smallholders producing coffee who are accurately reflected by the narrative of farmers struggling to make coffee growing stack up, the majority of the super high-end, boutique producers in Latin America, are very well resourced businesses. Farms such as these are often owned by the owners of several other businesses, allowing a strong access to funding and with strong brands and good access to the market because of a privileged position. It would, for example, be odd to buy a premium wine and describe it as ethical.

I think these producers focusing on excellence are a great thing, and I am in support of these successful businesses. It is highly valuable to ask how, from a business point of view, more agricultural businesses and individuals in disadvantaged positions can be supported to develop similar successful coffee growing business models. The same narratives are at play throughout the supply chain, around small and craft versus premium luxury. It would also be fair to make the point that the majority of coffee grown and sold over 80 points is not from a wealthy premium producer. There are multiple dynamics at play in boutique specialty coffee, which means that we have to be careful, in each case, to properly frame what we are actually talking about.

Another challenge here is that in claiming one thing to be ethical, there is the implication that "the other thing" is not. Larger estate farms that pay above legal minimum or local living wages and produce commercial and specialty coffee at scale are not inherently unethical. They are not small and boutique, this is true, but that doesn't make them unethical. Not respecting autonomy of other countries is often a problem of white saviour behaviour, broad ethical messaging can be disrespectful in this way.

For downstream coffee companies there are some challenging ethical aspects of working, with a variety of international political considerations. One such ethical quandary is around the concept of boycotting. Any supply chain that considers doing business with certain companies and individuals over others, based on a set of criteria, is essentially performing a type of business withdrawal, which is a soft form of boycotting. A more direct form of boycotting in the coffee supply chain would be to withdraw from business with an entire country as a way to protest and refute the behaviour of that country's government, such as discriminatory laws or human rights violations. Equally, a form of boycott can be explored directly on the grounds of a bad actor intervention in that country's supply chain. The conundrum here is that in pursuing a coffee buying boycott, you may be making a stand, but you are also choosing to not support the farmers and growers, who are not behind those policies, and are directly negatively impacted by the boycott. In the case of a coffee business boycott, I think there are often other options that can allow a business to find the most constructive way possible to still buy coffee.

Any claim of impact must be contextualised. I believe that contained quality-driven business stories are highly important and should be celebrated, but should also not be used as an example of widespread impact.

Often, in this part of the book, I am digging into the grey and challenging nature of discussing ethical topics in coffee, which leads to questioning several positions that can often get taken in specialty coffee. But please don't get me wrong, I am in favour of pursuing and promoting equitable supply chains in all industries, and particularly in coffee. The difficult questions and conversations are often the ones worth having.

There really are some wonderful projects throughout the supply chain that look to understand the specific industry dynamics in a given region and work on ways of doing business that support sustainable coffee growing. This can be done both economically and environmentally across the supply chain, top to bottom. For specialty boutique businesses downstream to be contributing to an improved coffee business landscape upstream, it is my view that we all need to endeavour to better understand the supply chain and what constructive solution can look like, whilst showing respect to the different businesses in the supply chain, and also abstaining from making broad claims about ethical superiority.

What is a Fair Price?

Perhaps this should be reworded as "what is a sustainable price?" The subtext when addressing the concept of "fair" or "right" price is that the price achieved needs to not only not be loss making, but also needs to make enough profit for reinvestment to optimise the business, and to pay owners and workers a "reasonable" income.

Fairness is a tough concept to discuss when broaching terms of profit and making money. One person's reasonable profit is another person's excessive profit, and trying to draw a line will open up a can of worms around political beliefs and how people think wealth should be accrued and distributed within a societal system and economy. One sensible way to approach this topic within the coffee world could be to benchmark different businesses in the same industry, much as we did at the beginning of the book. In addition, we must build an understanding of the concept of a living income for a given country or region into any calculations we make when discussing the topic.

Let's say we agree on a 20% net profit goal for a business, build in reasonable references for labour and create a model around this. We would then need to project various business scenarios regarding scale and customer spread to fully understand the cost of production. There are many business factors that impact the price and profitability that one business can hope to achieve. Chapters such as *The Cost of Production, The Impact of Scale*, and *The Sweet Spot - Volume and Price* all reference that the price that "works" for a given kilo of coffee of the same quality, and the price that will be paid, is variable across businesses. The dynamics of specialty coffee also demonstrate that there is an achievable premium based around cup quality.

Differentials (a structure that I talk about in the *C Market and FX*) also allow for a different achievable price per origin. For every origin there remains to be a variance as to what price will work for a given farmer. Caravela released a white paper in July 2019 titled, "A Study on Costs of Production in Latin America" in which they benchmarked the cost of production across several Latin American countries in which they work. They utilised a three hectare farm model operating at a high efficiency of 30 bags per hectare. In this study they clearly demonstrate that plot size is crucial to having a sustainable coffee growing business. At one hectare there isn't a feasible per unit price that works. At three hectares with high efficiency there starts to be a more plausible business income with an individual farmer. In the majority of countries where coffee is still hand-picked, to manage the harvest labour force and quality, a business around 30 hectares looks quite optimal in scale, and has the ability to be quite profitable at market prices and more so with a specialty premium.

In these examples the solution, paralleled by my wine friends, who told me that if I started a vineyard and didn't have enough land that I wouldn't have a business, is a focus on minimum viable farm size, with resources around consolidation of land to hit these tipping points,

Pricing is a really interesting dynamic in coffee, particularly specialty coffee. Many boutique importers found themselves in the position of being price setters in the market a decade ago, meeting producers, cupping the coffees and suggesting pricing for the different lots. This has completely changed, and now, in almost all cases, the producers are the price setters. This is a great change, it demonstrates there was an area where producers could benefit from market awareness, and that there has been a big improvement there.

Climate change and volatile weather patterns completely change the price that "works" and with both heavy rainfall and periods of drought having huge impacts on what a sustainable price looks like. Farmers are beginning to model these impacts into their business forecasts. Essentially, if your land is producing less coffee because of climate, then the minimum viable plot requirement increases, and the price needs to increase.

Access to finance and government lending support in different countries will also dramatically change the potential opportunity and profitability of a given agricultural business.

The challenge of pointing out the wide variety of context is that I worry it can result in a defeatist attitude. My intention is to point out the contextual realities around understanding viability in coffee business with an aim of improving the conversation, not avoiding it.

For businesses downstream trying to understand the upstream business of coffee, they will need to put in the work to learn and understand the business dynamics of the suppliers they are buying from in the countries they are buying from.

I think for coffee brands looking to build equitable supply chains and display an understanding of the coffee's origins, they need to build a contextual supply chain policy that understands the different variables per origin and per grower type. Too often I hear roasters and coffee brands pointing out that this complexity is too much for them, and also that it is too complex for their customers. This attitude is highly problematic, and in this case a company should not be referencing what it is achieving in its supply chain if it is not putting the work in. It is fully aware of the limitations in its own approach, and has not endeavoured to fully explore the topic to the best of its ability.

Although specialty coffee can achieve a higher price per lb, and does offer business opportunity, the ability to build a sustainable profitable business at the farm level is a business challenge that cannot purely be solved by a downstream brand buying specialty coffee. In several countries, commercial grade coffee can and does produce profitable businesses with correct scale, location and operations. For a coffee brand that wants to contribute as much as possible, and to make claims about how their business is addressing challenges in the supply chain, there are specific concerns that can be remedied with buying behaviour, mainly by committing to fixed pricing and volume across multi-year contracts.

Benchmark pricing still has value in the industry, as it encourages all stakeholders to discuss pricing with context, but collaborative buying models, such as the formal relations contract referenced in *Adversaries or Partners?* are more desirable in most businesses where they can be achieved. A farmer may not wish to tie into fixed pricing, and may wish to speculate against a market if price is likely to ascend. Obviously, this comes with higher risk, and for this reason, a hybrid approach, combining these two concepts can also be desirable.

Part Four. Values

Transparency, Traceability and Direct Trade

The concept of ethical or sustainable coffee has often just been a moniker for pricing, rather than a holistic reference to business practice, particularly in specialty boutique coffee.

A typical narrative given by a business may be the following: "we focus on transparent sourcing and pay a premium for great coffee." Another might be, "ethically sourced, direct trade coffee that pays two times the fairtrade price." The first statement seems fairly representative, depending on what transparent actually refers to. The second statement sounds impressive on the surface, but has a few things I would like to pick apart. I think it is misleading.

To justify a claim of transparency, the roaster could say that the coffee is either traded directly with open pricing or that the supply chain is clearly traceable back to the farm or grower. The value that is placed on this idea is based on a deliberate rejection of the lack of transparency that occurs through many traditional supply chain mechanics. These have occurred, not only due to a lack of industry or consumer engagement, but also due to the challenges that come with a global market. Lots of coffee from various smallholders and farmers are often blended into regional lots or country specific grades such as Brazil Santos or Colombia Excelso making the beans much less traceable. These products allow commercial companies to source coffee of a certain profile in volume year on year.

There are a few potential benefits to transparency. In the first instance it may better be termed "traceability." This refers to the ability to trace the lot of coffee back to a specific piece of land. The desire of specialty coffee to pursue this sourcing approach, isn't just linked to ideas of fair trading, but rather to a culinary focus on provenance. If you are interested in understanding and experiencing the specific flavour characteristics that a specific provenance can create, then you must avoid losing the coffee in a generic, graded blend from a country or region.

Parallel to traceability, is an added opportunity for growers to realise a higher potential price or value for their coffee. This relies on the coffee being of higher quality than the average of the larger lot or region. Traceability in and of itself also has commercial value, a

174

single estate lot of the same quality as a regional or blended lot will cost more. There is also a potential commercial benefit of cutting out some supply chain stakeholders, although this can also increase other risks.

The key here is that the coffee needs to be good. This is why the second example of a statement made by a roastery sounds questionable to me. It would suggest that a higher price was paid, but for the same kind of coffee and to the same kind of producer or grower that would otherwise be receiving a lower price. In this case that isn't what is happening.

I presume however that the roastery is referencing a premium specialty coffee, which is not the same as a coffee that would warrant a baseline Fairtrade price. This is a coffee of a higher value, and in buying it, the roastery is not addressing any issue surrounding lower prices in commercial coffee. They are partaking in a transaction at a higher price, for a higher priced product. If the coffee was not purchased by this specific buyer, it is likely another buyer would have paid the same amount.

As I mentioned in the last chapter boutique specialty producers in our maturing marketplace are more aware of the value of their own products than ever before. After different companies in coffee identified a problem with market pricing knowledge and introduced an effective solution, the problem has become less prominent. In this case the obstacle was making sure that premium prices are paid for high-quality coffee. Now this is really the key claim to success that specialty coffee has: it has, and will continue to have, contributed to maximising the market for premium coffee. It is creating routes to market that allow coffee to achieve a quality premium.

Specialty coffee's price premiums are not, however, solving an industry wide pricing issue, it is just a widening of the boutique end of the market. Yes, if the market for specialty grows, this will have an impact, but specialty shows no signs of becoming the dominant type of coffee traded. To this end, it is frustrating that this type of claim is so often made across specialty coffee. You will not hear the high-end wine industry claiming that it can address issues around the prices paid at the low-end of the market. Similar to coffee, cheaper wines are more susceptible to global price fluctuations and are more likely to be presented as Fairtrade or equity conscious wine.

There are exporters, green traders and roasteries that have identified opportunities to increase value in a particular growing area, or to improve a coffee's route to market and sales network. The Cup of Excellence programme effectively helps connect producers with buyers. Again though, this needs to be rare, high-scoring coffee. There is an argument the programme can have a knock on effect in the country, though many dispute the reality of this.

Some roasters and or importers have invested at mill level, which can help to improve a farmer or producer's coffee quality. This can be a quid pro quo business relationship if managed correctly. For a roastery to do this they need to be operating on a certain scale and profitability, or to have good access to finance. If you look at boutique specialty coffee as an industry though, these examples appear to be the outliers. Boutique coffee generally is too small, and most roasters in the space can't undertake these kinds of initiatives. It is also arguable in many cases that it isn't their place to do so.

Smaller roasteries and cafes will always need to rely on industry networks and structure to achieve anything within the coffee supply chain. In this sense the green exporting and importing companies are the true backbone of specialty coffee. As we have touched on earlier in the book, these green companies are the banks of the industry; they finance the whole movement. They typically have the buying power and access to the market to commit to multiple lots from growers and producers, for which they then find an audience. They take on a lot of risk, and many of the narratives and stories specialty roasters tell about their coffee's origins are only possible because of programmes created and implemented by exporting and importing green companies.

Actors within the specialty boutique scene are often surprised to learn of the impressive programmes that are run by many of the multinational coffee companies. Nespresso is, in particular, very impressive. I have witnessed this first hand as part of a Mozambique project I am involved in. The company has a policy of contributing resources in new or re-emerging origins, whereby they put experienced personnel on the ground, free of charge, with no commercial obligation, and no request of anything in return. This wider play to support the coffee industry is clearly impactful, and it makes sense that the larger corporations are better placed to create this kind of initiative.

When it comes to making claims of traceability and transparency in specialty, there is quite a bit to unpick. There is no singular platform upon which specialty coffee is "transparently" traded. The majority of the trade can be characterised as a series of individual business transactions, which are typically product and relationship based.

This will all begin with a buying assessment made by an individual, whose decision is based on coffee quality and either a first hand experience of the origin, or a verbal description made by a stakeholder close to the coffee's production. Typically the way this coffee's information makes its way through the chain to the roastery or café is via marketing materials that outline the specification of the coffee, and a description of the grower or producer business.

In this instance there is a well meaning chain of information, but nothing more robust. There is no requirement for verification or audit of this information, so it is typically a chain of marketing information that has been passed on.

Now this is a generalisation, and please take it that way. It seems fairly typical to me. but there are also more robust initiatives and intertwined relationships at play in specialty coffee. Algrano is a Swiss software platform that allows the coffee farmers and small roasters to connect without passing through the green traders that traditionally sit in the middle of the relationship. This definitely achieves more directness, which doesn't necessarily mean it is the optimal sales route for all different businesses in coffee.

There are also roasters that are committed to buying from the same producers regularly, and have been in a buying relationship for many, many years (this is also often the case with many non-boutique and non-specialty, commercial enterprises). There is clearly some transparency in these relationships, however, even then in most cases a financier (likely the green trader) is still involved, so this is not direct trade.

When talking about the merits of direct trade, I would note that, in my experience and in my research, importers are not piling on a huge profit, as we can see from their GP and net margin referenced earlier in the book. They can only seek to achieve large profits through scale. Bypassing the green traders and importers does not necessarily mean that you give more to the producer or farmer at the end of the chain. It simply means moving things around and often comes with negative consequences, as green traders are set up to do their job well.

On a similar note, whilst direct trade would, on the surface, appear to be good business for a roastery, it will require access to finance, and accrue risk. In addition, selling directly to roasters who can't fill a container increases logistical costs to the producer, costs that they would not incur selling direct to a green importer who can move more volume. On this same note a producer starting an importing office in a strong consuming country is achieving a more direct route to the roaster and this is the other more direct route at play that has become more common. Multiple producers explain that they have taken on more challenges in doing this and that there are many benefits to utilising an importing partner instead.

The logic regarding consolidation of a container here is no different to why it is better business for my roastery to sell coffee in full cases that fill a full pallet. I can make more profit on that coffee at the same price per unit if maximising a shipment. Breaking that order up and selling it in many different cases to different clients and locations costs a surprising amount.

Direct trade does not need to be solely profit motivated on either side, there are, of course, lots of good reasons to have a direct connection with your supplier.

It can give both ends of the supply chain an opportunity to learn about and better understand each other. The connection between people is valuable and important.

Multiple producers and exporters I have spoken to have outlined a desire to agree multi-year contracts at fixed pricing. Without this kind of structure, the roaster is simply another client buying in the same way that a trading house would. So it can be the case that offering a differentiated, collaborative buying model is not necessarily about direct or transparent procurement, but rather about the type of commitment and buying relationship that is possible. Words like traceable, transparent and direct don't guarantee this.

So in essence, I want to bring into question what transparency is solving. Is transparency the goal? Or is it a tool that can be used as part of an endeavour to build sustainable supply relationships.

It is becoming increasingly common for specialty boutique roastery businesses to publish price transparency reports in order to signal the "fair" prices that they have paid for coffees. A common issue with such a report for a roastery sourcing programme, is that the prices are all FOB (freight on board), and even if they are not, different coffees in different countries make their way through to market in different ways and have different associated costs that are not shown in the report.

Does the report change the prices that are paid for coffee? Who reads the reports? How are they assessed? When considered in this light, the transparency report in coffee appears to be in danger of providing more benefit as a marketing asset for the coffee brand, than as an equitable proof document.

Perhaps the most common criticism of this transparency report trend around pricing is that it is often lopsided in terms of expectation. The same roasters who use and publish transparency reports do not tend to break down their client accounts and disclose commercial prices and agreements that they have agreed for each of their customers. I don't expect the roastery would want their clients to see the different deals they have agreed, as there is a lot of context in each relationship, informing the pricing that is in place. Through this process the roastery would also be displaying their commercial relationships to their competitors. However, they request this transparency and disclosure from their producer partners. And with all of this, the farmer or producer may not be receiving a contracted multi-year price or committed volume in return.

The marketing benefit for the roaster is also not necessarily clear cut. The end consumer likely doesn't fully understand the pricing, and only those in the industry who have good knowledge of green buying will have full context. The highest marketing value is likely proffered when tendering for a B2B account that has a CSR initiative, for which this may tick a box.

I can't help but feel that the pricing transparency reports themselves don't really address the underlying mechanics to which they relate around acting as a proof of equitable business interactions. I think it is useful for other businesses in coffee to be aware of pricing, much of my book is about improving understanding of the business and economics of boutique coffee. Pricing transparency can support this, but the prices I see are what one would expect depending on the current market.

There is of course a lot of energy that goes into debating how to prove these numbers, with suggestions of potential use of blockchain and other models. Although it is 100% correct to question how verifiable claims are, it is also worth asking whether stakeholders should spend lots of money, time and resources to verify a transparency initiative that actually appears to have limited impact.

Price is not the only transparency and traceability criteria in coffee, though it has become one of the most prominent ones. An open business culture can have many benefits, and transparency of process, values and intent is laudable. I think traceability is clearly a key criterion of compliance, and a food company should be able to provide reasonable traceability that the thing it is selling is what it claims it is. Specialty coffee talks about a lot that cannot actually be proven. At the moment it is easy for a boutique coffee brand to make a broad statement such as "transparently directly traded ethical coffee." An industry peer of mine challenged teams in companies with slogans such as these to each, individually describe the exact meaning of the statement. The question is of course rhetorical, as most will not be able to agree internally what they mean exactly, let alone share that defined meaning with customers.

Many people I speak to in specialty coffee who have been in it a while are wondering what their goals actually are. Many sign up to be part of a movement that presents itself as a cause achieving certain things. After working in the industry and questioning both the methods and the goals, some are left wondering whether their loud mission and goals are often simply hot air. Terms like direct and transparent have been adopted in the movement and it is right that there has been a lot of cynicism attracted by these claims.

The intention to do work in coffee with integrity and consideration of equitable business relationships is highly positive and I don't wish to suggest otherwise. Transparency as a basic concept is, I believe positive, and one of my goals with this book is to help make aspects of how the industry functions more open and transparent. Knowledge and information surrounding pricing and transactions has benefits for all stakeholders if it can inform how to run a better business at each level, but transparency in and of itself is not the solution.

Impact - Specialty Versus Commercial Coffee

The definition of specialty coffee, and by extension, commercial coffee is tied to scoring. The idea is that if a coffee obtains 80 points, it has reached the specialty threshold. A 79 point coffee, however, has not. This line in the sand has always felt odd to me, I would rather that we didn't have it, and instead recognised the situation for what it is - a gradient of quality. Without getting too far into what scoring represents from an industry wide point of view, what is clear, is that scoring is impactful.

I think naming and categorising coffee below that line as commercial, and coffee above that line as specialty has created a disproportionate perceived separation. Couple this with the perceived superiority of specialty coffee with regards to ethical impact, as well as flavour, and you can end up with a good versus evil narrative at play that isn't particularly useful.

I have been in coffee for many years, digging into and trying to understand how coffee works, and to me this separation is a misrepresentation.

Hitting a sweet spot of volume and quality is the goal in all coffee businesses, regardless of where they sit on the spectrum. A higher quality product does not necessarily lead to a more sustainable or profitable business. Something that is referenced over and over again in this book is that boutique premium food products cost more to make. There is not a parity with a fashion label's ability to raise the value of a low cost fabric.

It is true that if you are able to produce boutique, high-scoring coffee, and perhaps more importantly, find a sales channel and resulting customers for it, then you should expect increased revenue opportunity per gram of coffee. Perhaps more importantly, this gives you a point of differentiation that helps you to achieve a business that is at less direct risk of the fluctuations of wider supply and demand in the market.

There are geographical specifications that will help to achieve higher scoring results, the "terroir." It is sometimes overlooked that this applies equally to efficiently grown, high volume coffee. All different costs that are part of seeking a boutique sales channel also have a deliverable margin challenge. If the coffee is sold in smaller lots, and doesn't maximise efficiencies, these costs all come out of the FOB price.

In most countries, it is pretty easy to supply cherry to a commercial mill. It needs to be this way, as a bigger commercial market requires a lot of cherry. Colombia, for example, is known for having a very "liquid" coffee economy. There is a higher density of mills located around the country who will buy cherry on the day of picking. During the higher prices of the C Market in 2022, many growers elected not to go to the trouble of milling and preparing their coffee, and instead simply sold their cherries, avoiding added cost and time.

In all of this, I do not mean to imply that large mills do not produce 80+ point scoring coffee, they do. There is a higher volume of 80+ coffees coming from large multinational coffee supply chains than most people realise. The reality is that the coffee industry as a whole is much more connected than branding narratives around commercial and specialty make it appear. Specialty, as a "labelled" market, has been growing steadily over the last 20-30 years.

The 2022 jump in the C Price (not the first by any means) meant that the C Price combined with differentials went above the premium base amount that many specialty roasters and or green importers had set over the past 10 years.

To clarify, not all coffee makes the C. It is important to reiterate that the C is not a minimum but rather a global value average.

Lower grade coffees will have a minus differential on the C Market.

A market for all coffee is important. It provides the opportunity to sell coffees of varying grades, all from the same farm, so that producers can maximise their land, growing at different altitudes and on different soils, and not waste any coffee.

Specialty coffee is the boutique, premium end of the marketplace. It is not an alternative market, and it is not separate. Once you have recognised this fact, the following question becomes crucial: how much impact can specialty coffee really have?

The truth is, it is inherently limited. High-end specialty coffee that rewards quality will always be the pointy end of the industry. If, theoretically, the whole market could move to better coffee, the specialty boutique end would simply shift and continue to be differentiated. If Gesha was the norm, it wouldn't be special. Delicious, yes, but differentiated, no. Oversupply would bring the price back down.

In reality this can't happen as coffee is a geographical product, and there will always be a wide range of terroir and therefore quality. This means that there isn't enough specialty coffee to be truly impactful on the scale of the whole industry. It is true that advancements in processing and cultivars could increase potential coverage and opportunity for specialty premiums, but the extent to which this could happen is still highly speculative and as above, the lack of differentiation that could happen in any wider production of specialty limits its adoption relative to market appetite. Essentially the growing opportunity is limited by market demand and not just production.

There will not ever be the same size market for specialty boutique coffee that there is for commercial coffee. The increased price of specialty coffee limits its adoption. There is a strong argument that specialty is already starting to become a little stretched across the growing number of boutique businesses, as it is just a small part of the coffee pie. The global market continues to want commercially priced coffee.

Looking at any market and saying that the people producing a lower value product should all move to the higher value version is ridiculous from a supply and demand point of view. The only event that will cause all coffee prices to go up will be a shortage in supply (not an increase in quality). It is most likely that Robusta production would also increase to fill this need. However, with climate change Robusta will be affected too.

It is clearly the case that there is not a high cash profit margin in any of the seed to cup businesses, and for there to be more money at a growing level, the price of the cup at the end of the journey needs to also be higher. The natural follow-on question: do customer prices need to go up? In *Part Eight* of the book we explore the price of coffee in more detail in *The Price of a Cup of Coffee*.

I think specialty is still exploring its price ceiling, but it has also been starting to see its limits. It's pragmatic and realistic to predict that there are thresholds to pricing of any product sold in volume that are not far away from current prices.

In summary, commercial coffee represents a significantly larger part of the market - most of it, in fact. This in turn means that any ambition to impact the sustainability of growing coffee, whether it be based on prices or environment or other sustainability goals, needs to actually be focused on commercial coffee as well.

As with many statistical topics in the world, the larger picture often gets lost, hidden under individual and anecdotal stories, which are more relatable. Specialty coffee particularly focuses on telling small-scale, individual, contained stories. There is a lot of value in doing this, but it can also cause us to miss the wider picture. In essence, all farmers can (and do) create different grades of coffee product. The market opportunity varies for each of these products depending on competition.

Specialty is, as we have explored, not lightyears away from commercial coffee, and the commercials are all quite close together, especially when contrasting 80+ point coffee with high 70 point coffees. As we explore later in *Is There a Coming Divergence*, this could change if supply changes.

There are, and will continue to be different operators in coffee growing, just as there is throughout the chain, and indeed in all other industries. Different businesses exist to cater to different parts of the market. It is true that as a small operator it is very hard to compete in the commercial or commodity coffee market, and the dynamic around where you focus your business in the marketplace ought to be based on your strengths and weaknesses, some of which are inbuilt and some of which are decision based. For this reason, it makes sense for smallholders to focus on specialty coffee grades, rather than competing with commercial scale operations.

Certifications

There are multiple certification bodies in coffee, and boutique specialty coffee has mixed feelings about them. As is the case with all compliance-based initiatives, the businesses involved have to undertake some amount of work to implement the certification and become a part of the verification programme of the individual certification body. This means that if the certification is an agricultural certification aimed at coffee farming then the producer must undertake the necessary costs and work to become certified. In this chapter the certifications I will mostly be talking about are third party programmes, this is a separate topic to internal programmes run by an individual business in the supply chain.

The value of certifications gets heavily debated. They have an unenviable challenge! How do you create something that can only achieve a lot if it requires a lot of its participants, but that is still accessible for everyone to take part in? Certifications are always an opt in. How can small businesses take part if participation requires resources, infrastructure and cost? None of this is easy.

It is worth starting with Fairtrade. Fairtrade started as the ICA came to a close. With the end of the quota system, Fairtrade sought to address the volatility of the competitive market, and to provide a price floor that prevented the lowest prices. The certification also provides a premium for development projects, and prioritises multiple other behaviours for improved coffee business.

It is important to point out here that Fairtrade is seen as a commercial coffee certification body, and not a specialty coffee mechanism. Specialty coffee achieves a premium for its quality and this means that in most cases the Fairtrade price is not desirable for a specialty producer. There are specialty grade Fairtrade coffees, and theoretically, a really low market could still make that premium desirable, as specialty pricing is not as far above commercial coffee as many people assume.

In 2011 Fair Trade USA split away from Fairtrade International based on differing visions and ethos of how to achieve the most impact. Most recently the two organisations took a different approach to the minimum price. With inflation and growing costs, Fairtrade International increased their minimum price per pound significantly, whereas Fair Trade USA decided to maintain their price due to concerns that too high a price could dry up demand. This particular point illustrates the challenge at hand. Certifications are not a market wide regulation or policy, so they need to compete for sales, which means that like specialty, the impact is limited by the market share that can be achieved based on company and consumer behaviour. Importantly though, Fairtrade is largely focused on achieving impact in parts of the market where the higher priced specialty coffees do not.

In the UK market one of the most consumer-recognised certifications is now Rainforest Alliance, which is focused on a variety of farming practices based around sustainability, and which has a premium attached, rather than a specific price floor. Many producers speak positively of Rainforest Alliance as it is not overly onerous, and the result for them is positive. It is, at the same time, limited in what it achieves.

Conversely, the Smithsonian Institute Bird Friendly Certification is considered the most stringent certification in coffee. It is a certification based on ecological goals. For a coffee farm to achieve the certification, many highly specific criteria are required to be in place (from shade management and structural diversity, to polyculture and organic certification). The conversation about how much a certification body stipulates, is at the core of how much adoption the different certification bodies can achieve. If a certification is very stringent and precise, many farms and producers will not be able to take part (or will not want to). However, if the criteria are too loose and broad, then the certification will not have enough impact or value to be of interest to the industry and consumers.

I do understand why, when a customer in a boutique café asks if the coffee is Fairtrade, that the question can be hard to answer. Simply denigrating the programme can be the easiest way to deal with that conversation for roasters and baristas, but this doesn't seem appropriate or constructive.

Evaluating certifications from a business standpoint is useful in understanding how and why business in the coffee supply chain may or may not adopt them. Most of the time, there has to be a positive business impact of some kind for an individual business to consider and take part in a programme that adds cost and uses resources. Beyond paying for an audit or a membership fee, internal systems need to be put in place and paperwork is required to be able and ready to have an audit. Being able to prove that things meet certain criteria always costs a business money.

At our roastery, we made the decision that we wanted to pursue achieving BRC (British Retail Consortium) food compliance. We did this in order to begin a new partnership. The process cost us tens of thousands of pounds in resource, team time and physical alterations to our facility, and the partnership was for a new product with no existing sales. This meant that at the time of investing, we were spending money, but had no increased income to show for it. Even if the product turned out to be successful, it wasn't likely to be of sufficient size to make the investment economics stack up. In this case, we were hoping that achieving this level of compliance would open up more business opportunities to us in the future.

With this in mind, imagine that you are a producer who has a fixed plot of land. You are managing to achieve a decent yield and a productive quality spread. You already have routes to market and clients for your coffee. What would be the commercial incentive to undergo certification? It would need to result in an increase in the value of your coffee. Or similar to my roastery certification, it would need to stem from client demand and an opportunity to spread your client portfolio at a time when that was useful to the business.

There are of course longer term commitments to sustainability that mean a certification could be a part of a company's vision.

A coffee farm may wish to commit to various sustainability initiatives based on its desire to build and run a sustainable business. The main incentive is not always commercial, but you also cannot ignore the commercials. It is also important to note that you don't necessarily need the certification body to be sustainable, a certification body is simply a third party verification of the things that you may already be doing.

This is perhaps why specialty boutique coffee businesses are less interested in the use of certifications throughout the chain. The stakeholders on the seed to cup journey are smaller, and the stories and initiatives for each farm or co-operative are more individual. This all makes sense, but also can mean that you run into problems of potential greenwashing or unsubstantiated claims. Trust is the only mechanism in place. In a commercial world, this is a flimsy thing to fall back on unfortunately. This dynamic leaves specialty boutique coffee in a strange place. It is an area where technological advancements could, perhaps, fill the gap in auditing and verification of claims.

The popularity of B Corp certification amongst existing and new specialty boutique coffee companies shows that there is a desire amongst these companies to explore a means of verification for working in a considered and positive way, and to get a stamp of approval for the values that they wish to represent. It is also true that pursuing a certification such as B Corp is not done only to prove that you do something you already say you do, but rather as a way to commit a company to a process of evolving and improving. B Corp, in particular, is presented as a framework within which you can run a better company. Although B Corp has some supply chain elements, it is more of a company behaviour programme that builds checks and measures into company culture and commercial behaviour, as opposed to a supply chain verification. Organic certification is perhaps the most straightforward certification, although like all of the programmes, proving you are adhering to and meeting requirements 24/7 is challenging.

There are internal certification initiatives within large companies that can be very impressive, though they are naturally met with scepticism, as the process could be conflicted and open to bias in a way that a third party verifier is not. A different problem for those taking part in this type of programme is how they tie you to one customer.

As we have explored in this chapter, it costs money, resources and energy to put in place any process and qualify for a given compliance programme. In these cases all of this is being done for one client, and if that client doesn't purchase, then it represents a lot of work for nothing. All companies are recognising the need to have more robust verification in place in their company as part of doing business with a wide range of clients.

I often wonder if the specialty aesthetic behaves as a certification of sorts in the customer's mind. When buying boutique coffee from a business that registers as independent and quality-focused, the customer may infer that the business is run well and has a considered supply chain. This obviously is not robust, and as many businesses begin to utilise the specialty aesthetic in a hollow way, this assumption can be problematic. There's probably some kind of study to be done here to figure out whether, on the whole, brands with these narratives are achieving better outcomes, even if with a lack of certification or verification.

The discussion around what certification processes can and cannot achieve continues to be a current one that is worth considering for specialty boutique coffee, especially at the larger more scaled end of the space. I think there will be more programmes and initiatives put forward, maybe not full certification bodies, but technologies and processes that allow verification of claims and participation in certain goals based initiatives.

Sustainability in Coffee
Whilst sustainability as a core concept does recognise the need to meet economic needs, sustainability and business often have a fractious relationship, and a challenging alliance. The often referenced four pillars of sustainability are:

Environmental
Economic

Cultural
Political

I used to offer coffee courses in the downstairs area at our shop in Bath. The courses often served the purpose of being a gift for a curious, explorative, hard-to-buy-for partner or friend. I found it to be a correlation that the people who came on the courses did all sorts of interesting things in their day jobs. This was great for me, I got to meet a lot of interesting people, and I felt guilty in some cases, that I was learning more in the session from them about what they did, than they did from me about coffee.

I once had a coffee course student whose day job was at a sustainability NGO. They advised large companies like PepsiCo on improving their sustainability. I peppered the student with questions about achieving sustainable solutions in food agriculture. They pointed out that you need to achieve solutions that consider and benefit all the key fundamentals of sustainability, rather than only addressing one of them. Not an easy task at all. The two fundamentals that typically compete are economic and environmental goals.

A great example that they had been involved in was potato farming in South America. Every 3 years landslides would cause the farms in question to lose their entire crop. A mapping of the root systems across the land showed that it had been over-farmed and lacked diversity of ecology. Root systems that had previously helped stabilise the land were gone.

The result of the project was to instigate a diversification of the ecology in the area. Whilst this meant that the farms had to plant less potatoes, by reducing the regular catastrophic landslide events, the reduction in the ultimate output per hectare was compensated, and the average production yield over a period of several years hit a higher average. It was quickly pointed out that a scenario like this, in which everybody wins is not commonplace, although one can compellingly argue that all you would need to do is stretch the timeframe out for this to be true in all cases, due to the onset of climate change. Volatile weather patterns and an underlying environmental change are certain to hinder the long term success of most agricultural crops.

We have talked about price at length throughout this book. Price and economic sustainability continues to be the predominant pillar of sustainability that demands attention in coffee. Without legislation, it is natural that the decisions being made around biodiversity and environment will be driven by microeconomics. The focus on price still takes the spotlight. Culture and politics will also be a focus of attention in certain coffee producing origins, either through government intervention, or political and disruptive cultural change.

All this having been said, if you could make coffee farming more profitable, would there suddenly be a focus on more environmental sustainability? The answer is clearly "no." An abundance of growth in more profitable industries has clearly not transitioned the earth to a biodiverse, permaculture haven. Whilst lack of profit may have hindered the ability to explore and implement sustainability initiatives, the presence of profit tends to deliver the same result in all industries, for a business the natural behaviour is to protect and maximise that profit.

For these reasons consumers and businesses look to find other ways to prioritise sustainable practices. These can be third party certification programmes or, as is becoming more common in larger corporations, the development of their own internal programmes. There are limits to these systems, such as internal commercial bias or simply ambition. This isn't to say that some of these structures are not beneficial and constructive.

It is unsurprising that companies can sometimes fail to self-police effectively, which brings to mind the question of legislation and government policy as a means to enforce adoption of sustainable practices. At the time of writing this book there is a legislative process underway in Europe. Businesses are preparing for "the regulation on deforestation-free products" that will come into effect in the EU. The policy is focused on wood, cattle, soy, palm oil, coffee, cocoa and rubber. The regulation will put the onus on the business that imports the product, who will be responsible for demonstrating that the product does not originate from land that was deforested after December 31, 2020.

Interestingly, I think this will be a shock for independent, specialty businesses that at least at the moment, often appear unaware that this policy is coming into place. Larger coffee companies are all allocating resources and energy, developing processes and changes that will allow them to be online and ready as the enforcement comes into place. Once the law is in force, smaller companies will be given a longer window to comply - 24 months rather than the 18 months allowed for larger companies. Countries will be graded from low to high risk, and proving an area of land is not breaking the regulation will rely on GIS mapping location data, and the production of polygon mapping.

From a carbon footprint perspective, there have been many lifecycle studies looking at the impact of a cup of coffee. A life cycle study simply maps the journey of a given product from its inception to its end of life, and potentially its continued use in the case of a reusable or recycled product. For products with a long winding journey to market, these studies can provide perspective on where their point of most impact is.

Carbon is only one metric of course. There are many other environmental considerations such as deforestation, water use, or plastic waste created. In addition, carbon footprint studies are always based on a model, and the inputs that were used can be fallible, so of course one needs to consider this.

Contrary to wide perception, small craft operations are typically not efficient models, and likely have higher footprints per unit made than larger companies within the same industry. In coffee the two ends of the supply chain typically are the biggest carbon creators. This is coffee farming, and coffee brewing. Transport between locations in shipping containers is a relatively efficient and low impact part in the chain, and roasting and packing are also not substantial, although this can depend on the setup.

Brewing typically has high energy consumption due to the boiling of water. With this in mind, the brewing formats that have the lowest footprints are those that maximise yield and can therefore use less coffee per cup made. Instant coffee produces a very high extraction from each gram of coffee used, and therefore does this better than any other format. I am referring here to commercial instant coffee and not boutique instant, which is actually one of the most energy consumptive methods.

I am somewhat surprised at the lack of focus on efficiency and reduced footprint at the brewing end of the coffee industry. Better grinders, more efficient brewing systems and reduced coffee waste all can have a significant impact on carbon footprint. The other big consideration in a market like the UK is, how much milk is being used.

There are carbon neutral coffee farms as well as numerous other farming practices that look to build sustainable ecosystems around coffee production. It is often pointed out that coffee can be a symbiotic crop, as it is a forest floor shade shrub. Research scientist Mandi Caudill undertook research on the impact of shade cover on coffee farms with a focus on mammal populations as well as benefits to bird life (which at this point, is more widely understood). As with many topics of this sort there is much complexity and nuance, but Mandi pointed out that 40% shade cover is a simple but effective goal that a coffee farm can aim for, and that will create significant benefits to the land's biodiversity. This goal is also appealing, because it is achievable. Of course, this more diverse environment will not allow as many coffee plants per hectare, which reduces potential yield, but it should be noted that coffee can grow very productively in an environment like this. Mandi mentions that she has visited many farms that have already achieved this kind of diversity but haven't sought certification. Finding simple and accessible ways to certify this kind of farming would be valuable.

Grant and Nicola Fleming, co-owners of Finca Santa Teresa in Panama, have been on a journey of discovery and exploration ever since they took on the farm. They explained to me how they have been learning, not just about coffee farming, but all farming. They have visited a variety of innovative farm projects around the world that put alternative and sustainable farming approaches into practice. Some utilising older methods, and others choosing to implement cutting edge technology and new concepts. Their farm is an evolving project. Recently they had the farm reviewed and analysed by a coffee expert who informed them they had an excellent coffee farm. Naturally they were thrilled, but Grant was keen to point out that they don't just want a great coffee farm, they want a "great farm." Grant also spoke to me about the groundswell that he sees around the world, demanding improved sustainability.

Sustainability is undoubtedly one of the key topics of our times, and coffee does have an opportunity to be an everyday relatable product that can achieve sustainable models of business, but there is a lot of work to do.

Independent Business - Small, Local and Craft
Specialty coffee has in many ways been coupled with the concept of independent business. This means that the concept of independent business is often part of the specialty boutique value set.

There is a lot of potential value in small, passionate, owner operated businesses. It is a format that often creates unique and characterful experiences and connections that just can't be matched by larger organisations. I believe that you could open a coffee shop almost anywhere in the world, and so long as it is opened and run by passionate, service driven people who care about their products and their customers, the business will be a success. The human element, done well, is really not commonplace, and creates a competitive advantage and a sticky business in most environments.

There is a human connection that comes with smaller stories and smaller businesses, and more than this there are strong arguments to be made on several fronts that small and independent businesses need to be championed and supported. Independent businesses (not just in coffee) can act as a positive counter to larger businesses in several ways, whether in a bid to counteract the tax avoiding financial behaviours sometimes undertaken by large corporate enterprises, or to break up high street monotony. Local, independent businesses are likely to be owned and operated by people who are part of the local community and can make a considered contribution to that community.

Even though we live in a globalised, neoliberal capitalist economy, our courts still oppose mergers that endanger competition in the market and create monopolies. In the coffee shop market, large companies can throw their weight around in a number of ways, and consumers who see this often choose to support independent business as a means to combat this dynamic.

Independent business supports diversity in business and on our high streets. A variety of hospitality businesses in locations aid in creating a unique identity and sense of place. The independent coffee brand space has allowed for a lot of creativity in storytelling and environment creation, and has given many people the opportunity to explore the same ideas of quality and taste in coffee, but each in their own way. I guess you could compare it to open source technology and IP.

However, I also believe independent businesses should not rely on the fact that they are independent to fuel their success. I remember when we opened our shop in Bath in 2009. As a Bath-based, independent coffee shop we were often approached with programmes that were aimed at supporting local business. At the time I used to get frustrated at the idea of giving a discount to get someone to come and buy a coffee from us, just because we were independent and local. I was, and still am, adamant that they should come to us because we are doing something of quality and creating value, and I don't want to put a discount on that. Independents have an opportunity to create special businesses and differentiated experiences and products for customers. But, if you run an independent business, and think you are owed trade simply because you are independent, then you're in trouble.

There are all sorts of assumptions that circle around not only the idea of independence, but the idea of size. An inference often seems to have been made that smaller is better. Small businesses are unique by virtue of the fact that there is only one of them, and if this is what you are searching for, the independent sector can provide variety in this way. This, however, is something that consumers drawn to known brands tend to shy away from. They feel that they don't know what they are going to get from the unknown independent, whilst the larger brand can offer familiarity, and can build trust. Meanwhile, the exploratory nature of the specialty coffee lover makes them a natural fit for the independent scene, as they can search out the best cup and the best experience across a wide and varied landscape of independent coffee business.

When it comes to cafés, I think that some of the best experiences can be found in single site operations. However, it quickly became apparent to me when starting out in coffee, that being a small coffee business does not prime you to pursue quality. Yes, I could do what I wanted in my shop with coffee, just as long as I could find a way to charge what I needed, and find customers who wanted to pay for the drinks and experiences. But, as we moved back through the supply chain, this logic didn't really make sense. Being very small creates many hurdles, and getting capital is challenging, so it makes sense for a lot of businesses to explore investment, which ultimately can mean not being independent anymore. This all depends (to an extent) on how you actually define independence - on whether it is a technical assessment of the ownership structure, or some sense and feeling of business size. On the other side of the coin, multi-generational family businesses have traditionally been able to achieve a large corporate size, so scale is not just for heavily invested businesses with large shareholder registers that have been sold to private equity or gone public.

Part of the success of the B Corp certification, and its growing adoption, is the recognition that as a company grows and is successful, there is a likelihood that decision making can be driven exclusively by maximising profit. B Corp designation can help to apply a set of values regarding how a company is run, independent of size or ownership structure.

Although there are success stories of businesses that have gone through the independent cycle and come out the other end, the funnel is constantly being fed with new independent operators. Boutique coffee is well set up for independent businesses and entrepreneurship. There is more and more of this throughout the supply chain, but particularly in countries where there is support and funding of these endeavours. Throughout parts of the coffee supply chain there are clearly baked in challenges for a business that is too small. It would not, for example, be easy to move into the green trading space as a small independent. I think that a healthy marketplace has a balance of smaller, independent businesses alongside larger businesses. Great initiatives and improvements can be made by both large and indie companies. I don't think it is a bad thing at all however, that specialty coffee encourages the smaller operator.

Greenwashing

"Greenwashing is the exaggeration of a company's environmental credentials. That is, marketing communications impress business operations to be better for the environment than they are in reality."
- The Green Business Bureau

In this chapter I am using the term greenwashing to not only look at the propensity for misleading environmental claims, but for the wider remit of virtue driven marketing narratives that deceptively leverage conscious consumers.

I think that in specialty coffee the greenwashing that occurs is more often than not done without a real intention to mislead. Many companies engaging in this thought process have approached their marketing with the narrative of "we are a small company with good intentions." The lack of audit and verification culture in independent business makes this problem worse.

The recent surge in online marketing has provided a great opportunity for businesses to play around with different words and messaging in a quick fire way, hoping to find something that sticks. This is quite different to a conscious and carefully arrived at set of messages, that a company feels confident it can stand behind.

Typically an in-house role, freelancer or agency will use a variety of scenarios to play with pay-per-click and ad spend methodologies. This can often involve trialling a large range of words, with the goal simply being to find something with a good conversion rate relative to cost, and that connects with the right customers. Too often marketing in the ethical or green space is driven by the realisation that there is an audience to be connected with and sold to based on their values, rather than communicating a set of values that the company really lives by. This phenomenon is not unique to coffee at all, but building a company because there is an opportunity to be pursued is a) not a bad thing if it still achieves the values it espouses and b) is very different to actively marketing false claims.

Perhaps a bigger issue in this space is the ability to actually prove a given term, especially as the terms can be broad and hard to pin down. Can something be called greenwashing if its claims don't really mean anything when you break them down. As we looked at in the first chapter of this part of the book, labelling coffee as ethical is problematic because what it is referencing is unclear. Ethics vary, and the labelling doesn't pertain to anything specific. In the world of intellectual property, broad terms can be good and bad. If you are too broad, then you do not have a claim to IP, as your ideas and fundamentals will overlap with those already in the public domain. The types of marketing messages that we are looking at presently are often sweeping, and work in the opposite way to IP. Vaguery means that it will be hard for a person to argue that the claims aren't true.

What does "direct trade" mean? There are many different scenarios that the term could equally apply to. The same can be said for coffee that is "transparent" or "traceable." At the same time, there is a reasonable inference that the words appear to create in context.

To get more muddy, I have spotted the use of statistics in coffee branding in a way that is not relevant or helpful. One such example might state that something is 50% more than something else. But if that other thing is very small then 50% is an imperceptible change in reality. This is not really greenwashing per se, just misleading context, and if it pertains to a suggestion that something is purportedly achieving a sustainable result, it could still fall into the category of greenwashing.

Often in coffee, one product's supply chain or impact is used as an example of how the company works, when in reality it is only a small part of the business's sales. These specific project products are used in the same way that a concept car is used, to drive the perception of an automobile company's wider range. Again, this is okay in principle, just so long as the consumer realises that the concept car is not what they are getting when they pick up their run of the mill model. This kind of marketing plays on expectation and suggestion.

As may be becoming clear, this topic is highly context specific. There are companies who are making earnest claims, but would struggle to prove them under scrutiny. There are others who actively and knowingly push their luck. In fact if the reaction to industry meme's produced by the likes of @50percentarabica on Instagram are anything to go by, there is already a recognition in the coffee community of the greenwashing in specialty coffee. Interestingly to me, this humorous dynamic implies that this is all seen as normal, par for the course. I often wonder if this is a negative side of a generally positive community dynamic. If everyone is doing it and the defence remains to be that "we are all good small companies trying to do something positive with specialty coffee" then this can stop appropriate, self-critical assessment within these communities. Speaking to operators, there is often an underdog mentality at play here also, whereby they expect the bigger company to be held accountable for their claims, whilst they don't expect to be held to the same standard.

While I do think that the expectations on companies should be different based on their size, resources and market advantages as a form of business equitability, I do not think that this should result in such extremes of obligation. The topics around sustainability are complex and grey. There are no clear cut rules to be followed. It is a work in progress for us all, as we seek to find pragmatic solutions and improvements. However, when challenges are used as an excuse to absolve the need to prove and verify claims, there is a big problem. These challenges will only get worse as these topics become more and more important in society and business. Whether through policy changes or consumer pressure, I don't believe misleading or unverified claims will continue to be so easily made. As a boutique community we should be more critical of ourselves in the language we use and the statements we make. This is a positive side effect of the success of growing specialty businesses, who now need to evolve and adapt their behaviour and approach to marketing when they get bigger. At these points, simply being a small independent no longer cuts the mustard as an excuse surrounding greenwashing.

Equality, Equity & Diversity

We live in a diverse world full of both inequality and inequity. Equality refers to each individual or group having access to the same opportunity and resources. Equity recognises that people have different circumstances and that to achieve equality there needs to be a varied and appropriate distribution of opportunity and resource in reaction to these varying circumstances.

The beginning of this part of the book looks at the most common equity discussion in coffee, which surrounds the price paid per pound of coffee per producer. As we have explored in the book at multiple points, the market tends to benefit those at scale and with business efficiencies. Speciality does achieve a higher price but requires a greater quality in return and is a smaller part of the market.

There is inequality at play as a product of geopolitics. Climate change typically compounds this, creating more inequality and inequity for people in regions and countries that are already at a disadvantage. Although there is broad agreement globally surrounding the need to reduce climate change, initiatives from wealthy nations around restricting land management behaviour in poorer subtropical economies are in danger of further adding to global inequality.

There are many value-driven companies and people in coffee. The global community we refer to in specialty coffee is diverse and perhaps it is this diversity that also brings to our attention many ethical and moral topics that exist not just in coffee, but in business and society everywhere. Specialty businesses looking to tackle and focus on certain ethical issues face the challenge of properly understanding what help really looks like and what good solutions are. Following this, is the challenge of actually implementing an initiative into a supply chain, or even verifying that a specific claim is being achieved.

The more complex conversation is around whether the specific outcome is itself an outcome that is supporting equity and equality. When speaking with Andrea Otte, who has worked in numerous roles throughout the coffee supply chain, she mentioned the challenges of building programmes around equality, whereby a company is looking for a prescriptive outcome.

The women's cooperatives she worked with in Guatemala as part of a 50/50 women's sourcing programme were created less through choice and more through circumstance, as many of the men in the families and local communities were moving to the US. In raising this case, she demonstrated to me how being prescriptive from a distance regarding an outcome you are looking for, is often not particularly empowering. Many supply chain programmes struggle due to this kind of box ticking, which causes them to take an oversimplified approach to their objectives, which then in turn do not actually achieve equitability. You can of course see where the goal comes from, actual representation is a logical metric to judge success.

There is an unfairness that can come from a strict idea of what fairness "should" look like. Supply chain ethics are very challenging in the same way that international political policy can be. On the one hand you may be rightly interested in building an ethical and considerate supply chain, ensuring no human rights violations or environmental damage, but you are also in danger of showing a colonial attitude, telling people and businesses in another country how they should behave in their approach to a number of topics, and it may not be your place to do so.

This is a huge and complex topic. Some ethics and morals appear to be universal, at least in terms of how humans think about each other. Humans (without psychopathy) agree that it is morally wrong to murder another human, this concept is innate and not learnt or culturally influenced. We do not, however, have agreement across the world regarding a variety of moral and ethical points from culture to culture, and for that matter, even within one country where the population will voice different ideas of what is right and wrong.

I spent six months travelling India when I was 21, and I read a variety of books about the country in order to better understand what is a complex multicultural nation, and a very different one to the United Kingdom where I had grown up. I later read a book called *The Righteous Mind* by Jonathon Haidt. The book's premise is centred around arguing that those on the left and right of the political spectrum largely want the same things but that they disagree on the means of how to achieve it. The first half of the book, however, is a treatise on morals and ethics across humanity, whereby he looks to ascertain which moral and ethical concepts are innate and which are learnt.

In the book he uses North America and India as two examples of cultures in the world that we live in today that display significant cultural differences which feed into moral norms. He posits that North America represents a culture that epitomises the celebration of the autonomous right of the individual. This is contrasted against India, which is an example in which the rights of the community are valued above those of the individual. India is not really culturally one country. Following the exit of the British Empire it became one nation, but, like other countries around the world, it was until relatively recently, made up of many different countries.

The conceptual thought experiment still works though. Human cultures do have varying ideas of what "correct" behaviour looks like, which often depends on whether that culture puts the community or group before the individual in the context of a number of societal constructs. Western interventionist behaviour, even in the form of aid, is often guided by a set of cultural morals and ethics from the aid giving country, which are applied to another culture without an appreciation of the differences.

When it comes to coffee pricing, approaching this with any one size fits all solution will always fall very short of obtaining an equitable outcome. Any sourcing policy that actually addresses equitable pricing will need to have context not just for each country that they buy coffee from, but also for each producer with reference to their size and background. This type of in-depth approach will need to be applied across everything a sourcing policy is looking to achieve, right down to its ethical and moral framework.

The concept of boycotting is a particularly interesting topic of debate. When a challenge is identified in a supply chain, this can often be addressed most easily by the procuring company simply not buying from that country or supply chain. However, this attempt to exclude bad actors from a business's supply chain typically results in also excluding many people who are not at fault. It can also often mean a move to a better resourced supply chain that has started off in a more privileged position.

In situations such as this, it is very easy to feel overwhelmed and defeated by the complexity and greyness of this topic. An approach I have been working on implementing in our roasting business is to map what we think the challenges are for each country or producer type, and to create a contextual framework for each. We need to know at the outset, what "better" looks like in each situation, as progress is relative to where we were before.

I have been involved in ongoing work on a project in Mozambique. It is a national park based in what was formerly a conflict zone. The coffee project is improving year-on-year. It has not hit the standards of the most developed projects around the world yet, but based on where things were several years ago, it has shown remarkable progress. This approach requires constant revision and benchmarking, and the development and review of success metrics in each instance to properly monitor progress.

Christopher Feran, who has written in detail on sourcing relationships in the coffee trade, has shared with me that he thinks it requires openness, empathy and collaboration to work on building equitable sourcing relationships that show an understanding and respect for all in the supply chain.

There is of course a desire for easy solutions, but in this area, they rarely exist. The intention is derived from an earnest aspiration to achieve a positive outcome, but also because there is a marketing incentive to tell a straightforward and catchy narrative that resonates with consumers. When discussing greenwashing and verifiable sourcing claims, we are not just asking whether the claims on the pack are being achieved, but whether they are even the correct objectives.

As we move downstream, we ask questions about the equality and equitability within the organisations that sit between coffee farming and the cup of coffee itself. This is an important point; the development of fair and equitable business practice is not solely a supply chain objective and is in fact something that all businesses should proactively pursue. Whether it is patriarchy, white privilege or race relations, there are many challenges to overcome if we wish to offer fair and equitable opportunities and places of work. As with some of the other big and complex topics touched on in this book, I recognise the limitations of my attempts to talk about these subjects, as well as my position as a white privileged European man, however I believe these are important concerns to talk about as part of the business considerations of the coffee industry.

Boutique specialty coffee has shown some grassroots movement behaviour, and can in some circumstances offer the opportunity for less directly nepotistic routes to success, allowing for a wider range of people to be a part of, and find success in, the industry. However, many disadvantages still naturally exist in the field. Entrepreneurial industries such as this allow those who are well resourced and from backgrounds with support structures to succeed more easily. Many of the better paying jobs and opportunities, as well as jobs in larger companies display the same challenges as in other industries.

A company's size creates a specific dynamic in this regard. Small start-ups are often made up of just a few people. These could be some friends, or a couple starting a business together. At a certain point the first employee will need to be hired, and then another. During these times a business is not really thought of as having an employee culture as there are not enough people. There is no HR department or company structure. At some point the team may grow to a stage where it could no longer be characterised as just a few friends, but rather a business with employees and a culture, and the founders need to think about this. Often this transition gets missed.

As they grow, businesses will start to have to think like an organisation and to regard themselves as an employer, putting structures and systems in place. I think it is easy for owners who are working really hard, and who are stretched, to grow their business in the model of the tiny team, and hire more people like themselves. Just because a company can easily develop a poor culture easily, this doesn't make it good or acceptable.

I really do believe that diversity in specialty coffee companies can be beneficial to the company as a whole. A lot of small and independent businesses are lifestyle businesses, and can fall into the trap of hiring the people that the founders and managers would most like to hang out with. A team needs to be on the same page in terms of mission and goals, but a work environment is just that, a professional environment, not a friendly get together. I think that camaraderie and great team spirit is important, but this is quite different to friendship. A diverse team that comprises people who see and think about things in different ways is valuable.

Societal inequality means that a lot of individual disadvantage starts right from the get go, flowing through childhood and education and into the world of work. This means that simply approaching a business as a meritocracy will likely fall short. Those who have been in a more privileged position from birth are also likely to more strongly meet several criteria. These challenges need to be addressed through multiple societal constructs, enacted through public policy and education, as well as wider cultural change.

Employers also need to recognise the challenge, so that they can start thinking about how to create constructive behaviours in reaction to it. Hiring is an area that can be more directly addressed, introducing blind assessments and hiring protocols that look to combat bias. Employers can also develop themselves by undertaking an analysis of their own cognitive biases that they bring to work. Perhaps more challenging is to make sure that the inter-stakeholder behaviour is constructive and not discriminatory day-to-day and month-to-month. A company needs operational behaviour that creates feedback loops and check-ins to guide and manage team behaviour. You need a good business culture and reliable systems if you wish to catch and combat inequality. This topic is not just unique to businesses, but also to the events, projects and programmes that take place across the industry.

For all of us looking to work professionally in coffee, this topic is part of our professional development. Many boutique businesses are learning how to be better businesses and to develop what they have built. Learning about how to create and build fair and equitable work environments is a key part of developing a good business.

Values Driven Initiatives Inside and Outside of Coffee
In this values segment of the book we have mainly been focusing on the values that surround coffee as a product and the people it touches. The specialty coffee market broadly is an area of creative and

passionate people who think about how to run better businesses with a positive impact. You can see this through a number of new and ongoing initiatives and programmes that are not solely driven by direct coffee work, but by models that target a wider array of issues.

B Corp, which we have mentioned already in this part of the book, is a commitment to trying to run a better business. 1% for the Planet offers a resolution to allocate revenue to a positive project that extends far beyond coffee. One percent of revenue may not seem like a lot from the outside, but for most businesses in the coffee industry that is between 5-15% of profit. With this in mind, it is clear that a coffee company needs to be run with a keen business focus if it wishes to allow for these different initiatives to be funded.

Coffee companies around the industry also participate in many different contribution and collaboration based charitable projects. Cafelumbus, a multi-farm producer/exporter in Colombia has initiatives, supported by their coffee business and its partners, which provides aid for different causes. One such programme is called Watchers of the Land. This is a programme working towards the preservation of a variety of bird and mammal species that inhabit the mountains of Ciudad Bolivar in Antioquia. They also support a brain damage charity in Medellin.

Businesses also often seek to utilise part of the coffee supply chain to create positive change. There are many programmes within the industry that offer opportunities for people in disadvantaged positions or those undergoing rehabilitation. The hospitality side of coffee can offer a route to work and an engaging profession for a diverse range of people. There also often can be staffing requirements across these parts of the industry. However, there is still a barrier to entry for many. SEND Coffee in London is a social enterprise business that works with people who have special educational needs and disabilities. Through their mentoring programme, they offer participants training, focusing on both coffee skills and soft skills. Following this, many participants are able to work in the company's own cafés, and for businesses run by wholesale partners. In the coffee industry there are a variety of initiatives of this ilk, which look to pair business with positive and enabling impact.

I often think that coffee is an interesting industry in this regard. It is not structured by traditional education formats, and with the right level of support, the industry can offer opportunities to a diverse range of people. It is also an interesting and engaging industry, which can provide a desirable place to work, making it suitable for encouraging and supporting employment initiatives.

The specialty coffee industry is clearly not perfect, but it does appear to be an industry that contains many value driven businesses that genuinely seek to have a positive impact through the work they do. From a business perspective, the lesson is the same as bringing a passion project to life around quality coffee. For any causes to be sustainably pursued, the underlying principles of the business need to be successful.

Burnout, Mental Health and Physical Health

I have always identified as someone who likes to work. I still do, but after burning out, I had to rethink this a little bit. I enjoy creating things and being busy, but I created projects that became responsibilities, and continued to load myself to the brink with work for a very prolonged period of time. Being a business owner can be a lonely place at times, the buck stops with you. There are pros and cons to the employer and employee dynamic.

I didn't really notice the stress, as I felt driven, and enjoyed much of what I was doing. This led to a situation where I was "on" too much, running on adrenaline. Moderate, but daily, alcohol relief didn't help either. It wasn't just work, I had some big personal stresses as well. I got very unwell, picked up a bunch of ailments and had chronic fatigue for months, which forced me to dramatically slow down. I had to put a stop to a lot of the side projects that I was working on, and only to give a few hours a day to the core businesses that are my livelihood. I was in a fortunate position where I could take the time to slow down and rethink things. It also actually marked an opportunity for my team to take on more responsibility and autonomy as individuals.

I had found a limit that I didn't know I had. This journey is not uncommon, and it is for each of us to discover (or, hopefully not). Working hard, and for long hours, is generally rewarded in business.

Though you have to work smart and focus on impact, rather than just being busy.

It is also possible that combining a passion with work may cloud the picture. The saying "do what you love and you will never work a day in your life" is unfortunately untrue. This crossover of passion and work is interesting. I am very grateful that I get to work in specialty coffee and I really do love it. But it is still mainly work as opposed to play. Because you love it you are also likely to work harder and put a lot of energy into your work and derive a sense of wellbeing from it (or lack thereof). Setbacks can hit harder, and it is also clear that nearly all roles are dynamic and complex, with a mixture of bits that you love, but also stressful or less enjoyable tasks.

To be clear, to run a successful business you need to not simply pursue the bits you like, but to figure out how to engage with everything that needs consideration in order for you to do a good job. I think it is clear that work can contribute a lot to an individual's sense of purpose, and it has the potential to be very rewarding and a part of positive mental health, but for the majority of people, there has to be a balance that is sustainable in the long term.

Although I have shared my journey here, and have therefore touched more on founders and business owners, this is clearly a phenomenon that can happen in all roles. The exact factors that inform mental health vary from person to person. There are ways businesses and workplaces can support their employees' mental health, both through wider company initiatives and culture, and also in taking the time to understand the individuals in each role, and doing what you can to support each person. Businesses can promote environments and management styles where team members are able to share how they feel and what they may be struggling with.

I felt it was important to acknowledge and include this chapter in the book as these themes are part of the world of business, but I realise this is only a light touch on what is a complex and important topic. Businesses after all are typically nothing without people. With this in mind, it isn't a surprise to find that from a business success point of view, positive states of mental and physical health in teams results in higher degrees of business success.

Many of the jobs throughout the supply chain can be very physical. I enjoy chucking green coffee sacks around, but I realise that this is because my hobbies include strength sports. The average coffee sack size far surpasses the recommended UK manual handling weight limit of 25kg for men and 16kg for women. Smaller craft roasters typically don't have the infrastructure in place to easily address this challenge. Lifting heavy things is really about how adapted one's body is to it, so for someone training to lift heavy things, 25kg is very light, for those not doing this, an injury can be easily sustained.

Agricultural harvesting work is extremely laboursome also, but can be invigorating and rewarding at the same time. With topics of this nature the balance is what is key. Hospitality roles can mean long hours on your feet, and normally injuries are incurred from repetitive movements conducted again and again, day in and day out.

The dynamics around physical and mental health are often specific to the individual, which means that there needs to be a meeting in the middle approach where the company considers how it can accommodate and support individual needs. Specific roles have requirements such as specific tasks that the individual must be able to undertake in the role. However, businesses should also be considerate and understanding of each employee, where they could need help and support, and where reasonable adjustments to the working environment can be made.

Boutique specialty coffee can be a wonderful place to work, but often the jobs in the industry are hard, and like all work and business environments, a consideration of and focus on promoting physical and mental wellbeing is hugely important.

Part Five. Branding and Marketing

Introduction to Part Five

Every company has an identity, some simply pay more attention to their identity than others. How you present and communicate this identity to the world is your brand. Your products or services are part of your identity and they are how your customers experience your brand, and it is these that you market to the world.

This subject is complex and far reaching. It is as much about human behaviour and psychology as it is about an advertising and branding structure.

Sticky Brands and Sensemaking

Every company wants not only to win new customers, but to keep them. Ideally they will not only retain them, but will subsequently build an optimal relationship with them. This is particularly essential in coffee, as throughout the supply chain, the sustenance of a business requires repeat purchases over time. This dynamic is at its most extreme in a coffee shop, which will need to not only sell a coffee for £3.80 to hundreds of customers in one day, but every day thereafter, all year round, barring a bit of time off at Christmas or for a mid-January lick of paint.

It is easy for a customer to move around coffee brands and companies. If the product isn't an end-to-end system like Nespresso, then there is no tie in, and in a competitive marketplace, brands need to keep customers in other ways. I have always believed that this is where the complexities of specialty coffee become its strength, affording the opportunity to build sticky relationships.

Michael Beverland is a professor of marketing who has authored multiple books on marketing and branding. He used to prop up the bar at Colonna & Small's, which was great on two fronts; firstly, he drinks a lot of coffee, and secondly, he was curious to discuss the specialty coffee space from a marketing perspective.

Prof Bev, as we called him in the shop, co-authored a paper called "Co-creating educational consumer journeys: A sensemaking perspective" in Journal of the Academy of Marketing Science. The paper looks at the idea that specialty coffee presents an opportunity for businesses to engage in an education dynamic with customers. The paper asks the question: "what practises enable the co-creation of meaning and value for customers during educational journeys?" Sensemaking, simply put, is the process an individual goes through to make sense of something they are engaging with, and of their collective experience. The two preceding concepts of sensemaking are, sensebreaking and senseguiding.

Sensemaking is an interesting term. It focuses on the customer as a participant in the co-creation of meaning, which is opposed to the more traditional idea of education, in which there is a one way knowledge transfer, much like the regurgitation of the dates of English monarchs like a parrot in history class. Instead, sensemaking presents the idea that the individual builds their own understanding, maybe through a light bulb moment where they "get" what coffee can be or how specialty coffee is different.

A business can encourage and guide this process, but it needs buy-in from the customer as well. I have never liked the term education when thinking about engaging customers with specialty coffee. When I got into coffee I didn't feel like I was being educated, I felt like I was actively engaging in a subject, and as a result, I was thinking about it and learning through experience.

This opportunity to be a part of an individual's re-framing and sensemaking around coffee is powerful, and it creates a strong connection between the business and the customer. That moment, where a person thinks "ah, interesting, coffee isn't as simple as I thought it was, how fascinating" only happens once, and over time the opportunity to illuminate coffee in a specialist way will likely diminish, as the concept reaches pop culture status. However, the benefit of specialist fields is that sensemaking is ongoing. I have been in coffee for 16-years, and I am continually experiencing a sensemaking process whilst writing this book.

This connection to a learning and reshaping process is very sticky, it keeps people coming back. It also can become tribal, and people start to identify as a coffee nerd, or something to that effect. There are a range of levels of personal commitment here, but an element of sensemaking can be seen in specialty coffee, even at the lighter touch points with a "typical" customer who may learn the origin they like best, or the drink format that they prefer to order, and so on.

Sensebreaking refers to the moment when the individual's existing idea of how something makes sense is challenged and confronted in some way. This forces a reconsideration of how the individual thinks about the subject. It is from this point that sensemaking can take place, allowing the building of a new and iterative idea of meaning in the topic.

Senseguiding is a process that aids sensemaking. Essentially, the position of a knowledge-driven brand that can present reasons for how and why its products are what they are, acts as a senseguiding influence. This most often comes in the form of a recommendation of how to best make or drink the coffee, but there are any number of scenarios and interactions that specialist boutique brands have with customers in which senseguiding could occur. This dynamic creates meaningful experiences and relationships between the business and its customers.

These sensemaking processes are most powerful in-person, and physical interaction affords opportunities throughout the supply chain to engage in this valuable process. This does not occur naturally in a café interaction, in fact most cafés struggle to engage in sensemaking journeys within the constraints of the fast food service model. These interactions happen throughout the coffee supply as a supplier and buyer at each stage of the process engage in sensebreaking, guiding and making.

Many coffee companies will engage in a similar process through online platforms, such as video content or newsletters. The benefit of creating a discourse between a business and their customers in specialty coffee is recognised across the industry, and is perhaps one of the defining aspects of what we think of as the specialty coffee movement.

Physical Experiences - The Value of Bricks and Mortar
In the previous chapter I looked at the immense value that can be created through a collaborative coffee experience between customer

and business. It may sound like an obvious thing to say, but for this coffee experience to be possible, we need to drink the coffee. And where we drink it, has the power to drastically change how a person feels about a product and a brand.

A lot of coffee will be brewed and enjoyed at home or at work, and sometimes in transit, but I have always felt that the heart of the specialty coffee movement is often in coffee shops. The sensemaking element of the business can be at its strongest here.

I was once discussing coffee with a Master of Wine, and he shared his envy of the barista role, lamenting that on the whole, the wine industry does not enjoy the benefits of a similar position. Of course, there is the sommelier role, but this role is not often tied into the preparation of the drink. There are many great sommeliers, but on the whole this duty simply denotes someone opening a bottle or picking from a list or shelf. The Master of Wine's argument was that in coffee the drink needs to be prepared, which creates an opportunity for an engaged and passionate server to interact with the customer when crafting and selling their coffee. This dynamic relies on the prevalence of manual systems, which as fully automated systems keep getting better, may diminish in certain stores. It also presupposes a great barista who wants to talk to customers, but I do see his point.

Even if a shop is making use of an automated machine, considerable value can be derived from creating the right environment in which to experience the coffee. Nespresso boutiques are a prime example of this. Even with their significant online marketing power and opportunity, in coffee, a physical experience continues to be the most powerful. Many brands look to utilise coffee's physical aspects to connect with a customer, who may then connect with the brand outside of this physical experience, by buying coffee online or starting a wholesale relationship.

A question that gets posed to remind passionate baristas of the importance of service and environment goes as follows: "would you rather have a great coffee and a bad experience, or a great experience and a bad coffee?" Die hard, fully initiated, coffee obsessives tend to pick the former, but for most, the latter wins out. This question is a reminder that the two are inextricably interwoven at a consumption level. Of course, there are times in the supply chain when people taste coffees in an environment that is as experienceless as possible, by creating blind tastings that try to take bias out of the sensory assessment. However, in marketing exercises, the experience factor has an impact and can be seen throughout the supply chain in group cuppings held by importers, or visits to farms and mills at origin.

I have spoken to a few producers who are exploring the creation of on-farm stays as a tourism business and not just a way to host potential green buyers. One producer cited the disproportionately large size of the Texas wine industry in the USA, noting that the reason the industry was so large wasn't to do with the wine itself, but to do with the vineyard experiences, tourism and hospitality.

I would argue that it is its sheer variety of physical interaction points that contribute to coffee being perceived as much more than a commodity. Specialty boutique coffee definitely puts a focus on weaving product and experience together. In a busy world where brands compete for our attention all day every day, physical touch points allow a brand to remain in the line of sight, and to maintain a connection and sticky relationships with customers.

This may sound like an obvious point, but when a brand takes on a physical space this gives them the ability to provide a great example of how their coffee "should" taste. If the brand controls the details of preparation and presentation, everything can be demonstrated in just the way that the brand wishes. Customers may then look to replicate these experiences in other environments. This can apply to a retail customer looking to make the coffee at home, or a procurement team from a wholesale customer, who might bring some of this coffee brand's experience into their business. Coffee brands that don't have cafés often create experience-driven spaces to support interaction with their wholesale clients. These can be showrooms or training spaces, which allow the client to become involved with the brand through an experience around coffee. Tasting events are another classic example of sensemaking touchpoints, which allow the brand to connect meaningfully with its customers.

Examples are plentiful. Whilst there are businesses in coffee that are able to build success without the need for sharing physical spaces centred around their coffee, it is undeniable that physical experiences shared between brand and client are a cornerstone of coffee marketing and consumer engagement.

Expertise, Trust and Word of Mouth

I think it is fair to say that most small specialty coffee companies' marketing relies on the most ancient form of publicity - word of mouth. This is the simple act of one person recommending or making another aware of something. This is a fabulous aspect of specialty coffee, it means that small brands without huge marketing budgets, can grow to build a reasonably sized business. More budget and resources in this area can create advantages, but it's also very easy to spend money, if you have it, especially on branding and marketing initiatives.

I have long wondered if the affiliation between word of mouth and specialty boutique coffee is caused by the complexity and difficulty of learning about the product. As we have discussed, many derive a value from the experience of an educational process that may be provided by a shop or brand. Many, once they have realised the full complexity of coffee, will stop short on that educational journey. They will essentially learn some basic principles, but also now realise that there is much that they don't, and probably will never, know.

Don't get me wrong, it is now easier than ever for a person to learn about coffee, but it requires time and inclination. As professionals and experts continue to delve deeper into their coffee obsession, they typically are distancing themselves more and more from the perspective of their average customer. This isn't because people can't learn about coffee, it is because unlike us, they haven't decided to dedicate prolonged periods of their time to the subject.

This is the thing about complex subjects. Whilst, at the heart of it, you can work on ways to make the topic as approachable, accessible and engaging as possible, ultimately you are asking someone to dedicate time and energy to it. I am a curious person, and I have a lot of varying interests. There are a wild amount of subjects I would enjoy studying. The ones that really catch my attention are the complex ones with a journey to undertake. If you were to use the idea of game mechanics and map out the topics that appeal to me, you could say that they are the ones that are hard to "complete." These hobbies can provide a lifelong interest because of this dynamic. Coffee displays this potential complexity, and this is both a strength and a weakness from a marketing and branding point of view.

For these reasons, the audience that specialty coffee has grown is not made up of individuals who self-identify as experts. Many market research studies wish to segment the specialty boutique coffee audience. They ask "do you have experts? Coffee geeks? Connoisseurs? Foodies?" And so on. This has proven to be extremely challenging. Many people drink coffee, and the lexicon is not well-defined, potentially leading to confusion rather than answers.

For me, the key mechanism at play is the recognition of expertise and complexity. A huge swathe of customers have become aware of the idea that coffee can be interesting and complicated. This means that they know that they don't know everything about coffee. They also know that they want the good stuff. The easiest way to find it, is to look for recommendations, and the easiest way to do that in a world packed with advertising, is to ask real humans.

Online review systems may help us know if a company can deliver on its promises, and not completely drop the ball, but these aren't good systems for understanding specialist fields or the companies or services within them. The world's most prestigious restaurants don't have the best Tripadvisor ratings. This is because they have a product which challenges their customers, this is often part of their mission. The businesses that successfully deliver on an established idea and norm are more likely to achieve a higher rating on an aggregated review system. These businesses have a more "classic" customer proposition.

All of this is to say that word of mouth is perhaps, more than ever, one of the strongest marketing tools at play in specialty boutique coffee. This was demonstrated during the pandemic, as brands with established strong reputations in the industry saw massive upticks in sales. One imagines that people at home asked their coffee loving friend where they should buy coffee from, and the trusted, established brands benefited the most from this behaviour.

As an industry, we aren't able to tell people how to decipher the best product by simply using the information on the pack. This isn't unique to coffee, but does mean that a customer will need another means to find a quality operator.

The word of mouth phenomenon is strongest at the consumer end, but is also at play elsewhere in the coffee industry. I do not mean this as an attack on the abilities of those working in coffee, but rather an observation of something that occurs naturally. Most coffee roasting businesses represent a vast range of expertise and experience levels across the business. Unless the founders or core team members have a wealth of experience, they are likely learning on the job. This means that there is a desire for recommendations, and also a more subtle validation process happening throughout the supply chain.

Buyers who are looking to gain confidence in their green buying could choose to buy predominantly from green importing brands that they feel they can trust to give them quality coffee. This is a great example of the need to trust a brand. A lot of brand trust flows throughout the specialty coffee space. It also plays out as viral mimicry, in which certain brands or individuals start trends that come to represent what's recognised as "good."

I have often wondered if the specialty space is as much driven by a community of businesses looking at and mirroring one another as it is based on exploring specific customer interactions. A lot of businesses in the space show great concern over fitting into a scene made up of their peers, at the detriment of reviewing whether a product or approach fits their values and mission. This can be part of a sensible approach for brands who are questioning how their product fits their brand perception and audience, but I also can find it disheartening when a brand appears to act only to preserve their perceived image in relation to other coffee brands, rather than basing decisions on their mission and values. The relevance of this kind of approach to a business really depends on what they had established from the beginning, and the customer base that they have built along the way.

Word of mouth can also be part of big, funded marketing

approaches. In these cases, the eventual goal is to accelerate and expand the word of mouth process. All brands want to be discussed at the water cooler, or over coffee. Technology definitely plays its part as a platform for word of mouth, but coffee often appears resistant to the way that online platforms can be leveraged. The influencer model doesn't seem to work particularly well in coffee as, for the most part, coffee influencers don't become Instagram influencers. And conversely, whilst your average Instagram influencer may be able to shift an item of clothing, in specialty coffee, people will question why they would be interested in which coffee a sports person or celebrity is drinking.

The success of how an influencer can grow custom for a product is specific to how people view and engage with that influencer. There absolutely are coffee influencers, but they will tend to have industry influence, which then flows through to industry peers and coffee geeks, and then potentially to a wider audience through the ripple effect of word of mouth and reputation. I have often wondered if the social media typically made by coffee brands speaks more to the industry than the end customer. People working in other coffee companies definitely engage with these profiles and posts, but they don't appear to drive end consumer engagement directly. If they have an impact it is through the word of mouth effect, down the road.

In the case of B2B coffee businesses, this social media audience is of course, the right audience, and the exposure can help. This still is not a substitute for in-person customer relations, which are likely to be more impactful in the long run. For this reason, you see a lot of coffee businesses that are very successful despite little use of social media.

A great shop will benefit the most from engaging its local customers, and building a reputation that (again) goes far beyond social media. Reputation, such as that of the Colombian producer or Ethiopian mill that you should be buying from at the moment, is also spread through social media, perhaps even more so than the end bag of coffee.

Whilst the coffee community engages with each other at trade and competition events, creating a lot of opportunity for word of mouth marketing, digital platforms allow discussion and awareness of who's doing what in coffee to carry on all year round. A coffee that does well in a competition or is bought by a well-known and respected roaster, is validated, and other coffee companies will want to get hold of a sample to see what the fuss is about. This is a sort of virality that is at play in specialty boutique coffee, and that can be seen throughout the supply chain, which is an ongoing feedback loop, circling around the pursuit of quality, scarcity and novelty. Word of mouth is clearly at play in nearly all industries, but it does seem to be particularly potent in specialty coffee.

Premium and Luxury Versus Craft and Local

Is specialty coffee bought by a narrow customer cohort? Or put differently, are specialty coffee customers all very similar people?

I think the answer is no. I suspect that one of the reasons that the market can be challenging in terms of online ad spend, is that the target customer is so broad. This circumstance is often described as a segmented market. Experts on online ad data often pick out cycling as an example of an industry that has a very clear target cohort. The behaviour and profile of those who really get into cycling is quite easily defined. When this is the case, a brand can utilise different marketing campaign techniques in an attempt to target these potential customers.

There is a stereotype of the specialty coffee person, or identity, but when you think about it, this typecasting is more reflective of the baristas than the café's customers. Whilst it may be fair to reflect that most specialty coffee customers can be represented as a gentrified, trendy demographic, the actual appeal of the product is much broader than this.

So, the super easy question: "who is your customer?" Is actually surprisingly hard to answer in specialty boutique coffee. Obviously it isn't for everyone, but who exactly should you expect it to be for?

The question can be a bit easier if you narrow down the product type. An espresso machine manufacturer aiming at the home market, for example, potentially has an easier job. Their product has a very high ticket price, and they might target a predominantly male, "gear" driven customer cohort.

The third wave café movement, on the other hand, has a very broad customer base. One may argue that a lot of the drinks sold in these environments aren't really that representative of specialty coffee, and that's a fair point. These shops will have their coffee geek customers, and potentially a committed community, but they also require a wide range of quality-seeking customers. These could be the customers we talked about in *Expertise, Trust and Word of Mouth*, who recognise something of quality, but may not want to dive down the rabbit hole or identify themselves as being a "specialty coffee person." This does not mean that they don't want to drink specialty coffee. There is also an association and connection between a brand and its people. Specialty coffee operators often have passionate owners or staff, and this can be a draw in itself, in which case the customer may not be too particular about the coffee.

One of the interesting customer separations is the divide between local and craft, and luxury or premium. These concepts are prevalent in specialty coffee. However a customer seeking local and craft may not have an interest in the product's premium nature, and vice versa. Whilst these aspects do have a crossover, they can also occupy quite separate spaces.

Nespresso may be a mass-market brand, but it has arguably done the best job of appealing to a premium-minded consumer. Their focus is on a luxury coffee experience, with a chocolate box-like presentation, and the convenience of making coffee with the push of a button. The brand does not tell a local or craft story, rather a luxury or premium one, and with annual revenues of several billion, Nespresso is definitely not boutique. It is, however, a premium luxury position in the wider coffee market. Compare this to an independent café and micro roaster who are putting forward a narrative of local, freshly roasted coffee.

It surprises a lot of people to learn that Nespresso buys a lot of specialty scoring coffee. So, both companies start with specialty coffee, and do vastly different things with it. Of course, it may be argued that the way Nespresso's coffee is presented when roasted as dark as they do, means that it no longer displays the attributes that it was graded on.

Questions abound about what customers do and don't want (and this includes a light or dark roast profile). The answer is that no individual flavour profile pleases all customers. The bigger the brand, the greater the need to please a larger, broader customer base by meeting their expectation or at least only challenging it slightly. I have always been a proponent of the idea that specialty is not for everyone. I see it as an opt-in or opt-out space. However, perhaps the opt-in and opt-out is based more upon a company's style and offer, than it is for specialty coffee as an ingredient.

One could argue that the success of Nespresso shows that there is an appetite for a premium product narrative that retains a more commercial flavour profile. We often link narrative to flavour in specialty boutique coffee, but it clearly isn't always necessary.

Back to the indie, local, craft coffee business. Does it resonate with customers because it serves specialty grade coffee, or because of the other values it represents? It could well be both. It could also be that the business utilises a perfectly nice 82 point blend, roasted to a quite developed point, and makes some good milk drinks that are only slightly different to their commercial counterparts. This business has less of a flavour-driven narrative around specialty coffee than Nespresso does. Whilst many would argue that it is vital that specialty prioritises origin characteristic and therefore avoids roast profiles that cover this flavour up, there are customers who want a darker profile, and also have an interest in provenance.

I was recently speaking to Paul Arnephy, a coffee consultant and trainer who was involved in the fourth edition of The Coffee Guide by the International Trade Centre. When putting the guide together, a conversation was had about how coffees that score in the low-80 point range, no longer reflect specialty coffee as a concept. This debate is one that will continue and continue, I am sure. There is a natural tendency to want to segment the scale further and stratify more, for example, premium coffee, mass premium, specialist and so on. An 80-point coffee is very much a different product than a 90-point coffee and they do have very different positions in the market.

For as long as the 80+ point scoring system continues to be

commonly used to define specialty grade coffee, I think that in business, specialty coffee will remain to be anything that manages to score past that arbitrary line at some point in its production journey. However, I am not sure that more detailed definitions and segmentation would be an improvement. I can understand many examples in which it could be useful to have further clarification, but I don't think that these delineations should be up to any one person or organisation to implement or control.

As I have mentioned earlier in the book, I don't see myself as someone who runs "specialty coffee companies," but rather "coffee companies that explore a range of premium and high-scoring coffees." As the founder, my business is driven by my preferences, and naturally we work more with the flavour profiles that I enjoy the most. In some of the business's collaborative projects I am more explorative and open minded when it comes to achieving a high-quality product specification that varies from my personal preference.

In examples I have given throughout this chapter we have looked at how companies working with specialty coffee can have a variety of brand narratives, some of which are more closely related to the actual coffee than others. This, in turn, returns a varying customer profile and marketing approach. The desire to categorise specialty coffee more simply is natural, but it is clearly a complex product that has different appeal in different parts of the market, and can therefore also appeal to a broad or segmented market. This versatility can add complexity to discussion around specialty coffee, but it is also one of its strengths, and this plays out in branding and marketing in the industry.

Semiotics - Specialty as an Aesthetic

Aesthetic: "**A set of principles underlying the work of a particular artist of movement.**" - Oxford Dictionary

Semiotics: "**The study of signs and symbols and their meaning and use.**" - Oxford Dictionary

Whilst it is fairly easy to talk about and to attempt to define some of the values that thread through the specialty boutique coffee movement, there are valid questions about whether these same values are really the key drivers for customer and business behaviours in this market.

How often are a coffee brand's values cohesively realised? And in some cases would it be more realistic to say these values have only been summarised into a mission and values statement when one needed to be written?

It is also tempting to string together some commonalities and to summarise the whole area of the specialty coffee industry under one defined banner. In doing so, we fail to recognise that although all businesses in this sphere are buying higher grade coffee, the businesses are not collectively the same, as I explored in the previous chapter.

A branding and product designer once mentioned to me how interesting it was to see the level of segmentation of the end customer who partakes in specialty coffee. By this they meant that there are a wide variety of motives that actually drive engagement, rather than one customer mission. Certainly, in the case of specialty boutique coffee, the impetus goes beyond just a convenient caffeine hit. You can see this customer variety in the sheer range of equipment and formats that now exist in coffee, as well as the multiple formats in which you can buy your coffee. The many different brewing devices all tell a tale of a different customer. Some appeal to precision, some are more about experience and ritual, some are automated and convenient, and some are deliberately complex, and require mastery. You can take this further, and look at the reasons behind buying behaviour, and think about how people connect to a coffee or a business that sells coffee.

The community aspect of the specialty coffee industry leads us to feel that it is a shared values movement. In many ways this is true, but as specialty coffee represents a collection of values, it can often be surprising for people to find the ways in which these vary throughout the space. At a coffee event or trade show, there is definitely a lot of passion in the room for coffee, but when you dig, you will find a multitude of reasons that people have been drawn to, or are working in, specialty coffee. As we have explored, a premium consumer is not necessarily the same as a consumer looking to buy from independent, local businesses. These two values are not mutually exclusive, but they can also be separated when it comes to buying habits and company culture.

One roastery may be focused on building producer relationships and another may prefer to scour the specialty world for the most intriguing and exciting coffee they can find that year. Both approaches are valid, and they come with different pros and cons. Committing to buying the same coffee in advance can actually create a quality risk, for example.

All of this eventually has to lead to the discussion of: "well what is specialty coffee about then?" The answer is, of course, that it is a collection of different things. If you work with the definition of the coffee's cup score (something I have already reproached multiple times in this book) you must bear in mind that a lot of coffee that scores well can be bought and roasted and presented by companies that don't fit the specialty feel at all.

Some claim that specialty provides an alternative purchasing model. It is true that there can be some differences in supply relations, but this claim is too strong, when in reality the coffee likely has various routes to market, some of which may be identical to those of non-specialty coffee. Even when these routes to market are different, the distinction is rarely drastic.

Whilst there can be some benefits of transparency, this has the most significant impact in the context of the provenance of the product. By this I mean that if the goal is to find a unique and distinct flavour profile, often tied to a specific location, this demands more specific traceability.

All of this being said, there certainly is a "feel" to the specialty segment of the coffee market, which leads me to the question of whether specialty coffee is a movement of businesses doing things in a certain way, or whether it is more of an aesthetic, rather than any particular set of objectives.

Joshua Tarlo, the founder of Headstand, put forward an interesting perspective to me over a conversation on Whatsapp.

He said that "when coffee first adopted certain design choices, it was signalling something or the absence of something. For example, minimalist café design signals a rejection of cluttering. It also signals a reduction of noise to more clearly showcase the product. The transparency of the space signals transparency in the sourcing of the coffee. These design choices while at first were meant to signal values, they themselves (the design principles) become something. As the design is deployed in various businesses, it is adopted not only as a principle by those who share the value in which it is signalling. It is also exploited by those that wish to profit from the consumers it attracts. Over time the principles behind the signals lose meaning, and the signals matter more than what they were originally meant to represent."

As Joshua suggests, I think that the marketing of many coffee companies in the space can rightly be accused of propagating the specialty feel or aesthetic without a focus on the behaviours that created the visuals in the first place. This creates a situation that can be misleading, as those who take part believe they are fighting a crusade for a virtue-driven coffee cause, only to find out that there is no robust substance behind the rhetoric, and that actually the business is just tapping into an aesthetic that they think will sell.

Joshua also took to social media recently to question if people working in coffee were experiencing a form of "moral injury." The crux of this argument is based around the idea that people choose to be part of something they believe in, and understand to be achieving certain things. However, over time, or through specific experiences, they find out that this is not the case.

I do think there is an interesting consideration here and I think that the situation can cause coffee companies to feel driven to make bold or overblown claims that aren't fully substantiated (see *Greenwashing*). The independent nature of the boutique space means that there is little audit or need to prove what is written on a pack or in marketing materials. Maybe more importantly, there can be no immediate need to prove these claims within the business either. As this situation plays out, specialty coffee is in danger of only being an aesthetic - just a set of marketing initiatives and branding ideas.

However, I do think that there is a collective passion that draws people to specialty coffee, even if the term (or any term) isn't fully suitable or cohesive in representing the collection of people, coffee, and businesses. As is the case in craft beer, maybe specialty coffee won't ever be clearly defined, and maybe it doesn't need to be, but the term will still be used and have meaning for most people. The shared thread for those who work in the industry is passion and enthusiasm for coffee as a drink, a supply chain and a cultural device. As we explored when we talked about sensemaking I also think that this idea of building an understanding of coffee and its complexity is at the heart of what we call specialty coffee.

The idea of an aesthetic as a central aspect of specialty coffee is perhaps most triggering to those working in, or drawn to working in the industry. It would be more comforting to think that high-quality, fairly traded coffee products will speak for themselves, that they will shine through, and that authentic companies will be honest with themselves, and question realistically what they are achieving and where they fall short. I don't think this is easily achievable or realistic though and semiotics are clearly a force in specialty coffee. All branding and marketing in the space engages with the semiotics of coffee, whether intentionally or not.

When we first started our café in Bath we noticed that the environment we had created wasn't aiding the experience we were trying to build. Our premises looked too much like a "normal" café. We made several changes, which I now realise could be termed semiotic decisions. We took away the typical visual signposts (window dressing and street level visuals, the normal drinks menu, etc.) and created some positive confusion, which we then used to create a differentiated and curated coffee shop experience.

Many businesses in many fields won't be looking to subvert the semiotics at play, but rather to use them to help tap into a visual language and target the customer base, and it must be said that although we actively removed some of the semiotic signals, we also included many that are associated with specialty boutique coffee.

With semiotic theory you can look at the visual signposts that flow through an environment, in this case specialty coffee, and notice the inferred meaning of the different visual cues that exist within it. In branding these can also be called "cultural codes" and are category specific. In this case the category is coffee, but the same process can be applied to whisky, for example.

I do think that semiotics are also highly likely to be at play in both complex and subjective taste-driven fields, and that customers make decisions based on semiotics all of the time. Semiotics are clearly a part of any brand, and each company should carefully consider its aesthetic. I also think that getting the semiotics right in specialty coffee can only go so far, and that an inauthentic brand will struggle in the specialty boutique space long term, but I know this can also be argued to not be the case.

I do think that there is a differentiation challenge in coffee, and fields like coffee, whereby messaging and aesthetics can be quite pervasive across many brands. How can a customer tell the difference? How do they choose? There are ways a brand can tap into the cultural code whilst also retaining a unique identity.

Josh Tarlo is right that the semiotics in coffee can also develop into less useful and potentially misleading signposts and that this is another reason that the value and behaviour we explored in *Expertise, Trust and Word of Mouth* can be so important in spaces like coffee. Semiotics are a limited guide.

Speaking of semiotics and cultural codes that guide customers, this brings us neatly to the next chapter.

Design and Differentiation -
The Chain of Independent Coffee Shops
As the specialty coffee independent café movement was spreading throughout the UK I remember hearing people commenting on the similarity of many of the shop fit outs. The comments were meant in a derisive manner, and I understand where this comes from. It is an interesting observation. I think that this circumstance can also be seen in a positive light.

Remarks that I heard included a lamentation of the lack of originality and creativity in shop fit outs, as well as (unsurprisingly) the suggestion that a lot of inauthentic businesses were opening up, exploiting the growing opportunity by copying the shops that had done well.

At the same time, aesthetic similarities are likely to exist in any movement that feels cohesive, just like in a genre of music. Specialty coffee, or third wave coffee, or whichever term you prefer, is often described as a community. This community really does exist and it's rather wonderful. In essence, it is a business community; it is a collection of businesses and individuals working in coffee that share an interest in and passion for the product. For the most part they also share some preference in terms of what is rewarded in the cup, even if this is still somewhat varied.

You could discuss specialty coffee as a subculture of businesses, especially in its early days. Subcultures all have strong identities, usually accompanied by behavioural and visual markers. When the industry was in its infancy in the UK, you would often notice that a business with a certain espresso machine and grinder, perhaps alongside a certain aesthetic, would also have a recognisable focus on specialty quality coffee. This did not mean that these were the only environments that could make good coffee. When the roasting scene was smaller, and certain roasters were very picky about where their coffee was served, this also could be used as a guide.

As with all movements, there tends to be an identity that evolves out of an interest in the product. Some interests have wider identity appeal and participation. If you were to profile those drawn to working in the early specialty movement, you would find a lot of counter cultural, creative and independent types. Many customers may also have fit these criteria, but most coffee shops require a much wider range of customers to be successful as a business. You can't operate a closed club when the ticket price is as small as a cup of coffee. In general, the customer cohorts attracted to these coffee businesses are all curious people who are interested in a passionate, quality-focused approach to food and drink. I think this is actually a very wide range of people.

In the early years it wasn't just a shop's environment or staff that signposted the type of coffee shop it was, but also the latte art on top of all the milky drinks. Latte art really wasn't everywhere, and it definitely was not as widely adopted as it is now. Drink types were also key. The flat white was rarely seen outside of these third wave coffee shops. As with latte art, it has now been adopted by large chains and in the UK, and has become one of the highest selling drink types in all shops.

I diverge, but my point here is that it was not a surprise to see some aesthetic similarity between independent coffee shops. It makes a lot of sense, and it likely positively contributed to the feeling of a growing coffee movement.

However, direct mimicry has its own problems. There is a natural friction within a community of businesses. They may share a lot of enthusiasm for the product, and when it's all new and there can be a lot of market demand, so much so that a bunch of businesses can support one another, whilst all continuing to succeed and grow. This allows everything to be quite friendly. However, it is also unavoidable that they are in competition with one other. I think this is why it's very enjoyable to be at international coffee events, where people can connect with other people in the business, and who share enthusiasm for the product, but who also are not in the same domestic market, and therefore are not in competition.

Although this theme of a connected movement has threaded through the look and feel of many brands in the specialty boutique space, there is also a natural need for differentiation. In reality there has always been. As the industry originated in this country, often a specialty boutique café was naturally differentiated from its local competitors simply by being different to what was there already. As more specialty operators open in the same locations, that differentiation has become more diluted.

In Lani Kingston's book *Designing Coffee* she considers the variety of design and branding around the world and looks at how "design is one way that cafés, roasters, coffee shops and producers can differentiate themselves in a saturated market". With more people and companies looking to develop and communicate their brand and identity in coffee, there is a wider breadth of visuals and branding than ever before in coffee, and indeed more variety than many other industries.

Differentiation is indeed a challenge in specialty coffee when many of us are telling very similar stories. As per the *Expertise, Trust and Word of Mouth* chapter, I believe that a brand's following in the boutique space is driven as much by word of mouth as by achieving a specific design result. Of course, the design itself can feed into the word of mouth marketing, as it forms part of the experience and feeling that the industry and the customers get. I guess, what I am saying is that stunning design won't do it on its own, but neither will great coffee. A coffee shop is a holistic brand space in which many factors contribute to the company's success.

With these different notions in mind, it feels as though branding and identity in the space needs to both conform and stand out. Brands need to hit a brand communication and tone that signal that they are a specialty boutique coffee company, and yet differentiate themselves within the community to demonstrate that they are not a copycat, and that they are an authentic company with unique identity and value for people to engage with.

Design in all areas of our lives is a transient thing. On the whole, and especially in a space like specialty boutique coffee, there is an ever changing design aesthetic thought up by many many different companies and creatives. What constitutes something that feels unique and differentiated can very quickly change if some of the style and signalling is adopted by multiple other companies in the space. A design also can become dated if it tapped into a wider aesthetic in pop culture that came and went quickly. Interestingly, as specialty boutique coffee matures, there are also brands doubling down on their own history from a design and brand point of view, choosing to communicate that they are not new and trendy, but rather recognised and established.

If we step outside of the specialty boutique space, and look at where specialty coffee is being served and how it is being framed, the context is wider than ever before. There are almost certainly companies looking not to tap into the boutique aesthetic on purpose, as they are keen to attract a more mainstream consumer. In a way this represents a coming together in the middle of the coffee space, where some specialty coffee companies are looking to adopt communication with more mass-appeal, whilst at the same time, mainstream brands have begun adopting some of the specialty coffee messaging and design aesthetic.

Coffee is quite an amazing product in terms of its cultural significance and its wide appeal across demographics. This creates a melting pot of design and branding across a wide spectrum of styles and themes. For consumers and buyers in the industry, design is key to how they interact with the business, with split second assumptions made about what the company is trying to do, based on its visual signposting.

Lifestyle and Merchandising Coffee Brands

When discussing design and branding in coffee with Lani Kingston, (*Designing Coffee*) we talked about the variety of branding and design that can now be seen around the world. An interesting point that came up was the propensity, in different countries, for coffee brands to go beyond talking about coffee itself.

The UK has a pretty literal brand relationship with coffee. This has most likely arisen from our recent history. We have only in the last few decades identified ourselves as a nation of coffee drinkers, and since then, our go-to format has overwhelmingly been instant coffee in the context of a jar of caffeine granules. Until the mid-1990s coffee hadn't really been pervasive in British culture (barring its original British boom in the 17th century, before making way for tea). There is also a cynicism in British culture, which perhaps leads us to treat coffee businesses as coffee businesses more so than some other geographies. Whatever the exact social and cultural reasons, we do not really see lifestyle coffee brands here in the same way they exist in other countries.

For the most part, the different coffee brand identities across the UK market, generally focus on what the brand is doing with coffee. Dark Arts coffee is an interesting exception. This is a UK coffee company that focuses on quality coffee, but that has an identity that isn't just about coffee. The brand engages with its tribe of customers and followers using humour, memes, and merchandise.

231

Brad Morrison, founder of Dark Arts, explained to me that they look to speak to their customers in the language that they use, which is, the evolving language of the internet. They use memes to communicate, because people use memes. They look to the trends in streetwear and other spaces for design inspiration. Brad understands that Dark Arts merchandise has become crucial in the way his brand engages with customers. This is notable, as the brand has become part of East London's pop culture.

Brad explained to me that when the company traces its merchandising sales, their customers are not always on their website to buy coffee, but that in their business, increased merchandising sales do correlate with increased coffee sales overall. These strategies allow Dark Arts to have a strong differentiated identity with a ton of character, and it is super interesting that a person's relationship with coffee can be much more than a simple food or drink supply transaction.

People often appear to have really connected relationships, not just with coffee, but the companies that they buy their coffee from. There are not many other food and drink areas that can claim this same connection. Craft beer can, and this has created another special market.

There is clearly an identity element at play in coffee branding. Some coffee companies tie clothing lines into their brand journey or other products and experiences. For these reasons you could argue that most specialty coffee brands are as much lifestyle brands as they are coffee brands. Whilst, in some cases this would be a fair assessment, most are still very much seen as a coffee company first.

Around the world there are more and more examples of integrated brands that tie coffee to an identity, and these brands may well diversify beyond coffee within this brand. Other food and drink items can be introduced into the brand ecosystem, such as artisanal baked goods and doughnuts. Perhaps as each market matures, and the brands that focus on quality tasting coffee and a provenance narrative are pervasive, the need for differentiation may drive more lifestyle brands in coffee.

B2B Branding

Outside of the world of cafés and coffee retail, most of the coffee industry deals in B2B transactions. Branding and marketing is also key in this area, and not just at the consumer end. In fact, I think a lot of what we have explored in this part of the book is even more relevant in a B2B sense. B2B brands need to appeal to their clients in the supply chain, and some need to appeal to multiple parts of the supply chain all at once. A roasting machine company, for example, needs to appeal to the roasting community, and will need to build trust and credibility around its technology.

However, for coffee producers and roasting brands there is a pull-through strategy at play, as they may still benefit from resonating with an end consumer, and creating a demand loop throughout the industry. This could play out like the following scenario. A brand begins to build some momentum and starts to be recognised by a smaller group of coffee people. These people then put the product in front of their customers, and also in front of other coffee businesses. The brand may then reach a point where it has awareness amongst end consumers, which drives further B2B opportunity, as the end consumers show a desire to engage with the B2B brand via another company. This effect can play out for a coffee farm. If end consumers are desperate to get hold of the farm's best lots, a roastery can become a conduit for that farm's coffee and brand.

Likewise, a roaster's reputation with customers can develop to a point where customers recognise and ask after, or search out their brand. Whilst the demand stems from the end consumer, it is pulling B2B sales back through. This brand demand phenomenon is very clearly at play when it comes to products like oat milk, where customers may not ask for just oat milk, but for their preferred oat milk brand. The same can be true for certain brewing devices.

This phenomenon is contrasted by those businesses that have a curated approach. In this case the business may choose to present only new and curated brands, avoiding any need to react to brands of which customers are already aware. This type of business prides itself on being able to present new and different brands as part of its own value proposition.

Those businesses that have a curation position in the market allow a funnel of new brands and companies. Some of these will move from being a "new" or unusual discovery to becoming an established "name." Many boutique roasters, for example, have cult-like followings. Their customers are looking to be guided on what coffee to buy, how to brew it, and to an extent, how to think about it. The roaster in these instances, can act as an introducer of brands, and give them credibility simply by representing them.

"New" brands can't be new for very long though, and luckily they don't need to be. In specialty coffee lots of companies are selling to lots of clients across the market. Many brands in the space are not looking to present new, unheard-of companies, but rather to work with brands that have a proven ability to produce a good quality product. With recognition and connection comes a growing customer base for the brand. This could perhaps lead to a pull-through strategy, and so the cycle continues.

As we explored in *Physical Experiences - The Value of Bricks and Mortar*, engaging in a physical experience with people and coffee is key in B2B business. These environments in B2B interactions are often driven as much by human interaction as they are with an experience of the coffee itself. Success may come from securing a relatively small number of commercial relationships, which will often be built on human interaction between key stakeholders in the businesses who are transacting and collaborating. This leaves the business open to key man risk, and over time the goal will be to to develop a brand that is less reliant in this way.

Part Six. Strategy

Introduction to Part Six

Strategy "**A plan of action designed to achieve a long-term or overall aim.**" - Oxford Dictionary

With the wide array of levers involved in running any given business, each business navigates its own path with the use of strategy. Some strategies are more comprehensive and complex than others.

A strategy will need to understand the business's current and potential proposition in the market, utilising both an understanding of micro and macro economics to strike out on its path to success. A clear mission statement can help create a "North Star" for the business, a guiding light that you can pin a strategy to.

It is often noted that many organisations lack long-term strategy, and instead are more short-term tactically minded. Tactics can, and hopefully should be, the daily and weekly behaviours that allow you to achieve your strategy over time. *Part Two* of this book is essentially an exploration of business operating tactics. However, being "in the weeds" of making immediate tactical decisions in a business, can mean that over time strategy drifts. This isn't to say that strategy shouldn't change and adapt when necessary, but this process should be deliberate, and not accidental.

In this section, we explore some of the key strategic thought processes in business, and how they play out in specialty boutique coffee.

What is Your Why?

Leadership expert Simon Sinek pioneered the Why, How, What approach within his book, *The Golden Circle*. Essentially, the approach explains how these simple questions are able to effectively inform strategy and the correct company culture to allow you to achieve the strategy. The idea is that you start with your "Why," your purpose for why you are running the business. What are you trying to achieve with the business and its products? This is followed by the "How." This refers to how you go about achieving your "why," which actions do you take to get where you want to go, to fulfil the "why." This naturally leads to the "What." This is the thing you have made, your product or service. Sinek's theory claims that successful companies start with "why," and he contends that many companies don't know their "why."

The Golden Circle by Simon Sinek.

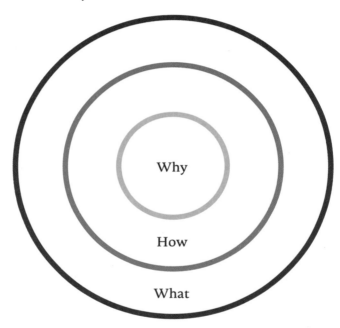

Business author Dominic Monhkouse argues that although the "why" is key, the "who" is just as important. Essentially you need to know "who" your "why" will appeal to. In coffee this can be somewhat challenging, as most coffee companies have a wide array of customers. In this way, economics also drives strategy, alongside the "why" and "who." In fact, economics can help to define the "who" and then question the "why."

Earlier in the book, in the chapter *Customer and Supplier Alignment*, we looked at this point through an economic lens. It was considered that a company needs to understand whether or not a product proposition is profitable in relation to a certain customer type and size. This does not sound as aspirational or inspiring as a purpose driven "why," but there are many "whys" in coffee that unfortunately don't work economically. A lot of this book is about explaining the constraints and challenges of running successful businesses in the specialty boutique coffee industry. These constraints need to be understood to result in more successful specialty boutique coffee businesses.

The "why" of many specialty coffee businesses is the pursuit of great coffee. This can be achieved by growing, moving, roasting or serving exceptional coffee. This "why" may have been strategically unusual twenty years ago, but is now quite prolific. At the same time, each company's idea of what exceptional coffee is, is different, and there is a clear market for lots of businesses pursuing these adjacent goals.

The company's "why" could be more specific. It could be focused on very particular coffee from specific producers, or specific flavour profiles, or a specific brewing format, and so on. This complexity in the space does leave a lot of room for variety, and essentially many company's "why" is to pursue their take on coffee.

When crossing the "why" with the "who" the strategy can become more concentrated on achieving a specific goal within the industry. It could be an importer representing specific origins or regions and seeking to grow access to the market for those coffees. It could be an exporter looking to represent and provide connection to the boutique market for specialty producers in that region. The list could go on indefinitely. Many coffee businesses in boutique coffee also outline a goal, not of pursuing exceptional coffee, but rather building experience and culture around good coffee.

Business author Jim Collins adds some further considerations to the "why" with his "Hedgehog Concept" outlined in his book *Good to Great*. Collins puts forward the three following questions that need to interact in order to hit a strategic sweet spot.

The question of "what are you passionate about?" (The "why") must be considered alongside two other questions: "what drives your economic engine?" And, "what can you be the best in the world at?" I think that the economic engine question is vital to all businesses. Your economic engine is the fundamental economics of the business from which you are able pursue your "why," "how" and "what." You need to be strategic about pursuing a commercial structure that sustainably creates profit if you wish to achieve your "why." The "being best in the world at what you do" mantra is less essential in my mind. I don't actually believe it is key to running a good sustainable specialty coffee business, though it may be key to running an exceptional one.

Three circles of the hedgehog concept

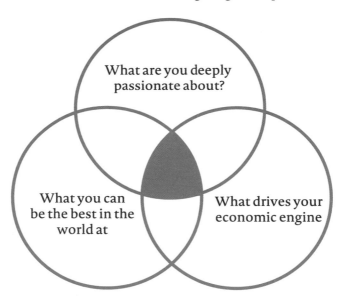

Regardless of the answer to the "why" question, your guiding north star can act as a focal point around which strategy can evolve. A wonderful side of our industry is the passion that abounds, and many people I speak to who come into specialty coffee from another industry, point out how they have never worked in such a welcoming, collaborative, and enthusiastic space. I think that this results in plenty of answers to the "why" question. The key is to think about these answers strategically, and ask reflective questions about how a business can seek to achieve its goals, whilst critically assessing its own position.

Porter's Business Strategies

Michael Porter is an American academic who outlined a variety of theories and principles for strategy in business in the 1980s. They are commonly used in MBA courses around the world. Although they are in some ways quite dated now, there are some applicable concepts to discuss.

The Four Generic Strategies

This concept is based on two main axes of thought: cost and focus. On the cost side Porter proposes that a business is either looking to offer a lower price for a given product than competing businesses in the market, or that they seek to establish a higher price through differentiation that is recognised as value by the customer. On the focus side, the theory proposes that a business will either focus its attention on selected segments of the market, or aim broadly and industry wide. Each business must choose a strategy that selects two of these four generic principles - one from the cost axis, and one from the focus axis.

So how do these play out in coffee? At first glance it seems quite straightforward to allocate specialty boutique coffee to the differentiated cost option and the segment targeted focus. This would mean that the strategy is to pursue a differentiated coffee product that targets specific segments with whom the product's differentiated value and higher price resonates.

The most high-end area of specialty coffee is perhaps the most easily represented by this strategic positioning. At the coffee shop end of things, the analysis is more intriguing, as many businesses don't really have a place on the cost axis. Often these businesses do not aspire to achieve a higher or lower price point than the mass-branded coffee shop market. Instead, they intend to offer a differentiated product at a matched price. This strategy is driven by the desire to appeal to a wide audience, rather than a segmented one, however these businesses do still wish to capture the specialist segment.

In this way, many businesses are actually trying to incorporate a variety of Porter's Generic Strategies into one business strategy. Within one menu a specialty boutique café is likely to have products that have different relationships with the generic categories. A café operator may have a product that achieves a lower price compared to competitors in the area, such as a batch brew, whilst simultaneously showing a freezer menu of coffees, with differentiated, higher prices.

In most cases, coffee hospitality operators recognise a need for a base of customers, and will need to rely on potential customers with relatively close proximity to them to provide this. This entails appealing to a variety of potential customer segments, and therefore providing different products with different positioning strategies. This spread strategy is also seen in the case of green coffee producers or importers who often offer a range of products, which can appeal to a variety of needs. Brands are unlikely to cover the whole spectrum of coffee, but generally need to offer a broad enough spread of options to retain commercial relevance. There is a strong argument that a sustainable competitive advantage cannot be achieved and that it will need to change and evolve over time.

The power of brand is not really represented in this theory. Of course, the brand itself is a clear form of differentiation, but it isn't represented in the cost versus focus framework very well. The perception of how well a company's brand achieves its product or service goals is tied to its market position. There are many customers and clients who associate certain expectations with companies, based upon how they position themselves in the market.

The spread strategy is also operationally very difficult. This is due to resource requirements as well as team and personnel challenges and a brand commitment that makes it challenging to succinctly offer "everything." Companies typically end up tailoring their resources and operations to a more specific part of the market, meaning that although a form of spread strategy is common, it still has its limitations, and companies need to make decisions about where their strategic focus lies. The "why" and "who" are tied to market and operational strategic focus.

The Five Forces

Porter's "Five Forces" are a sort of market analysis process, allowing you to view how your company is positioned as part of a competitive landscape in the market.

1. *Competition in the market.* The larger the number of competitors, along with comparative products and services, the lesser the power of a company.
2. *Potential of new entrants.* This refers to the competition that has yet to become a part of the market. How quickly could more competitors impact your business?
3. *Power of suppliers.* Can suppliers increase the cost of inputs? And how able is a company able to utilise a competitive supplier market to keep input costs down?
4. *Power of customers.* A small cohort of high-value customers are in a position to push for better deals, whereas a wider range of customers allows a company to explore pricing and maximise profitability.
5. *Threat of substitutes.* What product or services substitutes exist as an alternative for a company's customers? Alternatives and substitutes provide a threat to retaining customers.

The Five Forces differ from the common SWOT analysis (strengths, weaknesses, opportunities and threats) as they are more focused on the marketplace, whilst SWOT is based internally on the individual company.

In the terms of force one, most parts of the seed to cup journey present themselves as highly competitive. The market contains a high number of businesses, and there are many comparative products and services in the space. Looking at force two, there is always also a high possibility of new entrants.

Force three is interesting in coffee. The global market of green coffee is very powerful, and if there is a shortage of supply then prices will go up. Price increases are less likely to be due to a supplier or farm making an individual decision to push the price up, as there is a competitive market, allowing companies to source beans elsewhere.

However, at the super premium end the power of the supplier is much stronger.

If I want a Geisha from Hacienda La Esmeralda, there is only one place I can get it, and as such the farm is able to set a high price. The same goes for the CGLE 17 Hybrid (Gesha and Caturra cross) at Café Granja La Esperanza, which produces a beautiful cup of coffee for which there is a growing demand in Asian markets. We bought all of this coffee for our roastery when it was first produced three years ago, and the prices have already more than doubled, as the supplier is exploring how rarity and reputation can leverage a higher price point.

As we move downstream, an importer will typically, but not always, strike a deal with a producer or exporter to represent their coffee in another market, and the importer then is in a similarly strong position if demand is high. A roaster and a coffee shop also can experience this dynamic. The likelihood of being in a powerful supplier position is low, and more often than not, the competitive market means that suppliers are not in a very powerful position, and will need to work hard to build brand and strong relationships if they wish to maintain a good price.

Force four is much like force three in that there are examples of both powerful and weak customers depending upon where you look in the industry. The most powerful individual customers are those with wholesale supply relationships. These are high volume clients, who can utilise scale to achieve lower prices. This is a good example of why a business would be wary of a single customer that contributes more than 10% of revenue.

When considering force five, in the wider market sense I would say that coffee feels pretty resilient. People want to drink coffee and there's a growing demand for specialty coffee. Lots of research has been done on the health impact of drinking coffee and although there are some arguments on both sides, overall coffee is seen as a positive habit (of course some people find this not to be the case). It doesn't feel like there are any likely coffee substitutes on the horizon. There are mushroom alternatives and other beverages which some will choose to swap in, but really coffee seems to be on solid footing in this regard. On the other hand, the tea industry in the UK could have cited coffee as a substitute threat, and they would have been right to do so, just as soy milk would have the right to identify oat milk as a substitute threat.

For individual businesses in the coffee industry there are a proliferation of substitute threats throughout the supply chain. Through the analysis of the Five Forces, the Four Generic Strategies and the SWOT concepts, coffee has shown itself to be a highly competitive market place, meaning that pursuing and achieving a strong strategic position is challenging. Perception of differentiation through branding and communication can be a big strength for companies in coffee. Strategic position for boutique specialty coffee companies can also come from capabilities, such as specific locations for stores, the ability to make desirable coffee from a revered farm, the best access to finance, or a flexibility and capability in roasting and packing. Whatever the points of difference are that a business chooses, this is definitely something for all companies to ponder, particularly in the competitive market place of specialty coffee.

Scale, Diversification & Vertical Integration

It becomes quite clear when looking at the fundamental business economics at play across the different parts of the coffee industry that scale is a key component of any strategy, for any business in coffee. Many businesses in coffee have a minimum viable scale. Due to tight margins, nano or micro businesses in coffee are often not sustainable unless treated as hobby businesses. The lowest margin businesses such as green importers have the greatest incentive to pursue a sizable scale.

As I pointed out in *The Impact of Scale*, scale does not have a one size fits all solution, formulas are contextual. However, clearly the lower the net profit of the business, the greater the need for a higher revenue goal. A boutique importer needs to hit triple the revenue (if not more) to make the same net profit as a café.

A lot of what we looked at when considering these topics in *Part 2* of the book touched on scale and the sweet spots of business in coffee, talking around how any business strategy needs to be keenly aware of the impact of different scales on the viability of the model.

Scale also comes with the likelihood of increased investment and risk, you cannot simply pursue scale in a vacuum. A successful strategy must consider different stages of scale and how the business will move through them. Pursuing scale as a means to address current losses is rarely a good idea. Nothing about coffee suggests that it can be operated like a tech business, in which you can establish the cost base, run at losses until you see exponential customer growth. As the cost base in this scenario is fixed, more customers can translate to more profit, resulting in a viable high profitability at scale. In coffee, as sales grow, so do costs. If you saw a model on an investment deck that showed EBITDA shooting up from 5% now to 30% in three year's time as a function of scale, this would seem a highly dubious pitch.

My friends in the USA note how there they have noticed a greater cultural desire for scaling specialty coffee businesses from the outset. In the UK and Europe a lot of specialty boutique businesses appear happy to either stay smaller or grow more slowly over a longer time period. Work by Caravela Coffee has both outlined the need to hit a minimum scale to make coffee farming viable, and also encouraged the business practice of pursuing routes to achieve optimal scale at a coffee farming level across Latin America.

Discussion of scale in specialty boutique coffee is tempered by the quality focus of the movement. With quality being a strategic focus in specialty businesses, any strategy that pursues scale, needs to understand and consider how that affects its core quality proposition.

Vertical integration is naturally woven into scale discussions, and it is often at larger scales that vertical integration can become a beneficial part of the strategy. Vertical integration in coffee is very much an extension of the value add conversation. The idea of vertical integration can be summed up with the following question: "shall we do that ourselves?" It is an approach to streamlining operations by taking ownership of various parts of the supply chain that were previously produced and supplied by external companies.

If vertical integration can ultimately lead to better business, you may ask why, if the scale is big enough, all larger companies don't vertically integrate their whole supply chain. The most significant answer is risk and flexibility. For each aspect brought in-house, no matter how big the company, there is more stacked up risk.

Another reason is focus. In fact, when companies get very large, and appear to have vertically integrated, the integration is often at an ownership level. If different processes and services are quite different in regard to infrastructure, expertise and process, then the structure will still involve relatively separate, autonomous teams. The goal is still achieved, which is to allow the company to increase their control over the supply chain by owning more of it.

The complexity of the coffee supply chain means that different modular approaches to integration are at play across different businesses in the industry. Vertically integrating can be a strategic approach allowing a company to take control of an integral part of the supply chain that would otherwise cause a company over reliance on a separate business. This reduces risk of the other company failing to deliver or becoming actively adversarial. In this way vertical integration can be considered a strategic direction in a company, but understanding the true costs and challenges of bringing a process in-house is fundamental.

Vertically integrating from an upstream position is usually more for the purpose of diversifying and gaining access to the market further downstream. I have spoken to many producers on this subject. The possibility of branching out beyond agriculture and exploring many of the other parts of the industry is a strategic question some are exploring, whether through an importing office in a high-consuming nation, a roasting operation, or even long shelf life products such as coffee pods, which could be sold globally by a coffee producer.

A business strategy such as this can be just as much about reducing risk and stabilising income and profit as it is about growing sales. Diversification in coffee is able to help spread risk, just so long as the associated costs of an increasingly complex organisation don't spiral. A diversification strategy should be approached like a balanced risk investment portfolio. There are only so many high risk endeavours that you can pursue at any one time, if you wish to avoid a "house of cards" situation, where everything can be brought down at once.

Scale, vertical integration and diversification each represent different tactile and strategic approaches that are common in the coffee industry and feel like fundamental aspects of many businesses in the market.

Growing a Business - Quick Versus Slow Growth

There are many different ways to approach the process of starting a business or taking business in a new direction. Success stories from the world of tech and Silicon Valley get people excited about the opportunity of a runaway, fast-growing company that can make founders and investors a quick return.

The speed of a coffee company's growth is not necessarily a simple choice, ie, "would I like to grow slow or fast?" You could intend for fast or slow growth, but there are other factors that will dictate how this actually plays out. For example, a company that creates a strong value proposition but without the strategy to grow fast, may find itself growing fast and having to figure out how to keep up with demand. In opposition to this, a company with the ambition to grow fast, may find that their strategy doesn't work, and the growth does not materialise.

For many boutique specialty coffee businesses, strategy around growth is either contained, or not there at all. I think many businesses in the sector have evolving growth plans whereby strategy is built around making the most of what they are currently doing or building the next part of the project. Moving from one project to the next is a very entrepreneurial approach to business, and is a tactic often employed within the boutique coffee space. Essentially, in the case of small and independent businesses with limited funding, it is often only possible to work on what is right in front of you.

The exact strategic and tactical approaches to growing will vary across businesses, and this discussion requires context. However, I hope that throughout this book I have been able to explore and document dynamics in the industry that inform this, through observing how different levers in the market work.

A fundamental obstacle to growing quickly in many industries is access to finance. The percentage profit available in the different businesses throughout coffee means that many business models are unable to fund growth through the use of their own profits. A coffee shop can take a few years to break-even, and then a few more to hit its optimal profit window. Depending on how resourceful the business is when opening stores, there should be enough money to open another site four or five years in from the success of the first. If the fit outs are really expensive then it could be a decade or more before that may be the case, so more funding from somewhere will be required.

Finding the right locations can be a big challenge when opening shops, and if a business has set some specific site requirements, such as maximum rent relative to location and size, then the possibility of multiple site openings will be dictated by the ability and time taken to find the right sites.

Likewise, coffee farming requires the ability to find the right site, the finance to acquire the land and the capital expenditure and working capital to get things to where they need to be. This will all also depend on the position of the land and whether it was already being used to grow coffee successfully, and at what quality.

Exporters and importers need to successfully find sales in the marketplace, and then have to keep increasing their ability to access finance to support their business of financing coffee. For them, more coffee quite simply means more financing. Roasteries need to build out their food manufacturing business both in terms of team and capabilities, but also in terms of equipment and infrastructure.

At the beginning of this chapter I referenced successful business stories, where a business is able to create something of value, and subsequently has runaway success. In this scenario the business ends up working overtime to keep up with snowballing sales. Many businesses that target this type of fast growth, proactively pursue and fund their growth. In these cases, the finance challenge is not around increasing the ability to make things or provide services, but rather a need to focus on sales. This could be through marketing initiatives or a more traditional, boots on the ground, sales approach. It is common for sales initiatives to have a lag dynamic, whereby a lot of work is put in without direct return. The expectation is that the sales will flow through later. This approach is costly, and many businesses will end up funding initiatives that don't work, whilst trying to find those that do. In this way a scattergun approach takes place, a lot of money is spent trying lots of things at once, with the danger that none of them will work sufficiently well. This is a high-risk profile, and trying to grow fast by chucking money at it has only one sure-fire outcome, which is to spend a lot of money.

If funding is achieved through dilution of equity there is also the challenge of where the business will be (or needs to be) in the future. Often growth has to be very high for everything to work in this strategy. There needs to be room for future fundraising and incentive has to be retained for all invested at each stage. The risk profile of aggressively funded models, combined with the obvious challenges, means that it's not uncommon for these approaches to fail. Valuations need to be high, and as we have explored, they are in most cases, more conservative.

There are of course other perhaps more tangible ways to use funding in the pursuit of achieving growth. One such approach would be the purchase or consolidation of other businesses. Good shop operators often keep an eye out for promising sites on the market, and are able to assess whether they haven't worked due to some clear tactical missteps by previous operators. They can then come in and utilise the foundations to grow and achieve success more quickly. A merger or collaboration can be a way to pool resources and combine success to hit some critical points in terms of efficiency and scale. Finding collaborative businesses that both want the same thing and share a vision isn't easy though.

The challenge of maintaining quality and value whilst growing fast is also very real, particularly in boutique specialty coffee. It is for this reason that a business may not only shy away from actively pursuing growth, but will purposefully limit and control any growth. We explore the concept of scaling quality later in *The Fifth Wave. Can you Scale Quality*? There are clear examples where trying to maximise volume or pursue growth make it very hard to maintain quality. Not just the quality of a physical product, but also the quality of an experience and the cohesive quality of a brand. The organisational challenges that come with growing a team are also a consideration, we touched on this when studying stages of organisational growth by Larry E. Greiner in *Part Two*.

Many specialty boutique businesses focus first on quality and experience, meaning that growth is contained in phases that are driven by a vision to achieve a specific idea. The strategy will be to build a specific idea, and the focus is tactical, whilst the founders and teams look to make a success of the business that they have mapped out. This could then be followed by the next strategic step to grow, diversify or vertically integrate. This more "organic" way of growing has many benefits. Risk is less likely to be high, and the operator can keep a handle on things that don't work and kill them as they go. It is a more iterative approach that is more likely to move through phases of sustainable growth, as the business does not have deep funding to dip into. Instead they need to have a strategy that allows them to use what they have built as a safe base to explore new growth strategies.

Whether the strategy is to grow fast or slow, or not at all, I think a strong understanding of how the coffee industry works is needed for success. Effectively, the levers that we worked through in *Part Two* of the book need to be utilised. I do also think that precedent in the marketplace suggests that specialty boutique businesses are less likely to be high-growth, and are more likely to be successful when built over decades.

Funding and Financing

As we saw in the chapter *Access to Finance - An Industry Built on Borrowed Money*, different forms of funding are key to the industry's ability to function, and almost all businesses in coffee benefit from finance, somewhere in the supply chain. Any strategic position taken by a company in any industry requires a consideration of the financial requirements.

Lean margins in coffee mean that a company typically will not have enough cash from profits to fund a faster growth strategy. This is typical in many industries. Investment for a younger or faster growing business will often come from external investment funding.

Perhaps a more interesting strategic approach to funding can be found in group business. This is based on a balance of different businesses, which are either at different points in their journey or operate different strategies. An example here would be that one business in a group is run with profit in mind. This business typically will have some form of maturity, and is therefore able to create profit. This business could be described as being in a "cash generative maintenance mode," which means that the owners are looking after the business, and not strangling it by pushing hard for a better bottom line, which may hurt the business in the medium to long term. At the same time, another business within the same ownership group can utilise the profit from the steady and stable business to fund a more ambitious growth oriented strategy. Faster growth strategies typically require more funding for both speculative sales and marketing campaigns, but also for capital expenditure and working capital needs. Even the lean profit of a bigger, mature company can provide a large amount of funding for a smaller business or project.

This strategy could take place in a group of relatively large SMEs, but the strategy is also common within smaller businesses and even within a single business that can use its more profitable customers to fund the growth of new customers.

A producer in Central America that manufactures plastic moulded products and also has coffee farms, may utilise the profit from the plastic business to fund diversification in the coffee farming business. This type of approach can also be commonly seen in the instance of a coffee roastery that also owns shops. People will assume that the roastery can fund the shop, but for me, it was the other way around for a long time. In the case where a brand has a more aggressive strategy for growth, this approach is often not enough.

An ambitious growth plan will typically require equity to be given away in exchange for funding. Debt may simply add more pressure and burden on the business as it tries to grow. A funded strategy in coffee is often set up to achieve a "tipping point" in the business. The brand strategy is aimed at reaching a point where the business has a large and sustainable recognition and engagement from consumers. This approach, to put a product everywhere at once, is quite a classic route that has been taken by large food and drink companies successfully. It is expensive and risky but with a lot of funding, it can work. It has not, however, been overly common in specialty coffee.

A strategy around funding also relies on the spend ceasing at some point. The scale must produce profit for the bottom line. Although this is strategically possible, I think that if the model is too far from profitability at its instigation, this won't simply turn around with scale. In product based companies, whilst there are some economies of scale that can be built into a strategic plan, a lot of the costs will scale with the growth.

A lot of financing, strategy and tactics in coffee are not tied to a fundraising campaign. An awareness of the importance of finance throughout the industry allows businesses to implement strategy with this in mind, either in their open business or as a competitive advantage to win customers.

A coffee roastery could work on developing a financing facility that allows it to lease machines to cafés, which is not dissimilar to a car financing arrangement. In this case, this is a strategic facility that can win and retain wholesale coffee customers. In the chapter on *Access to Finance* we looked at the tactile strategy of utilising back-to-back financing of commercial coffee to fund the export of specialty coffee.

Of course, financing requirements are directly linked to scale. A green importer's financing needs to increase as they get bigger, whilst a roastery's can improve with scale. If a roastery can move through containers of coffee regularly, it can negotiate a better price on the coffee it purchases. And for roasteries, the big saving comes from not having to finance and store the coffee over time, as the roastery is able to move through stock more efficiently.

Like many of the chapters in this book, the ideas covered here are not exhaustive, but hopefully they are illustrative of the factors at play. Funding and finance strategy is key to all businesses in coffee.

Part Seven. Business by Business

Introduction to Part Seven

The structure of this book has been built around the idea that the core mechanics of running businesses can be applied throughout the industry regardless of the business location or type. I wanted to think about each business as a business first and foremost as a means to understand how the sphere of specialty coffee works. I hope this analysis is useful for the reader and the wider community of coffee businesses and professionals.

For this penultimate part of the book I want to circle back to each of the typical and specific businesses in the supply chain, applying the levers we have looked at in order to consider perspectives of business in each of these areas.

Growing and Processing Coffee
Economics and Scale
Early in the book we mapped out some basic target summaries of the economics of the different business types that make up the coffee supply chain.

The smallholder grower is the most challenging to operate financially as a business, especially if the scale is too small. The *Rich Farmer, Poor Farmer* article written by Alejandro Cadena of Caravela coffee, from which some of the numbers are derived, maps out some scenarios of smallholder farmers based on data points from across several Latin American countries that Caravela works in.

Alejandro looked at the C Price against an average cost of production from 2010 to 2018 with a 30 cent differential. The profit made varied wildly as the C Price moved, from highs of 52% profit to lows of -2% profit. The average was 24%. This sounds high, and it is as a percentage, but importantly it is still a small cash amount, due to small production. In the article he shows that at one hectare the numbers just don't stack up at all, and that with good productivity on a three hectare farm, this profitability level results in an average of $2,227 profit per year. The need for annual reinvestment to deliver the following year's harvest will utilise much of these takings. This also does not account for the need to manage the volatility risk.

The work Caravela has done to map profitability potential against size helps with the farm-level discussion around coffee production in the countries that they are active in. This kind of insight can and is used to inform a farming strategy around reaching a minimum viable scale alongside a model of efficient production and access to market.

When looking at larger specialty producers who either have a big farm or multiple farms, who may or may not dry mill their own coffee, but who do export their own coffee, the business models target approximately the same percentage margin. With both a higher volume of coffee but also the full FOB price there is a higher revenue to draw the profit from.

Just as with the smallholders, the profit achieved is heavily influenced by both the global market pricing for coffee and the impact of varying weather conditions. Producers in countries all around the world from India to El Salvador report increasing climatic volatility, which reduces their yield and therefore reduces their income and their bottom line. Carlos Borgonovo has indicated that in Borgonovo Pohl's El Salvador coffee farms, increased heat and a lack of water has meant that the ratio of cherry to green coffee has consistently reduced year-on-year, over the past few years. This means that they need to start with more cherry, in order to get the same weight of exportable green coffee, which means a reduced yield and lower sales relative to the cultivated land.

Too much rain is a huge problem and can reduce crops by a huge amount. Pedro of Pergamino in Colombia has spoken to me of losses of up to 40%. In these circumstances, even a high price paid for the coffee is not a sufficient counterbalance. This volatility and risk brought by market pricing mechanisms and climate interference makes the business of growing and producing coffee more challenging and with a higher risk profile than other businesses in the supply chain.

An established coffee roastery and café brand has risk and may target a similar cash margin as a larger established producer, but the risk and volatility or not comparable. A consumer driven coffee business will be subject to price negotiations and tender processes, which means that their prices can change year-to-year. This dynamic doesn't remotely match the lack of stability, and the increased price variability of having your clients negotiate with you based around the C Price, which is how the majority of specialty coffee is transacted.

The collaborative "formal relations contract" concept we looked at in the *Adversaries or Partners?* chapter in *Part Two* of the book could model a positive arrangement that would help to address these challenges. This process would have to take place in opposition to the opportunistic lure of riding the market to maximise profit.

The market price for green coffee has come down since the highs of the ICO quota system. When adjusted for inflation, coffee prices have been steadily decreasing as a trend. The book *The Coffee Paradox* by Benoit Daviron and Stefano Ponte looks into this. The book was written in 2005, and the title refers to the paradox of the booming coffee industries in consuming countries when compared to the coffee crisis in many producing countries. In the book they look at business opportunities that could develop more value in the supply chain upstream, and also explore how new regulation solutions could support coffee farming.

In the book Daviron and Ponte demonstrate that many big coffee brands achieve added value through branding that isn't directly reflective of an increased price or quality of the raw ingredient. In specialty coffee I don't think this is as much of an issue. Although it is true that specialty roasters can use their brand to add value, and it is also true that, unlike the trading of green coffee, a roaster is held less accountable for what a consumer is getting for their money. In a growing and competitive specialty market, the businesses downstream appear to be more focused on hitting competitive prices to win or keep customers at a given coffee quality. The focus on transparency does help here, but as we have explored, it's not full proof.

Specialty roasters and cafés are working towards the margins I have outlined earlier in the book. If green prices are lower over time, the roasters on the whole use this as an opportunity to be competitive, rather than to flesh out their margins. During the recent C Market price increase most specialty roasters have not fully passed the increased price on, and instead have worked with reduced margin and profit. This is especially the case when combined with other inflationary costs. In a competitive market, businesses nearly always prioritise availability of product over profitability. It is, however, easier for companies that are running with sustainable profits to make the decision to pursue this strategy.

In *The Coffee Paradox* the authors reference the three Technoserve business suggestions for coffee farming: 1) promoting consumption in producing countries and emerging markets; 2) diversifying production; 3) promoting specialty coffee. This was written in 2005, specialty coffee has definitely grown since, and as I have posited elsewhere in the book, the specialty market has had success in increasing the demand for, and therefore the opportunity to grow, specialty coffee. This can be a positive for those who are able to produce it, just as long as the increased costs of production are reasonable. Specialty coffee prices are, after all, a high price for a more valuable quality of coffee, which typically costs more to produce. It is not just the production of specialty that has grown, but the knowledge of the product and its market value. Nowadays, most producers are acutely aware of the market value of different coffee characteristics and grades at any moment in time.

Diversification, Vertical Integration and Risk

Early in the book I chose to focus on the concept of boutique business. Throughout the whole supply chain there are large non-boutique companies producing and working with specialty coffee. The same is true at every step in the supply chain, including farming. However, it is also typical to see a lot of the explorative side of coffee production coming from boutique producers.

The concept of diversification in coffee farming is a notion that has been around for a while, but this solution can be easier said than done in many cases. For those well resourced enough, or with the support or grants, it is a valid business strategy that can be implemented in coffee farming models. As is often the case, the optimal strategy on paper requires funding and access to finance that may not be available. It is also true that, with the deferred nature of coffee crops, it isn't as easy to swap between crop types harvest to harvest as markets move.

Developing internal markets and economies in coffee producing countries has allowed a growing trend of farms diversifying with more consumption based businesses, and forms of agritourism. This is a form of vertical integration. This diversification from upstream to downstream can offer many benefits, increasing revenue and mitigating against C Market variance, as the business can effectively manage fixed coffee contracts with itself. It also can fit quite neatly alongside an export business, as domestic consumption activities are unlikely to be in direct competition with exporting clients.

The danger of building new business divisions in any enterprise is that it comes with risk, and spread focus has its own business challenges. However, for producers who have been building a quality-driven brand and product, leveraging this into consumption markets can make a lot of sense. A variety of producers have also been playing around with long shelf life products such as coffee capsules, allowing for an international sales channel with a farm to cup product direct from the farmer to customers worldwide.

There are very few operators anywhere in the coffee industry who are solely focused on luxury specialty coffee. This is equally true at the farming level. As we explored in the chapters, *The Ingredient Versus the Finished Drink* and *The Sweet Spot - Volume and Price,* the majority of operators in the specialty space are working with a portfolio of products. Small exotic lots are part of brand and relationship building, allowing the business to tie small, high-value lots to medium grade "staple" lots. Rare and expensive coffee does not represent large market potential for most producers, which is mostly due to the size and resource involved in producing, marketing and selling it. There are, of course, a small number of super premium coffee farm brands that are able to take advantage of a high-quality coffee product to sell exotic varieties and luxury coffees as their main sales focus, utilising the industry B2B branding mechanics we looked at in *Part 5* of the book.

Communication, Connection and Access to Market
The dawn of modern communication means that there are more
opportunities and avenues than ever before, allowing the supply
chain to connect around specialty coffee. Talking to Ric Rhinehart,
executive director of the SCA, he recalled the change that began with
the introduction of AOL. He was amazed that he could now email
coffee producers and exporters directly. He and Ted Lingle (Executive
Director at the Coffee Quality Institute) debated what this would
mean for green traders. Ric wondered if it may end their position of
power in the industry, whilst Ted pointed out that the real mechanism
at play is finance, and that the ability to connect was not the real driver
behind things.

I have not been in coffee as long as Ric by any means, but I have
seen a change in communications, and the continued development
of varying digital platforms allowing people to connect more easily.
I remember watching Hidenori Hizaki win the 2014 world barista
championships (whilst lamenting my fifth place finish) with a routine
based around a Facebook messenger dialogue, which allowed the
creation of a specific flavour profile process in Costa Rica, specifically
intended for use in the competition.

This type of conversation around coffee has become more and
more common, albeit with a requirement for both sides to speak or
understand the same language. There remains a need for financing
and there often still needs to be the support of an importer to help
make this happen. Some of the dynamics can lead to the shifting
of risk from importer to roaster. This phenomenon may not be
ubiquitous by any means, but it has been growing.

Ben Palmer, Head of UK and EU sales for Mercanta pointed
out to me that their company can be viewed as having the sole focus
of representing a variety of quality-driven producer brands in the
countries they import to, spreading and sharing their narrative with
roasters and clients.

In a complex subject such as coffee, trust is key. Good brands offer
exactly this. Whilst there are a lot of expert buyers in coffee, in a taste
driven industry that achieves any scale, a good proportion of buying
is informed by confidence in reputation and brand as much as it is by

blind tasting. At a shop or consumer level, there is also the potential to build ongoing brand loyalty to a coffee origin and or producer.

At the premium boutique end of the producer scale, it is more common to see farms or processing collectives discussed as brands, in the same way as a wine producer. As is the case throughout the supply chain, branding has the ability to add significant value. The boutique sector often wants to tell the story and sell the flavour experience of particular coffee from a specific place. The farm is that place and I think that as specialty coffee develops more and more the narrative has and will continue to move more and more to that of the producer or farmer.

Building a brand is not easy though. This is a truth in all businesses, and especially in the coffee industry. Coffee businesses are challenging businesses to start, run and build. Often it may be easy to assess from a distance the business models that appear to deliver profit, and simply to suggest that those are the ones that a farmer should pursue.

Research and Development, and Access to Finance
A repeating barrier for all coffee growing businesses is access to finance. This being said, it appears that wet milling and exporting can provide some key value points at origin. Dry milling is less clearcut. The investment and scale required makes dry milling too expensive to instigate for smaller, and even most medium-sized operators, however the need to control the quality and timing of this phase often drives a desire to bring this in house where possible.

A focus on experimentation and processing at the wet milling stage through controlling and manipulating a variety of factors such as temperature, yeast and bacteria in the fermentation stage is abundant in the specialty boutique world of coffee farming. Even though a lot of the coffees that make up the volume and business of the space are not processed in this way, these experimental coffees are having an impact.

At the time of writing this book, a lot of experimentation is happening within the Colombian coffee industry, and there is a very entrepreneurial spirit at play. All coffee is, of course, interventionist in the sense that human hands greatly shape the coffee that we drink. However, at the experimental boutique end, we are seeing lots of exploration into highly interventionist coffees. This has begun to raise interesting questions around when a coffee is "flavoured" or not. From a business point of view this trend is creating interesting opportunities for farmers and mills to target specific flavour trends in a way that is not possible through traditional methods and terroir.

As with all R&D, this process involves investment and risk. Some of the methodologies that have achieved the most success are backed by millions of dollars of investment. In this case the R&D is producing private intellectual property. There is also lots of R&D done in the agricultural coffee sector to support research around cultivars and agricultural studies such as the work conducted by World Coffee Research.

An interesting area of exploration is also other coffee species, and whether advancements in Robusta and Liberica farming and processing can provide alternative products that can be sold across the specialty boutique market. I am not sure about these myself, as they will have to improve a lot before they can compete with Arabica for the specialty client base. The success of wild processes does, however, suggest that there may be room for more variety still, and obviously if there were to be a shortage in Arabica, the market dynamic would change quickly.

People, Expertise and Talent

People are a key part of all business. There are labour challenges presented by both ends of the supply chain. The majority of coffee harvesting still requires seasonal labourers to help harvest the coffee. Much like barista roles the pay is often minimum wage, and there remains an important question to be asked about how this stacks up against a living wage. Seasonal work is also significantly different to full time employment. Finding pickers is not the only challenge, in many producing countries younger generations also increasingly do not seek to own or run coffee farms.

Initiatives such as those by the East African School of Coffee in Kenya, as well as those from the FNC in Colombia have been devised to help promote participation in the industry.

In the penultimate chapter of the book, *Is There a Coming Divergence?* I explore some thought experiments around how this could play out in the coming decades. I think specialty coffee is helping with this trend, although on what scale this is true, is up for debate. There are definitely many producers and farmers working in an integrated way in the boutique coffee industry, who have a passion for the product and the boutique side of the industry.

Throughout the full supply chain, coffee rarely represents the highest economic return for those entering the industry. Making coffee a desirable and passionate industry that connects people and provides a rewarding line of work is therefore key. This spirit does still need to exist alongside a sustainable income or profit, which for all specialty boutique coffee requires a focus on key business principles, which I have already detailed in this book.

A key part of the business of coffee growing is expertise. This can be in the form of experienced farm owners, or expertise-driven individuals who work on producing projects across the sector. Expertise is required to manage inputs and processes, allowing a farm to deliver a high-quality organic product. And just as is the case with all businesses in the coffee supply chain, many non-coffee functions and professional skills are also needed, from operational direction to marketing and commercial strategy.

Government Policy, Sustainability and the Future
As we explored in *Government Policy* in *Part Three* of the book, doing business at a producing level in coffee is typically interwoven with government policy and regulation in the region and country where you are based. Because of this, and the variety of subtropical macroeconomics at play, as well as the post colonial globalised market dynamics, the business of coffee growing is the most contextual part of the supply chain.

The specific dynamics and background can vary dramatically between businesses. A lot of current narratives in specialty boutique coffee are currently being driven by coffee farms in Latin America. The story of a specific micro or nano batch of a particular cultivar, processed in a certain way, lends itself to farm operators who process their own coffee, rather than cooperative groups. This isn't to say that cooperatives don't take part in the same narrative, just that their structure is less geared towards this. Small nano lots represent a typical story of premium boutique coffee, but are not actually the bulk of what we call the specialty coffee market, whether in Latin America, Africa or elsewhere.

The agricultural business of coffee is concerned with the same sales numbers and concepts as every other business in the supply chain. What is the market opportunity for different coffees of different qualities and flavours? What volume and price point are they able to achieve?

In part due to the subtropical positioning of coffee growers, a lot of the sustainability initiatives are being placed at their feet. Life cycle studies show that we should be focusing just as hard on reducing the impact of a cup of coffee at the consuming end. The new EU "regulation on deforestation-free products" is yet to be implemented, but undoubtedly will also end up sitting with the grower.

From a business point of view, the regulations are more likely to be seen as a core business need, depending on how they are enforced. This is very different to a certification body membership that can be entered into willingly by the coffee farmer, and in which the associated costs and resources required appear balanced by increased commercial opportunity or profit.

There are many small passionate growers whose mission is to grow coffee sustainably. It is part of their why, and in this case the business challenge revolves around helping clients recognise the value of this practice.

In countries like India there is already strong regulation in place around deforestation, meaning that nearly all coffee grown in India is shade grown. Simple, low cost technologies that allow growers to verify their growing conditions might be an interesting area for innovation and adoption in the coming years.

As coffee has an ability to be grown in a diverse ecosystem, it is an area in which different ecological models can be explored and implemented. The potential of a higher premium in specialty could support this, but at least at the time of writing, it is still very common for coffee to be sun grown. The lean nature of coffee growing business does, as it does throughout the supply chain, encourage a focus on efficiency and yield to hit a viable and risk mitigating scale.

Specialty coffee, as a term, covers a diverse range of producers and growers. It affords the opportunity for producers who are able to build strong business models around their crop to differentiate their business in the marketplace. As we have explored in the book, specialty is not about to become the industry norm, or a large-scale alternative to the commercial coffee sector, but it has been, and continues to grow.

In many ways, specialty and commercial coffee are much closer than is often realised. Many specialty producers sell their lower grade coffees into the commercial supply chain, rather than trading them under their own brand, much as a premium vineyard might do with its lower quality grapes or wine.

The specialty coffee market has been growing, continuing to show strong demand. However, associated operating costs have also been increasing for producer businesses, and in many cases, the premiums for specialty at reasonable scale are not highly differentiated. The producer is seeking to create a strong market position, and profitable business, by building a business that is able to maximise value.

I think that entrepreneurship and business exploration will continue to expand and evolve in this part of the supply chain, with a growing focus on the business models whose brand connects more closely to the coffee's consumption. For this reason, I anticipate many coffee growing businesses taking more downstream control of their product and brand. It is however also important to consider that for those unable to hit the right sweet spot in the agricultural business of coffee growing, it may not make business sense to remain in the industry. It is yet to be seen how this could play out. One prediction would be a growing split between commercial scaled operators and boutique premium producers, leaving a dwindling number of businesses in the middle.

Green Trading, Importing and Exporting
Economics, Scale and the Market

For any coffee scene to be developed and have breadth and depth with a flourishing mix of coffee businesses of different sizes, there needs to be a solid bedrock of importing businesses in markets around the world. The underlying financials of this finance and logistics based part of the supply chain are the tightest and typically require the most scale. With importers all relying on reaching a certain scale to make their lean margins work, the space is not as readily entered and doesn't consist of as many players as the two opposite ends of the supply chain.

To reference the numbers from *Part One* of the book, a specialty boutique importer is targeting 5% Net Profit (EBITDA). This means a fledgling boutique importer would need to achieve triple the revenue of a café opening to hit the same cash profit margin. There are some highly specific specialist importers that are targeting and hitting higher net profit margins, but the majority of specialty green coffee is imported by companies with a lean profit model.

This business is arguably the centre of the coffee world, in so far that it is where a lot of the money sits, even if that is in the form of debt. Large green trading companies typically like to set up an exporting office in key countries and tie this to an importing business in the country the coffee is headed to. These offices are subsidiaries of the main office that tends to be in Switzerland as we explored in *Access to Finance, an Industry Built on Borrowed Money.*

The necessity of financing in coffee is very clear to all in the supply chain, perhaps except for the coffee shop or the retailer, who don't really see the commercial interactions before that point, even though they rely on it.

Value is tied up in coffee during its journey from seed to cup, and before this point, when it is the potential product of a shrub planted in soil. At all points this value is leveraged in exchange for finance. Green coffee trading is the epitome of this pent up value. Futures contracts are a financial mechanism built around the idea of the value in something that is yet to be delivered, but is agreed to be delivered at a future moment in time.

Because a core function of trading and moving green coffee requires access to finance, this means that the barrier to entry is significant. Coffee can be traded as a commodity or stock, and there are companies trading coffee in this way, which is quite different to the physical process of moving coffee around the world between sellers and buyers, and utilising financial mechanisms such as hedging and FX facilities to mitigate risk and achieve a strong commercial position. Large producers in Brazil will often have a position utilising the same commercial mechanisms. A larger trader may only have 70% of its business tied up in moving physical green coffee with the remaining 30% split between carry (the market paying you to roll hedges) and speculation.

For smaller importers focusing just on specialty scoring lots, the goal is simply moving coffees that they have sourced, into a market where they can offer them to roasters. This changes as the importer becomes established. The challenges of being in this space means that these financial mechanisms become crucial to adopt at some point.

Finance and Risk

A boutique importer's coffees normally take the form of both a spot list, which is the list of coffees that have been imported with no pre-agreed customer, and of pre-sold coffee. The coffees on the spot list have been bought speculatively, they are selected, transported, financed and stored under the premise that the importer can find a customer for them.

These coffees are often listed by lot size and or quality. Clients of the importer can look at a spot list at any time and decide whether they would like to explore buying some of these coffees. The coffee is landed, so any samples will be indicative of landed quality. There are lots of obvious benefits to the roaster with this approach. Coffee is ready to ship to the roaster as soon as they have tasted it, the roaster is not taking a risk on the coffee, and so on. However, for the importer, this represents a significant amount of risk, and it is not a great way of planning and managing supply for the roastery either.

What if some of the coffees don't sell? As the days and months is the real threat that the coffee will degrade in quality.

This makes the timeline more crucial than in the case of merchandise that isn't selling well.

An alternative approach that a boutique importer can take is to build buying relationships with roasters, whereby the coffee is sampled and discussed whilst in the country of origin. The importer can then build a container's worth of coffee, or add the chosen lots to a container that they have coming up. The party who takes the biggest risk on this coffee is less clear. The roaster may request a right to approve the landed coffee as part of their contract, pushing risk back onto the importer. However, if an importer simply finances and offers the logistical service for a purchase directly between farmer and roaster, the risk will sit largely with the roaster when it comes to the coffee's landed quality.

Of course, any company can integrate the importing process. It can be the producer, a roaster or coffee brand. Some key brands in the consumer end of boutique movement have adopted this approach as part of a direct trade strategy. The challenge for all export and import is that, the more successful you are, the more financing you need to do. While you may be able to buy small amounts of coffee upfront and get them shipped to your roasting location, with success and growth, the likelihood that you will need financing support increases.

Interestingly the farmer or producer who opens up an export office in (for example) the UK, may utilise their own cash flow as part of the exporting and importing process. In effect, they ship the coffee from their farms and import into the UK, delaying payment to themselves back at the farm level. They will need cash flow flexibility to do this. Other producer or exporter groups with an import office may still utilise third party financing so that business or partner producers are not waiting for the roastery or client to pay before they get paid. It can seem a long way down the line to wait for the roastery to draw down, and use the coffee.

These financing options represent the different models that Anna Luiza Pellicer of Mio in Monte Santo de Minas in Brazil explained to me that they have been exploring and evolving in their UK importing business. Anna explains that transitioning their producing company into becoming an importer into the UK has required a lot of learning. Particularly challenging is managing the variety of qualities that they produce at different scales, and the range of different clients this requires.

I also spoke to Simon Brown, owner of Las Etiopes Coffee Estate in Peru. He outlined his reticence around importing, with the preference of focusing on a mixture of domestic supply and export. Before buying a coffee farm in Peru with his wife and family, Simon worked on the import side of the industry in the UK, so he has seen this part of the supply chain first hand, including all of the work, risk and stress involved. For him, managing the coffee contract, with coffee being drawn down and paid for overtime, all for a small margin, doesn't feel worth it. His focus is instead on maximising the domestic opportunity to sell the coffee in Peru, alongside pursuing the export side of the business, for which he is able to utilise relationships with importers around the world.

Osito a young start-up importer that also exports out of Colombia, started their business with financing support from one of the world's largest honey businesses, based in North America. When the pandemic hit and the honey business decided not to continue funding the growing coffee business, the founder, Kyle Bellinger, had to look for alternative sources of finance. Like most boutique importers, he utilised the financing available from large coffee traders. The large coffee traders know coffee and are the most likely to give the green light on a finance request against a shipment of coffee, as they understand and work in that space all the time.

The margins in the importing space are slim and require scale in order to work. It is challenging to only import from one origin, and most coffee companies are built around a variety of origins covering both regional and single farm offerings. In the boutique segment, an importer is more likely to offer specialism or unique differentiation. This narrowing can create an issue for roasters, who may have to take on a broad range of green coffee suppliers if they want to offer breadth to their customers.

The most obvious commercial aspects for both the importer and the roaster lie in consolidating supply to create a more meaningful business relationship between the two, as opposed to working with a wide range of importers, but not building a meaningful business relationship with any. This can mean first access to certain coffees for the roaster, or a better price on certain coffees as part of an overall volume of business and so on. Boutique businesses however, are not just focussed on the most efficient business strategy, and I think that the operators and teams in roasteries enjoy interacting and working with a variety of people, coffees and supply chains, and this means it is unlikely that a boutique coffee brand will only work with one importer, though it does happen.

Relationship, People and Expertise
The expertise required within an importing business is an interesting mix of financial competence and knowledge of coffee quality, the coffee supply chain both upstream and downstream and sales capability. The larger importers have a bunch of specific expertise to support the trading and movement of coffee and the wider business model, such as a weather team to analyse upcoming weather risk and its impact on the market. For the larger companies who are working as traders as much as coffee importers they will of course have financial traders who speculate on the coffee market, much as one would with any commodity, stock or currency. Larger trading houses can either have a specialty segment or as has happened in the space, fund or buy a more specialty boutique focused importing company.

The exact service importers offer to clients is differentiated based both on their supply chain and the producers they work with, as well as their target clients. Many businesses will have a list of top customers, something like a top ten, who contribute the majority of the turnover. This will often be followed by a long tail of smaller customers. This is an increasing phenomenon in the specialty space, with smaller high-value products sold across a wide range of businesses. This does mean that for many boutique importers managing the amount of resource that goes into any one business relationship (with many not delivering much value) is important.

It can be somewhat demoralising at times for importers who create a huge amount of opportunity and value for roasters and coffee businesses to find little appreciation or recognition of this in return. In fact, because roasters are often telling a story of a supply relationship between themselves and the farm, the importer can be seen as a simple middleman that they would rather not mention. The reality for nearly all the micro roasters (and even most larger ones) is that specialty importers are providing a very valuable service in the supply chain. Yes, there are examples where an importer is not involved, and there is a good business dynamic, but on the whole these companies are challenging to run, make little profit, and offer many benefits both downstream and upstream. An importer can offer access to a range of coffees and act as a connector between farm and roaster whilst also managing quality risk and utilising financial tools to help soften the market movements.

This part of the industry has a sales and marketing element that is very people driven. Coffee brands build strong relationships with importers and a lot of their success can come from having great sales and account management people as part of their team. The specialty sector doesn't, on the whole, respond well to more aggressive sales approaches, and the relationships need to be authentic and professional. These can be tough businesses to staff. Do you hire coffee people who know a lot about coffee and are keen to learn more, but need training on the logistics, planning and commercials? Or do you hire people with a financial education, but who need to learn the coffee side of things? I have heard tell of both approaches working. In the case of micro importers, they are often learning both skills as they go.

Many boutique and small roasters are not wholly confident in their own ability to select and navigate green coffee sourcing all on their own, and an importer's brand and industry reputation can play into their success in providing confidence to this type of client. This is very much the word of mouth and expertise driven marketing that we see throughout the supply chain. A boutique roaster wants to trust the importer in a number of ways, from transparency and quality of product to problem solving.

For many roasters, the importer is the connection to the producers, and boutique importers have excelled in promoting this in their work. Although, I have pointed out that there is often a lack of verification in terms of marketing materials, at the same time, importers often encourage and promote positive connection between the two ends of the supply chain.

Relationships between businesses at the smaller specialist end are often very transparent and friendly. However, for the specialty roasters who are bigger, the relationships tend to become much more commercial and increasingly price-driven. As the connection between coffee roasters and boutique producers rapidly evolves, it is also more and more common for importers to offer an open book financing and logistics service for transactions between growers and roasters. Of course, in this instance the quality risk is not taken on by the importer. This can be a big learning curve for micro importers, who quickly come up against the challenges of finance, and offer a long contract with favourable draw down payment terms, but also the risk scenario of who is responsible for coffee that doesn't deliver in quality on arrival.

Government Policy, Sustainability and the Future

Some of the most pre-emptive approaches to getting ready for the impact of the EU's "the regulation on deforestation-free products" are being taken by importers. This makes sense, as it is the importer who, at the customs point, is held accountable for compliance with new regulations. Small importers are likely to be caught out by these regulations, partly through lack of awareness and knowledge of what's happening, (as is happening all across boutique coffee) but also through a lack of resource and infrastructure required to build systems in the supply chain to comply.

Sustainability and compliance initiatives on the whole are being pursued more comprehensively by larger importers. This makes sense, as their larger clients are demanding more and more verification in their supply chains. Many of the big importers (who also export) have existing programmes, and are developing them alongside new programmes, providing a network of sustainability criteria that coffee brands can tap into in order to build their own sourcing programmes around.

The importing industry has changed a lot in the past decade. Importers are looking to provide a valuable service in the industry and specialty boutique coffee has changed the requirements somewhat. In many cases the importers have not simply been reactive, but have proactively pursued boutique initiatives in order to develop supply chain opportunities.

Certain boutique importers have done impressive work around identifying business challenges in the supply chain and working with producers and exporters to explore solutions. Some importers provide upstream finance, others for example, Raw Materials, actively seek out areas where they assess that they can add the most value as a partner.

Without specific regulation or subsidy, the most impactful and progressive solutions in the supply chain, the ones that can move it forward, are business based, and importers are often key in providing this.

Roasters
The Growing Market
Coffee roasting businesses often find themselves trying to strike a balance between acting as a regulated food manufacturer and the maker of a passionately crafted product. The target net profit of a coffee roaster, boutique or otherwise is roughly 10% pre-tax. As with each of the business models in the supply chain, there are examples that exceed this, but also many that are not able to consistently achieve this number at all.

Different cultures and economies have a different relationship with roasting businesses and how they either stand alone as product businesses or vertically integrate with coffee shops or producers. They can be brand-forward or service-forward businesses.

I remember when Sang Ho Park, who now runs Centre Coffee in Seoul, South Korea, left his job roasting at Square Mile coffee in the UK and headed back to South Korea to open his own coffee roasting business, only to be quickly presented with a distinctly different marketplace, whereby it was much more common for shops to roast their own coffee on a smaller scale, much like a bakery, baking its own bread.

This was distinctly different from his experience in the UK, which is typical of many markets across the world, with a broad separation between roastery and café. The UK roasting market is a wholesale market, in which roasteries supply cafés and other channels as a B2B transaction.

The growth of the UK roasting market saw a handful of prominent specialty roasters dominating the scene in the mid-to-late-2000s. These roasters supported the burgeoning specialty boutique café market, which saw new openings happening thick and fast. The market has evolved a lot since then, and there is now a wide range of specialty roasting businesses. International players from other markets, typically the Antipodean market, have entered the fold, and a growing range of sizable British coffee brands have emerged.

Multiple coffee shop operators have also turned to roasting coffee. In some cases this was a means to supply a small collection of shops, and in others it was part of a decision to make roasting and supplying coffee a core business proposition.

Heavily funded D2C roastery brands entered the fray later, and all the while more and more micro roasters have been opening up. In many ways this mimics the boom of small gin distilleries in the country. Many of the businesses are organic, passionate, independent businesses without a strong strategy beyond roasting some nice coffee and sharing it with customers. Other operators naturally have much more of a business driven ambition, and as specialty has achieved more market engagement, this continues to become more common. In addition to all of this, larger existing roasters have also assessed and pursued the growing specialty opportunity.

When you take the market as a whole, there continue to be strong indicators of growth. The market is growing overall. Green importers are seeing growing sales volumes of specialty coffee across a wider customer base than before, with larger and still growing established businesses joined by flocks of smaller operators. This means that, from a roasting point of view, the market has definitely become more competitive. This is a natural process, following a maturation of a market place, and the balancing of supply and demand. Operators who were first to the burgeoning specialty scene will muse over a beer about how easy it was in the early days. There was a greater demand for specialty coffee than there was supply, and if you took some nice coffee, did a half decent job at roasting it, and put it in a brown bag, you would have customers and a quickly growing business.

This may still work on a small scale, but it can no longer achieve the same level of growth, as the market has changed and matured. I sometimes suspect that business founders and operators forget that it is not only the scene that has grown, but their own businesses as well. Growing a business from zero to 500k revenue is very different to growing it to three to five million revenue. A larger company, looking to hit the same growth trajectory, will need many more customers, and will therefore be talking to a broader range of people as well.

Diversification and Talent
It may well be countered that many roasters choose to combine the production of a gourmet product with the supply of other services. In many cases roasters are as much a service provider as they are a food manufacturer. The services most often incorporated into a roastery's offering are those of barista training, and machine supply and maintenance.

It is easy to see why this combinational approach has come about. At the beginning of the specialty movement there was a deep talent deficit, not just in terms of baristas, but in terms of operator knowledge as well. To get the best out of the roasted coffee product, it needs to be prepared well. People needed training. This has been a fairly common industry wide undertaking when putting coffee into less coffee-focused environments such as restaurants and bars.

As someone with a hospitality background, I have always found it odd when the hospitality operator does not want to handle the daily SOP's (standard operating procedures) and product quality management themselves. Of course, professional development courses can be beneficial, and training in specific areas can add value for team members. However, it still makes the most sense for supervisor or manager roles, who oversee the daily preparation and serving of drinks, to develop the expertise and knowledge to train their staff. If the business ever hopes to achieve a consistent quality, it can't expect to achieve this via a visit from an outside company, once a month for a few hours.

The commercial reality of training and on-site support is also more expensive than most realise, and cannot be offered to a high standard, and with any regularity, without being paid for. In some very established markets around the world, this thought process is very much out in the open, and the pricing of the contracted price of coffee can be directly linked to additional extras. This is very much like buying a car before the seat warmers and special trim get added.

I often wonder if smaller accounts, that pay a coffee price that includes training, but who never actually use the services, help make the economics of the larger, high-maintenance accounts stack up. This is much like the well-worn example of gym-goers signing up and paying a monthly membership fee, but never using the facilities, or perhaps more aptly, paying to use all the facilities but only using the pool.

A company that delivers its own coffee to clients can tie this training into the delivery visits for each site. The model of having a fleet of delivery vans, with staff who act as delivery drivers, crossed with a machine mechanic and coffee trainer, is one that multiple coffee roasters have successfully implemented. This requires the business to become as much a delivery, training and maintenance business as much as it is a coffee roaster.

In fact, there are examples of roasters who have successfully offered this service, but didn't roast their own coffee for quite some time. The businesses chose instead to focus on service and supply, making the decision to vertically integrate roasting later. This is clever business, some scale needs to be achieved before roasting in-house can provide savings over white label supply.

A very successful model is also based around the ability to offer a finance-based lease service on equipment, which can help a coffee shop with its capital expenditure, and also work as a way to create a stickier sales relationship. These different business approaches, that tie a variety of services to the coffee supply will, for the right client base, provide a competitive advantage.

Finance, Growth and Equipment
Roasteries tend to have a capital expenditure growth issue, especially at the boutique end. A roastery can actually be started for quite a low set up cost. A lean start-up scrappy approach to both a coffee shop and roastery are actually quite similar in upfront expenditure. Let's say with a decent space that doesn't need loads of work you can get either started for £30k.

This would be a very resourceful coffee shop fit out, and most fit outs are many, many magnitudes more than this. A roastery doesn't need to look as good on day one, so in reality, a coffee shop typically costs more to fit out than a roastery. The roastery however, will have a much higher working capital need, with raw ingredients and packaging required from the off.

As the roastery grows, the stock holding and cash flow needs will become greater. But, the biggest challenge for the roastery is delivering enough profit to increase capacity and buy equipment. It is very challenging to make enough profit to have sufficient cash reserves to buy the next roaster when the time comes.

Roasting machines jump in price dramatically as you move from the five, 12kg or 15kg machine that most boutique roasteries get started with. Let's say a boutique roastery gets to £600k revenue in 4 years from opening. At this point, the 12kg machine is working overtime, as are the operators, to hit their volumes. If they have worked hard to save profit and put it aside over those 4 years, they may have been able to put away £80k in cash reserves. The next roaster is going to cost more than this. Some kind of finance solution will be needed. It could be debt, investment, grants or another solution.

The infrastructure side of manufacturing businesses is very challenging. If (as with coffee) the product value is relatively low in comparison to the equipment that you need to produce it, then the business will end up building an infrastructure that it is tied to, for long periods of time.

Roasting coffee can be pursued in a simple, manual way, or with a heavy focus on technology and automation. A weighing machine, or a form seal packing machine can be acquired to help break the inevitable bottle neck in most boutique roasteries, which is hand-packing coffee.

The nuts and bolts of the business of coffee roasting is very much in the sphere of food manufacturing, meaning that goals typically involve developing a business based around efficient and capable production processes and culture. In this way, milling coffee and roasting coffee are quite comparable. Small roasteries don't have as much need for these kinds of systems and structures, but for any roastery that grows beyond a few staff, this will become a huge focus.

People and Expertise

For many a passionate barista, the roastery represents what feels like a natural career step. However, the two environments, the coffee shop and the roastery floor, couldn't be more different. This is the difference between a hospitality environment and a manufacturing one. People who love putting on a show each day, love the café environment. Roasteries are less in the moment and much more about systems and structure. Of course, there are crossovers. However, roasteries don't typically have a lot of "coffee" jobs as more roles are based around the professional skills needed to run a production business. Increasingly roasteries are also brands that need a lot of resources and time dedicated to tasks such as merchandising and marketing.

Having said all of this, a roastery is also built around its core product, which is roasted coffee. The roasting technology and the coffee team who source and manage the raw ingredient, oversee the process of turning it brown and achieving a specific cup quality in the process. In this respect the business's taste aesthetic is down to a few people, those who make sourcing and roasting technique choices. In most boutique roasteries, this is the job of the founder, and this works well, as they roast coffee in a way that they personally enjoy. When hiring people to work in these roles I have always thought it important to find people who are on the same "taste aesthetic" page.

Technology and Access

The technology itself also plays a significant role in how flavour can be crafted. Roasting technology is evolving. Perhaps the most dramatic changes the industry is seeing at the moment is at the small end. Electric sample roasters and mini-production roaster technologies has proven disruptive, reducing the barrier to entry of coffee roasting, and allowing it to be introduced into many new environments. There have been little home roasters for many years, but this new wave of sample and mini-production roasters have been built for the industry, with heavily-developed software that allows for the tracking and sharing of roast profiles as well as auto-profiling.

These little roasters have now been used on barista competition stages, they have allowed producers and clients to roast and share profiles and they have allowed many people to play with roasting, when before it was something of an inaccessible dark art. Large electric roasters are yet to really come of age, but this development will inevitably happen at some point. Most production roasters remain to be a form of gas roasting whether they use hot air or a heated drum and air.

Roasting is still an area that can be hard to learn about, and there are multiple theories, styles and approaches. I suspect that roasting has more technological disruption to come. This will be in the roasting machines themselves, but also with the systems and apparatus around the roaster. Some of this may come in the form of new developments, but much will be borrowed from the impressive automated systems already in place in big commercial roasteries. If the technology becomes available, smaller versions of integrated silos and bean movement systems will be desirable for roasteries that can afford to implement them.

Software to run and document coffee roasting has developed significantly also, and will continue to evolve further. One of the biggest challenges in roasteries remains to be managing the different raw ingredients across many products. Whilst large roasters have developed and implemented complex and costly ERP (enterprise resource planning) systems, most boutique roasters are still using manual spread spreadsheets, paper, pen, and memory.

Part Seven. Business by Business

Traceability and Sustainability

The complexity of this process is compounded by compliance needs. Coffee is relatively low risk from a food compliance point of view, but compliance is required all the same, and for boutique roasters to sell to a variety of clients and into a variety of channels, they will have to achieve high levels of compliance and product traceability. On the traceability front, as we explored in *Greenwashing*, many of the claims and marketing made by roasteries simply don't hold up. What is on many specialty coffee packets is widely unverified. On the whole, the boutique roasting movement relies on the businesses of the last chapter - importers. More consideration in the boutique roasting space around claims being made is needed.

From a sustainability and product quality point of view, the biggest impact made by a roaster comes from the suppliers they look to buy from. A roaster is, after all, a middle business. The roaster can lessen its own impact. It can consider how to keep waste to a minimum and reduce energy used and so on. A roaster can select coffees and producers for many different reasons. A lot of coffee is still purchased utilising blind taste tests, where price is referenced against quality, lot size and scarcity. At the same time, there are now many boutique roasters who are building a sourcing programme with the intention of working with a selection of producers year-on-year, accepting that there will be variance in quality, and an evolving relationship.

Marketing, Merchandising and Lifestyle

Branding and marketing is significant in the roasting space as a focus and function. Roasting businesses tend to sell directly to the consumption market through a number of channels, and therefore need to put a lot of resources into identity and messaging. Some successful boutique roasteries I have spoken to say that they see their roasteries more as a brand-driven business than anything else. The way that coffee is packaged as a product in its own right makes this possible. Roastery businesses often appear to have a divide between operating as a production business and a commercial brand business.

Location does not feed as much into a roastery's access to market, as most roasteries in the UK can ship anywhere else in the UK. This makes for a competitive marketplace, which is why the focus on brand identity is key. Pre-Brexit, many UK roasters had a good degree of success throughout Europe. Many boutique roasters are still able to find a global audience, by tapping into the worldwide coffee community.

Where roasteries offer a service and support tie-in, geography becomes more significant. Roasters with this type of offering will often open multiple offices or support facilities in different locations, but will still have limited coverage.

As with coffee shops, there has been growth in the variety and execution of creative branding identities in the roasting industry, and many roasteries are now building lifestyle identities and branching out into merchandising, something I look at in *Lifestyle and Merchandising Coffee Brands* in *Part Five* of the book.

In the case of many specialty boutique roasters, the business itself is part of a lifestyle goal for the founders or small team involved. There is definitely value for roasteries in non-producing countries to go and visit the producers and farmers they work with and to learn and expose themselves to more of the supply chain of coffee. However, many of the trips taken by boutique companies are also not business critical, and represent a lifestyle goal that runs through the business.

This struggle between lifestyle business, and the realities of actually running a business, is a theme that runs through coffee, not just for owners, but for individuals looking to explore coffee by working in the industry. It has become common in the boutique space, for a shop or a "bracelet" of shops, (more than one, but not a chain) to move into roasting, not only because they think it could add some direct commercial value, but because they see it as a way to retain and offer development for staff.

In these instances operators may soon realise that they were taking on more than they bargained for. The project can quickly spiral into something more onerous and challenging than a simple retention tool. Some smaller roaster setups are interesting in this regard, as they model a way of exploring roasting, without the need to commit to starting a full-on manufacturing business.

The connection between roasters and producers is pivotal in a specialty boutique roasting business. Highly branded coffee blends remain to be a popular product, in which raw ingredients sit second to a branded narrative. However, beyond this, the space is becoming more and more of a shop window for quality-driven producers around the world. Roasters are both retailers of an agricultural product from around the globe, and artisans who have a hand in crafting the end flavour result of the product. For this reason roasters have the ability to build more of a sticky brand relationship with customers than if they simply acted as a gateway to access a certain producer's coffee.

Vertical Integration and the Future

Roasting is a task that can find its way into any part of the industry. After all, coffee can be roasted by anyone in the supply chain, sometimes even the end consumer. As a side note, I don't believe that home roasting is something that will take off, and will instead remain niche.

Being based in the UK, I often think of a roastery as a different part of the industry, and at scale, it is its own business, as it requires a manufacturing business to be built around it. Roasting is also something that can be engaged with by almost every business in the supply chain. Importers are the odd one out really, as their client bases are predominantly made up of people and businesses who roast. To add a roasting arm to their business would create direct competition with their customers.

For coffee shops, retailers and coffee producers, roasting coffee represents an accessible part of the supply chain, always worth considering as a business strategy. In multiple coffee producing countries the local market for specialty boutique coffee has been booming. This has opened up the opportunity of combining a roasting business with a producing business. This is one example of the growing exploration of diversification and vertical integration, as boutique producers evolve their brand position and business activities.

Formats like capsules allow roasters to develop international markets. New packaging formats, and changing approaches to what freshness means also allows for coffee to be treated increasingly as a transportable pre-made product. However, on the whole, the space is still dominated by a just-in-time manufacturing approach to coffee roasting. The roasted to order element of the market places a constraint on what is possible, meaning that most roasting businesses in boutique coffee are inherently domestic businesses.

Coffee roasteries and coffee roasting brands are some of the big storytellers in the supply chain, and act as a connecting link in the coffee bean's journey. In a developed market, the roastery marketplace hits a high level of competition quite quickly for the roasting business, causing specialty roasters to seek new channels, and alternative products and clients, alongside increased business efficiency. In this situation larger scale roasters are best able to solidify a strong position in the market. There is also lots of room for micro roasters, but that middle space is very challenging, and due to matters of funding and equipment, it can be difficult for a small roaster to transition to a large-scale opportunity.

The growing market for specialty coffee would suggest that there is continued opportunity for growth in this segment. As we have explored in this chapter, coffee roasting also appears to be a business area that will see continued diversification, adoption and disruption.

Online
Deliverable Margin and Outsourcing
E-commerce is perhaps the most distinct channel through which to sell coffee. Although it is typically integrated into a coffee business such as a roaster or coffee retailer, e-commerce can also operate as a "mover" of coffee, more like the role taken by green exporters and importers. Models, such as Amazon resellers or Shopify-based aggregators, are good examples of the latter. In these cases, a variety of coffee products are sourced and resold, in a way not dissimilar to an online supermarket.

As explored in the *The Ingredient Versus the Finished Drink* chapter, making the numbers stack up can be a significant challenge. E-commerce models owned by roasters or coffee brands appear to gain a lot more margin by selling their own coffee online, but often the margin leaks away in the process. So whilst e-commerce allows the business to achieve an increased gross margin when presented as raw goods cost versus selling price, in terms of deliverable margin (see *Deliverable Margin* in *Part 2*) most, if not all of that extra margin, gets eaten up.

If a business can profitably supply Amazon or a mainstream supermarket with coffee, they will mostly be safe from "further" costs that take away from net profit. The margin that these physical resellers will take, is in many cases the equivalent of Google, Facebook and fulfilment costs to the business, when operating their own e-commerce platform.

In all cases, a business only ever gives away margin to access something it feels it is unable to do on its own. Otherwise, why on earth would they do it? Most of the time this is a way to access a cohort of customers that another business either already has or is adept at reaching. You are giving away margin to gain the ability to access sales. There is normally a reason for this. As a supplier of raw ingredients, it can be because of market preference. In the case of coffee, particularly specialty coffee roasted in the country of consumption, they may offer the opportunity to buy locally or to get service and support.

The Pandemic and Word of Mouth Marketing

It is impossible to talk about e-commerce in boutique coffee at this time without recognising the pre and post-pandemic landscape. Without fail, every coffee company I have spoken to with an established coffee brand in specialty coffee saw online growth of several hundred percent during the early lockdowns. For the most part this was a relative swing, if you already had a larger brand presence in the space, you likely saw a bigger online uptake. This dynamic appeared to occur regardless of online ad spend.

The phenomenon appears straightforward. The specialty boutique café sector had become a significant force by the time the pandemic hit. When people were told to stay at home, there was panic amongst coffee connoisseurs who frequented boutique cafés and coffee shops. "How am I going to have great coffee whilst I am at home?" They asked. The sudden change in purchasing behaviour was pronounced for coffee roasters, who saw their wholesale sales all but disappear overnight, and their e-commerce numbers surge.

Equipment and machine manufacturers and brands perhaps saw this more keenly than anyone else in coffee, as a mad rush for equipment created stockout left right and centre, just as was happening with bicycles, home gym equipment and flour.

For me the COVID-19 online phenomenon demonstrated the core sales mechanism of the specialty coffee space, in action, in fast forward. This was word of mouth marketing, driven by the concept of expertise and trust.

As specialty coffee gets bigger, more and more of the people purchasing, brewing and drinking specialty coffee will not self-identify as coffee experts or knowledgeable connoisseurs, but rather coffee lovers who know when they like something (and when they don't). I think that, for the most part, this cohort recognise the complexity and specialism of the space, and seek out signposts for the coffee they like.

These signposts could be brands that speak in a certain voice, or specific pieces of equipment that they have seen in a café that they like. But, as specialty coffee gets bigger, and there are more brands that look the same, the most powerful navigation tool will be asking others (who you can trust). Consumers will reach out to someone they perceive to have knowledge on the topic, or someone who shares their typical preferences, or even to a brand that they already know and trust. Essentially, the brands that got the uptick during the pandemic had put in the hard yards, building their reputation beforehand, in an authentic way.

As restrictions slackened, so too did online sales, at least for all the companies that I have spoken to. However, there also appears to be a lasting legacy. The deep coffee dive taken at home by many, which in normal times a person might have seen as too time-consuming and too geeky, has resulted in customers that are more knowledgeable, engaged and appreciative of boutique flavour-driven coffee than ever before. Even though e-commerce sales have come back down from their heady heights, for most companies, the numbers didn't sink all the way back to pre-pandemic levels. This, combined with restored café and wholesale sales has resulted in a significant net gain for many companies.

Cost of Acquisition, Customer Relations and Online Advertising
It was easy during this time for the real cost of online acquisition campaigns to be lost in the growth, or even mistakenly correlated to it. There is a good argument that a lot more customers were online shopping for coffee during this online surge, and that ad spend helped capture some of these potential customers.

I am sceptical about the extent of this correlation, based on the trust and recommendation aspect of the boutique sector. Coffee isn't a one-off purchase. Most of us intuitively understand that a coffee brand's marketing will tell you that it is the best, both "ethically" and in terms of flavour and quality. Consumers are savvy enough to know that these claims are made by all companies, but that they don't like all coffee. This is the reason they fall back on third party verification of some kind.

Customer cohorts vary in loyalty. There are definitely both brand loyal and disloyal customers in boutique coffee. The customer base can have a tendency towards explorative curious buyers, who naturally have a lower likelihood of sticking with one brand. This is just one segment however, and there are also lots of customers looking for some consistency. In fact, these two behaviours can sit side-by-side. A customer can stock a go-to "house" coffee at home, and some accompanying coffees that allow for exploration of flavour. Disloyal customers are also the most likely to pick up online deals, and simply move to the next online deal when yours ends which is why using discounts as a way to convert new customers is not a foolproof strategy.

With quite a low ticket price (contextually) the coffee brand is after repeat sales. A lot of loyalty exists in the boutique segment. Customers don't necessarily need to move around roasters to try new coffee, as most boutique roasters offer a variety of origins and flavour profiles. In this way coffee is distinctly different from wine. Wine is built for the reseller. Vineyards or wine brands create the product in its entirety, leaving room for a world of merchants to display a collection of different wines at any one time.

A roaster is part producer and part merchant reseller. I think this is one of the reasons that online aggregator models have struggled in coffee. Customers are more likely to explore a few roasters and find the one they like rather than trusting a third party to act as a go-between. The tight margin that online sales create against a low ticket price, also encourages roasters to sell direct to consumers online where possible.

With all of this in mind, it will always represent a significant challenge for specialty boutique companies to bank on e-commerce as a singular channel, however as part of a diversified range of sales channels, it can be highly complementary.

Diversification in Bricks and Mortar

The whole food and drink sector faces the same challenge when marketing their products online, you can't taste them. At its heart, coffee is driven by the experience at the end of the journey, whether in a café environment, at home, or the desk at work. Initiatives such as giving away the first bag of coffee for free can help bridge this gap for the customer, but they can be very costly for the business, and the promotion is hard to pay back.

Just as Nespresso's boutique stores were instrumental in building adoption of its format, coffee shops are a key experience space for specialty boutique customers. Coffee brands that own shops, but are focused on their roastery operation as the core business, will often see the shops as engagement centres for the brand rather than simply as cafés. In these instances the business may take a slightly more relaxed approach to how profitable the bricks and mortar spaces need to be, as they feed the sales funnel via engagement and brand awareness.

Physical stores have the potential to add to both wholesale and end consumer business. When speaking to Tom Sobey of Origin Coffee Roasters from Cornwall, he described that the company sees a direct spike in e-commerce where they have physical locations. They have also noticed that they have created an ability to build relationships and drive wholesale through their physical locations. In many ways a café is the ultimate marketing space for a coffee brand - it can generate revenue, turn a profit and present one of the most effective ways of growing sales across the brand.

At the same time it is worth pointing out that physical locations can also hinder wholesale growth, especially local supply, where the roastery's store or café can be seen as direct competition, essentially putting potential clients off stocking the coffee. How much of a factor this will be, depends on local sentiment towards the company. It has not been uncommon for roasters in competitive market places to agree a minimum supply radius around their top clients. In this case, the roaster will agree not to supply a nearby competitor. There are of course a lot of other considerations for why a shop chooses a wholesale supplier, especially if service and support are part of the equation.

Lifestyle, Merchandising and Sales Models
The lifestyle coffee brands we touched on in *Part Five* of the book are typically best placed to maximise an e-commerce strategy as they are able to foster different buying behaviour. Buying merchandise doesn't require you to taste it, and the conversion metrics can look much more sustainable. Tieing coffee into this purchasing psychology is clever. The e-commerce numbers and insight I am referencing in this book are mostly UK based. Other markets globally do show some indications that online pay-per-click strategies can be more successful, but they will still face similar challenges.

A real challenge for many coffee brands is the amount of work and resources it takes to be online as a brand. Managing a website, email communications, creating content and running social media channels alongside implementing various marketing campaigns can take up a disproportionate amount of resource and opportunity cost relative to the sales that they deliver. A few coffee brands I speak to have decided to axe this channel altogether for these reasons.

As a counter to this, other coffee brands find e-commerce to be a very complementary channel, when combined with a wider ecosystem of sales channels. If you can marry up the SKUs across wholesale, e-commerce and shops, they can each utilise the same roasting schedule and marketing materials. In most of these cases, online sales represent growth for the coffee brands, who several years ago were doing hardly any online sales. There are also success stories of specialty brands that are e-commerce dominant in their sales and have managed to hit a sweet spot.

Subscription style business in the space is of course very desirable. Predictable and recurring revenue in any business affords many benefits, from increased security of sales to improved ease of production through pre-planned manufacturing. Global online subscription behaviours continue to show promising growth post-pandemic. Subscriptions and a longer lifetime value of the customer allow a lot of the lean e-commerce margins to start working. This model will rely on a company becoming the household staple supply. As a lot of specialty consumers are looking to explore coffee, many successful specialty subscriptions offer a changing curated list of coffees, to keep the customer engaged and stimulated.

E-commerce has clearly become a significant, valuable and growing part of the specialty coffee market. The key challenges to success in this area of the industry are manifold. It is a highly competitive space, and building an online coffee audience will either require wider brand building or a loss-making awareness phase of marketing. This will need to be accompanied by a knowledge and control of the associated running costs to make the sales profitable and sustainable.

Retail
Margins and Selling to the Multiples
Retail coffee shows many similarities to e-commerce in the way that it works. The ability (or lack thereof) to taste the coffee can dramatically alter the opportunity to convert a sale. Selling the coffee cheaper to get it into someone's hands, or mug can be effective. An online business may achieve this using a deal, such as 30% off the first bag, or a free coffee brewer. In supermarkets the deal is nearly always much more straightforward, a simple price reduction that is part of

most brand's annual calendars.

The price reduction will occur for a limited amount of time, and will typically happen on an agreed cadence, multiple times in a year. It is normal for there to be eleven offer periods throughout the year where the retail price of a coffee is dramatically dropped. All brands I have spoken to see a consistent rise in sales when their products are on offer. This is a core expected strategy for new brands. The theory behind the process is that it helps to get the brand out there, and when the product is no longer on offer, it will have gained new customers increasing its base rate of sale.

UK supermarket coffee isles are notoriously disloyal places. The repeated uptick in sales experienced by any brand that puts a product on offer suggests that there is a cohort of customers who simply hop around the discounted coffees. These customers probably can't be converted to the brand. Understanding revenue and profit within this model requires margin calculation that takes into account the portion of sales made when the product is on offer. This factor, plus a number of other costs, can make margin a struggle in the grocery space.

The UK grocery space is particularly interesting in that it hasn't, at the time of writing, been a place with much specialty boutique representation. This is particularly evident in the pricing of the coffee. Both whole bean and capsule coffee appear to be showing strong category growth in supermarkets. Historically instant was dominant in the UK market, with roast and ground coming in second. To be clear, those categories still rule the roost overall. It is noticeable that the highest prices of retail coffee seen in the coffee aisle remain significantly lower than the average price of a bag of roasted beans that you would find in a specialty boutique café, roastery or online.

The grocery channel is a very unique space. It allows larger FMCG (fast-moving consumer goods) businesses with sufficient budget to purchase at-till sales data to see who and what is selling well. This is really unique, there is no other channel that can afford this kind of open, comprehensive sales insight. Most companies of this sort have access to this data and utilise it to keep an eye on which new products could do well on the shelf, and to monitor current performance and pricing trends.

Grocery data shows the same trend in coffee that you find in any other channel, as the sales price increases, the sales numbers decrease. As in most markets there is a sweet spot of price and volume that represents a kind of bell curve, which informs the elasticity of the pricing in the space.

Price Elasticity and Shelf Life in Specialty Boutique Coffee

The intriguing discrepancy is that price elasticity in boutique coffee appears higher outside of the supermarkets. In the infancy of the boutique market it could have been speculated that this was simply an impact of scale, and that the market was so small that there wouldn't be enough product or customers to support a listing in the supermarkets. The success of boutique coffee in general in recent years has been such that sales rates in other channels for successful boutique brands can outstrip a successful supermarket listing for a single product. This calls this trajectory into question.

The implication is that customers have built up buying behaviours for specialty boutique coffee outside of supermarkets. The customers buying specialty coffee at premium prices are not wandering the coffee aisles in supermarkets at all, as they have already purchased the coffee either in café or online.

There are obvious reasons that the coffee has been sold through these alternative channels. The paperwork, margins and stock management required to supply a supermarket chain are onerous compared to selling bags in a local shop or shipping online. The boutique sector's focus on providing coffee fresh from roast also plays a key role.

I speak to many quality-driven operators in coffee who agree that the messaging around freshly roasted coffee is overblown. In a nitrogen flushed environment, with a good oxygen barrier, quality coffee can have a very healthy shelf life. The perception that more freshness is always better can put roasters in a strange position. Few consumers understand, as an industry professional might, that there is an optimal window post-roast that provides more ideal brewing conditions. Commercially this is challenging to manage and communicate.

The marketing and communication message that "fresh is best" offers an easy differentiator for consumers. Independent roasters cleverly spotted this point of difference early. They also likely realised that this narrative gives them the upper hand over larger competitors, when selling to local clients. Most boutique roasters run less optimal roast scheduling and batch sizes in order to meet the demand for produced-to-order coffee.

It is true that as coffee ages from roast, at a certain point it becomes stale and tastes worse. It is also true that a green coffee that has passed its best will taste worse, even when freshly roasted, than a coffee from good condition green coffee, which was roasted a few months prior.

The exact limits of packaging, shelf life and quality is a different conversation, but it's fair to say that the boutique sector has encouraged and pushed the narrative around freshly roasted coffee. This has to be playing into the challenge of getting more boutique coffee onto the supermarket shelves, and also getting more customers to engage with it there.

Coffee Pods and Other Drink Formats
Coffee Pods - Cost and Barrier to Entry
Every time you do something to coffee, you add a cost. Simply handling coffee adds cost. The more green coffee is moved around, the more cost is added. If you add extra cost, from a business perspective, you should also look for some value to be added, otherwise you are simply incurring unnecessary costs.

A recurring theme in this book has been the need to understand what things really cost. This is a simple concept, but surprisingly challenging to stay on top of, especially for small businesses.

Coffee capsules provide a good example of value adding. The specialty coffee capsule market has grown in recent years. At Colonna, we were one of the first boutique companies to start utilising the format. We put competition-winning coffees into the pods, and set the flavour goal of producing identifiable and individual specialty coffee profiles. At the time, the typical specialty offering that was being seen in beans had not made it into Nespresso pods.

Capsules are perhaps one of the best examples of IP implementation in coffee, as Nestle has used multiple patents to create an end-to-end closed system combining hardware and coffee. In 2012 a landmark court case opened the market up. At first it was flooded with plastic capsules mostly of poor quality, seeking to steal market share from Nespresso, predominantly by beating them on price. The market has since evolved considerably. Here in the UK, it continues to be one of the fastest growing segments in grocery and retail coffee.

I often hear it mentioned that Nespresso capsules represent a high cost to the customer per gram of coffee. For this reason it is surprising to many that the margin in capsules is lean, unless you are able to make your own. This is no easy task and the barrier to entry is enormous.

This biggest hurdle is how challenging it is to make pods well. Whilst, on the one hand, a pod is just some coffee portioned into a small container, on the other, it is a high-tech process that requires state of the art grinding and packing technology. If you wish the coffee to be of a high standard, in which the finished product achieves a good TDS, cup quality and technical performance when used with the market hardware, you can't cut corners. Making the capsule and packaging usually costs more than the roasted coffee that goes inside. This value add for the customer clearly hits a mark, which is why it is a highly successful coffee format.

For a roaster the coffee pod also represents an example of deliverable margin. The gross profit of the product may be lower for the roaster, presuming they are specialty boutique and need to work with a packing partner, but months of stock can be made in one batch, meaning it is retail ready and has a good shelf life.

This larger MOQ requirement is one of the aspects that has held back the more widespread adoption of capsules. Due to the nature of packing lines, there is a setup time and minimum run duration or volume requirement for the process to be worth doing at all. The exact setup of the packing business defines the point at which MOQ makes sense for them. In any case, this will necessitate some large upfront stock holding for a roaster or coffee company looking to make their own pods, or an enormous investment if they wish to pack their own capsules.

Coffee Pods - Marketing and Strategy

Coffee capsules are also a great example of the gap between producing a product and selling it. Access to market in this space has been more challenging historically, but the growing adoption of the format in specialty boutique coffee is now making it easier for new entrants to hit the ground running. Nespresso had to utilise its size and a huge diversified marketing approach in order to establish its system with a large customer base and drive adoption of the format. They did this over many, many years. The boutique experience stores that they opened were, when combined with effective D2C online sales strategies, crucial to their success. Typically, boutique companies are not in the position to roll out something of this scope and ambition.

Customer expectations of where and how (in which consumer marketplace) to buy something is linked to an established norm. Different marketplaces put different products in front of different customers. Sometimes the selection happens organically, and en masse. One such example would be the offer of retail beans at boutique coffee shops. These beans are supplied by the specialty boutique roasters who also supply the coffee served in the shop. Essentially, expectation is built up by customers about where and how they can purchase a certain product. This consumer behaviour is key for any business to understand. For companies that have built brands around selling beans it can be hard to access a capsule customer.

Some of the limitations to the pod format are not actually limitations based on the format's goals, but rather based on a desire to appropriate the format into a variety of environments, basically anything outside of people's homes. The system is at its strongest when used domestically or in similar environments like a hotel room or small office. The hardware does not translate as an alternative for producing high-volume espresso machine strength drinks. The shelf life benefit allows for specialty coffee to be sold differently into many channels, and can allow for higher value coffee to be consumed cup by cup.

The market these days has a lot more variation, and comprises compostable alternatives alongside aluminium offerings. The aluminium achieves superior quality results, both because that's what the system was designed to brew, and because the oxygen and moisture barrier of aluminium is still superior.

Coffee Pods - Sustainability and the Future

Interestingly, aluminium wins out on the life cycle studies around environmental impact, but only if it is recycled, and this is one of the main challenges of the coffee pod. Finding suitable disposal solutions that consumers can (and do) adopt is tricky. In the UK, a joint initiative from Nestle and Jacob Douwe Egberts called Podback has been launched. Podback allows other capsule brands to access their recycling networks for a fee, making this service available to their customers.

When it comes to pods made from compostable materials, the challenge is not only product quality, but the fact that the material is truly single-use. The composting is still not a preferable end of life to a recycle and reuse model, if it can actually be adopted. In this case the critical assessment that must be made, is the energy and resources used to create the product, more than whether it gets composted, which is simply a bonus.

Specialty pods simplify and take control of brewing, making them an excellent system for engaging customers around the flavour and provenance of coffee. Continued signs of adoption suggest that this is working. However, the commitment to stock and MOQ sizes combined with the tight margin does also add limitations to the proliferation of the format within boutique coffee.

Instant Coffee

Instant coffee as a format for boutique coffee has a lot of parallels with coffee capsules, but I think it is fair to say that it is a more difficult sell. Like the movement of specialty coffee capsules, it represents a novel format that doesn't historically have much boutique or specialty representation. In fact, this format of coffee felt very separate from boutique coffee before companies began to experiment with how it could be used as a delivery mechanism for specialty coffee.

Unlike coffee capsules, there is very little barrier to entry to having a go at making an instant coffee, albeit on a small scale. One can pick up a freeze dryer for a reasonably low cost. The jump between this, and producing instant coffee commercially, is very significant.

The customer's perceived value does not match up very well with the production cost of specialty instant coffee. It is very hard to make a high-quality, instant coffee product. The process, in effect, involves brewing the coffee, releasing all of the volatiles and then dehydrating the coffee, (in some way) so that it can be sold as a soluble version of the coffee that was dissolved into the original brew. Customers just need to add water to this already brewed coffee and hey presto.

Capsules are not so ambitious in this regard. They are a means of making coffee in the same way that most high-quality coffee is already prepared, utilising ground coffee, with water being added and coffee dissolved at the point of preparation and consumption.

In the field of specialty instant coffee, the goal is to make an instant coffee product that offers another way for existing specialty coffee customers to buy boutique coffee, or allows specialty coffee to reach a large existing audience that prioritises convenience in their purchasing decisions. Currently, the ability to achieve the level of convenience afforded by instant processing techniques, has also been shown to create a trade-off in cup quality and character.

To maximise the comparability of flavour to that of specialty and boutique coffee, a lower extraction is needed than is usually used in the commercial instant process. This further increases the cost of production on what is already a highly costly process. The commercial instant process is built around achieving the highest yield from the raw ingredient of any coffee format on the market. This approach allows the cost of producing and manufacturing instant coffee to be offset by increased yield, which can be as high as three times that of any other typical method (50-60% instead of 20% extraction).

A lab technician from a multinational coffee company once told me once that they were now able, in theory, to obtain a 100% extraction from the coffee bean, but that the cost of the energy required to do this was proportionally so high, that this yield is actually counterproductive economically.

Back to specialty instant. The value proposition struggles to stack up. At this stage of development, companies have to charge a higher price for a lower quality. The hope is that convenience is a powerful enough draw to make up the value shortfall. A solution like specialty instant is often touted as the most powerful opportunity in a situation where the prospective customer lacks access to the other coffee making methods. This scenario projects the customer taking out a sachet or jar of specialty instant when away on a work trip or out camping and hiking in the mountains. It is true that the product has the potential to service this situation well, but this is an atypical user experience, and as such, these scenarios present a reduced market opportunity. These occasions may occur several times a year, or less, in most cases. With coffee's ticket price, the whole industry is built on the premise of people drinking coffee every day of the year, not on the odd holiday, or work trip.

Will Little who runs both a specialty boutique coffee business and a family-owned, flavoured instant coffee business, was keen to point out to me that the instant coffee market is typically very happy with the product. "We've explored the question of tapping into the bigger market with better instant, but in our market research we found people were really happy with the instant coffee they are buying. So if you can't get existing instant customers to move to specialty instant then the whole premise is about getting specialty drinkers to give up their home brewing set up in favour of instant, which isn't going to happen".

The question around formats is a key one in specialty coffee. As the market matures, there will still be new companies looking for ways to get going, and existing ones looking for new ways to grow, but as Will pointed out, although specialty coffee has a lot of market potential to convert customers, it isn't for everyone, it is the boutique specialist end of the industry. This means that each format isn't simply waiting for specialty boutique coffee to come along and adopt it. The format may not be suited to the requirements of specialty coffee.

Cold Brew and Other Formats

Cold brew is a format that is newer to the whole market place, commercial and boutique alike. The question with a new format like this is whether it will be a success for both parts of the industry, one and not the other, or neither.

Cold brew displays many business strengths because it can be formatted as an RTD (ready to drink) product. RTD products are retail products that have been fully prepared. This sounds straightforward, but nearly all coffee in the industry is not sold in this way. It is sold with further steps required by the consumer or operator. Even in the terms of instant coffee, the customer has to boil and add the water to the brew. When in a can or a carton, all the ingredients are combined and prepared. This allows the company behind the product complete control over product quality and flavour. Although the caveat here is that the RTD product can only display the achievable quality and attributes that the format can afford, and like all shelf-ready products, shelf life is necessary, and this is hard to achieve without either pasteurisation or the addition of shelf life stabiliser.

Cold brew, as a method, burst onto the coffee scene and picked up some serious adoption quickly. Interestingly, this was counter to the consensus in specialty circles that it is very challenging to achieve a high-quality flavour profile using the method. The prolonged brewing times appear to cause loss of aroma and the introduction of oxidation. There has, and continues to be innovation in this format, with new techniques, devices and technologies that achieve better and better results.

For me the best results can be achieved when brewing a cold coffee more quickly, so that aroma is kept and oxidation is limited and the coffee still tastes clean. For full disclosure I am involved in a project that is working on this. This is also interesting to me in a commercial setting, as the need to plan and brew a batch of coffee over many hours is taken out of the equation.

In the existing scenario cold brew can be made very easily by anyone with a simple setup and some time. For cafés and the like, the process can be frustrating. You either have too much product that goes to waste or too little when the sun comes out, and no way of quickly creating more stock. It reminds me of when I worked in a cinema and you had to guess how many hot dogs to preheat for the upcoming showings. You were in big trouble if you overshot, but it was no better if you didn't cook enough. In short, a nightmare. It is this difference that makes cold brew different to the previous two formats that we explored. It is not simply a delivery format for an end consumer, but a drink format that can be prepared by B2B businesses, themselves.

Interestingly some of cold brew's flavour attributes that I am less keen on, also appear to play as strengths in the market. Cold brew coffee tastes less acidic and generally shows less origin characteristic. Both of these qualities are a key goal of specialty coffee in its purest form, but clearly a lot of participants who engage in specialty coffee are not in it for these specific reasons.

The addition of nitrogen into cold brew formats has proven highly successful. It can add visual and textural aspects to the drink, which add appeal, and work for both on-bar servings and on-shelf canned RTDs. The success of cold brew doesn't appear to match up with the regions and more specifically, the climates that would seem to make the most sense. The hottest regions are not necessarily the places where cold brew drinks have the most success on coffee shop menus.

The exploration of different formats and drinks on the menu offers a variety of opportunities for specialty coffee businesses. It should also be noted that expanding into more product lines for any business adds complexity and has risks, especially if the format requires investment to explore.

On the one hand, specialty coffee represents a purist approach to coffee, and on the other hand the specialty industry has begun to embrace combinational ingredient drinks, from cocktails to soft serve. As a commercial space, specialty coffee definitely finds value in novelty. The few drink formats explored in this chapter are only the commercial surface of the many options being explored in specialty coffee. Certain drink types, such as espresso and filter coffee, appear to stand the test of time, and will be menu staples around the world, whilst other formats will gain and lose popularity in time. The sticky interaction cycle that specialty coffee looks to embark on with customers requires engagement and will allow new formats and drink types to succeed in the business of specialty coffee in the future.

Coffee Shops
Location, Access to Market and Customer Relations
Coffee shops have boomed in many countries around the world. Multinational chain operators, swathes of independents, and some that bridge the gap, have all found success in the market. Coffee shops can be special businesses that create valuable experiences, ascend beyond the transactional, and venture into the cultural space, becoming significant parts of people's daily lives. Specialty coffee really wouldn't be what it is without coffee shops.

In the first several years of running our Colonna & Small's shop in Bath, UK, I used to write a blog. I expanded on and dug into the different aspects of trying to run a boutique coffee shop with targeted goals around customer engagement and specific boutique coffees.

As businesses, cafés are quite different to all of those that come before them in the coffee bean's journey. They sell an experience and an environment just as much as a physical coffee product. I don't think that coffee shops are easy businesses to run at all. The complexity of the business structure is greatly reduced in the sense of commercial complexity and operations. This is exchanged for a high focus on hospitality, product, service and environment. This is something that you need to be on top of every single day from open to close, I describe it like putting on a theatre show daily.

Of course, a robust understanding and management of the fundamentals is key, and in this regard, the starting point is perhaps one of the most important parts of making this kind of business work. Location, for most coffee shops, is clearly paramount. The requirement lies in finding a site that has a suitable cost per square foot, combined with availability and proximity to the customer cohorts and demographics that your business is looking to target. This doesn't necessarily mean high footfall, well executed specialty coffee shops will draw customers to them, as long customers don't have to travel too far out of their way.

The price that the business can afford to pay for location depends on the ticket value that the business can achieve (a ticket of just coffee is lower than a food and coffee combo, for example) and the amount of customers you expect or are able to serve over a week.

For a specialty boutique brand, the space also needs to successfully attract, communicate to, and deliver an experience to the customer cohort. The experience sought is varied of course, although many would argue there is a ubiquity here, just as there is in terms of the look and feel of specialty coffee shops, as I mentioned in *Part Five* of the book. Through a combination of these factors, a lot of the underlying, determining aspects of the business's success are achieved before the doors even open for trade.

Once operating, the success is about building, maintaining and maximising the environment's potential as a coffee shop. This can be different depending on the business's modus operandi. For example, one café may work towards building a reputation of having a limited and heavily curated menu, whereas another may be looking to offer a bit of everything. There are all sorts of other goals, and hybrid stores as well, which could, for example, be retail driven.

For many cafés, there is a specific key consideration regarding local population density - the audience with proximity to the café. It is often stated that the majority of custom for a given coffee shop location comes from within a one mile radius of the shop. As above, this shows how important location is. UK mainstream "grab and go" coffee and food chains will choose locations based on their offering and the target customer base. Greggs and Pret A Manger target different customer cohorts in the UK market, partially by utilising different locations. These same mechanics are true for independent boutique businesses. It is true that the independent's decision is mainly made more on feel than on a complex demographic analysis, which may be an option for a larger company.

This approach sits alongside the somewhat less common model of creating a destination café. In this instance, the business eschews higher footfall areas, and instead seeks to attract customers to it through reputation and word of mouth, among other marketing initiatives. Here a business can benefit from reduced rent and rates, but they need to create a reason for a customer to head out of their way to come and visit. Theoretically, specialty coffee should be better placed to execute this model, as the product has a differentiated quality and experience that appeals to an engaged customer. This demographic is more likely to seek out and make the trip, as long as the business is doing a great job.

As an overarching principle, every shop needs to have a base goal of meeting expectation, and a stretch goal of exceeding expectation. The shop is in the business of both winning new customers and retaining existing customers. Building a base of customers that return is normally key to the boutique café model. Businesses based in tourist destinations may be an exception, if a one time client is par for the course in their location. The danger in these monopolised environments is that price goes up and quality goes down, but not always.

Customer Feedback and Industry Perception
Specialty coffee as a movement has had a somewhat fractious relationship with meeting expectations. The idea of provenance-driven coffee products that are treated more like their well established food and drink counterparts, has become relatively well established in the UK market now, as well as in many other markets around the globe. This has led to the point where it is an "opt in" proposition for customers. Once a burgeoning movement is established, it is no longer a new, crusading idea that needs to be spread with the same fervour.

Specialty coffee represents an approach that people now understand and can decide if it is for them or not. A few years ago a national McDonald's ad campaign recognised this. The satirical advertisement showed customers who became bemused and unhappy with a boutique coffee shop experience, who then headed to a McDonalds to "just have a coffee." Naturally, afront was taken within specialty coffee, as the depiction was clearly not accurate, and was taking the piss.

I understand this dynamic. When we started recommending coffee in particular ways at our shop in Bath, especially coffee without sugar, we quickly saw people dramatising the situation, making out that we were acting like "The Soup Nazi" from the famous Seinfeld episode. In reality we worked tirelessly to find helpful ways to explain why we recommended our coffee one way, but also made it clear that the final drink was still up to the customer.

It is also fair to say that specialty coffee environments can at times be very unwelcoming, either because they are too "hip" for their own good, or because coffee geeks who want to make great coffee, are not always equally passionate about, or very good at, hospitality.

Putting to one side whether or not the content in the ad campaign was fair, the representation of the boutique coffee shop movement in a major UK-wide advertising campaign was a telling moment. One of the largest food businesses in the UK (and incidentally one of the largest coffee businesses) used this as a narrative that it thought would resonate with its target customer base. Simply put, the boutique movement is big enough for McDonald's to notice.

Their advert is indicative of the segmentation of the market, which in reality is much more segmented than just two sides. As consumers become more aware of the different options on the market, the market will become more about educated customer choices. For a café, success will be found in clearly and successfully targeting a customer segment, or as is most likely the case, several segments it can hit at once.

A challenge for most coffee shops appears to be the attempt to please everyone, to meet all expectations. This isn't possible, even for the biggest, most successful coffee shop chains. If you do start trying to please everyone you will become some kind of café mini-mart. In doing this, you resolve some customer requests, but at the same time, you will be displeasing those looking for a more focused specialist experience. This not only represents an unattainable goal in terms of customer satisfaction, it also creates a wide product range that is unlikely to be executed to a high standard.

For independent shop operators this dynamic is most challenging at the beginning, when they open, and a vocal legion of locals and early regulars explain what they think the shop should do. As we looked at in the *Customer Feedback* chapter in *Part Two* of the book, a business needs a way to properly process feedback and consider it against the company's goals. The need to find your audience is a reason a shop should build in some budgeting time to make those connections over the first 6 to 12 months, rather than basing all decisions around peak available business from day one.

This desire to meet multiple expectations is well founded though. As I have mentioned, a café can typically expect its customers to be in a one mile radius from their location, and each customer is likely to have a relatively low ticket price, so the shop needs to appeal to enough of this available audience to hit its minimum sales requirements and to be profitable. Typically, specialist focused businesses are not trying to offer a local service in this way. Many specialty businesses attempt to juggle the offering of a boutique specialist menu within the constraints of a fast food, local service business model.

Bricks and Mortar Economics

The economics of cafés are based around a few key factors. It is often commented that coffee in a café is a high margin product. Specialty boutique shops don't tend to charge particularly high prices compared to mainstream coffee chains. In fact, the trend on the whole, is a price that matches or is actually cheaper for a typical steamed milk drink (albeit a smaller version) than the high street average. The premise seems to be that the boutique café operator is offering a boutique quality proposition with a comparative price point. With their size and boutique ingredients, the cost of goods for an indie is higher than a chain store.

However, as the ticket price for coffee is low, even for an expensive coffee, the big costs are caught up in the running of the shop experience. Staff represent the biggest percentage cost, and with a lower average ticket price than other hospitality models, normally supported with some pastries and cakes, the rent is also a big factor. The business can't generate the same revenue that a food-driven hospitality site can achieve with its higher average ticket price. Your average indie shop will be targeting rent that equates to 10% of revenue.

Peter Dore-Smith of Kaffeine in London actively targets a 40% staff cost. In modelling a higher staff cost he is prioritising service, and to balance this he will only consider sites that have a considerably lower than average rent, this isn't easy to find. Once the "big three" of goods, rent and staff are covered, there are operational costs to incur, and this should leave the operator with a 15% net profit pre-tax. Managing product costs, utilities and staff is an ongoing requirement if you wish to maintain a sustainable profit. As with each of the target business models, the reality is that the majority of businesses don't attain these goals and actually have a lower profit.

There are various approaches to this modelling that can impact the results. A small footprint, high volume takeaway model that is able to achieve fast efficient order taking and drink making can, and often does, present itself as the most profitable model. The shop can be run with a small staff, as tables don't need serving or clearing, and the customer dwell time is low, so many customers can move through the business quickly, resulting in more coffee sold throughout the day. In the UK this model is pretty much London centric at the moment, and it requires high-density cosmopolitan areas and a large office crowd to support it. In this instance revenue goes up, and staff costs are a lower percentage of revenue. There are shops hitting 25% net profit pre-tax with this approach. These examples are few and far between, and most of the operators who have hit this, struggle to replicate it across multiple sites, even in London.

At the time of writing this book I stipulate that the following is broadly true in the UK specialty coffee shop space. A profitable established independent coffee shop that is coffee and not food driven will on average be making £50k profit per year pre-tax from a £300k revenue. This is a relatively "pure" number and doesn't account for investment in equipment and upkeep of the property, as well as other exceptional costs. With this in mind it makes most sense for owner operators to be present on the floor, reducing staff cost, and to take a wage from the shop, rather than relying on the annual profit. Like all of the businesses in the supply chain, the business models are challenging and typically very hard work, but can also be very rewarding.

The coffee shop model doesn't really stack up very well commercially next to a restaurant, primarily due to the low ticket price. A common mode in the space is a brunch driven café, the sort of thing that has been very successful in Australasia. These have been popping up around the world. A successful food and coffee operation can generate a more profitable business, but it also comes with many challenges and increased risk. If you build the space, team and resources to offer a food driven proposition, there will need to be enough covers turned over every day. For these reasons a brunch model will often prioritise a menu that is relatively easy to service from a kitchen point of view.

People, Expertise and Multi-Site Models

A coffee shop's focus is a challenge in numerous ways, not just operationally and in terms of customer engagement, but in terms of what it means for building, training and maintaining staff. A specialty barista role that is comparable to a sommelier role in wine, is actually very rare. This is because very few specialty boutique cafés are based around a complex coffee menu. The majority of the expertise required is around using a house coffee to make a variety of drinks efficiently and to a high standard, whilst showing great customer service and multi-tasking skills.

I personally find this work can be very rewarding, but in most environments, there is a point reached where the coffee curious and coffee passionate individuals are not able to develop or engage sufficiently with their interest in the subject. This is where the common desire for individuals to transition to roastery jobs comes from, and some shop operators, as we explored a few chapters back, choose to engage with the roasting process to help support this, and aid staff retention.

There is a natural staff churn built into this business model, though for most operators, it remains a key focus to try to keep the turnover of staff low. Even if you can consistently find experienced, capable staff, they need time to get up to speed in your environment, and to work well in your team. One of the biggest value points that can be created by a team that doesn't change too often, is a familiarity with regulars. I remember getting into coffee in the central business district in Melbourne, Australia, and if you could make good coffee, fast and remember people's orders and preferences, you could boost the daily numbers quickly.

In our Bath shop model, which prioritises knowledge around coffee and dialogue, we have a full-time staff only policy. This has its own challenges, and most shops are a mix of full and part-time staff. Many people take on hospitality roles as a stop gap or a job to support a different endeavour. I have always enjoyed the eclectic mix of people I could meet through hospitality both in terms of staff and customers. For those that catch the coffee bug whilst working in the industry, it is always possible that they may consider a career in coffee. This could mean moving throughout the supply chain and looking at jobs that orbit coffee, and just as likely, it can mean working towards opening their own shop.

As the interest in specialty coffee has grown, more and more different models of specialty cafés have appeared. Some operators choose to build highly curated specialist experiences, whilst others are aiming to be a fast-paced takeaway option. Then there are those looking to create crossover, hybrid stores. Specialty coffee is also making it into a wider array of environments. We are seeing more "roll out" models that look to emulate the success of businesses like Blue Bottle, who have created a large bricks and mortar speciality coffee shop brand.

As with most hospitality roll outs, this is tough to accomplish, but there is also precedent for them to succeed with the right strategy, good site locations and an overall lean operating approach. As well as this, there have been a growing number of businesses targeting the size between, which could be described as a "contained multi-site operator." This would be a business with a handful of locations.

One operator I spoke to in London recently said that the goal to hit a nice economy of scale was five shops in the past, but this is now perhaps ten shops. Multi-site operators all also explain how tipping the business from a single site into a collection of shops produces different operational needs, and leads to structures such as a head office, to help look after the fleet of shops. The financials of larger operators don't suggest great economies of scale. Often the savings are cancelled out by other costs. Of course, hitting the same EBITDA percentage across multiple sites does track as a commercial success. Looking at the available financials of the large chain coffee companies, it is hard to pull out just the shop numbers, but they hit roughly 10% net profit. This is lower than the more standard 15% goal, but 10% profit of a business with thousands of sites can be substantial. In this way a larger business, which has the growing costs of running its many sites and managing the brand, are better able to pursue a lower percentage profit as cash profits will be high due to volume.

A big challenge of operating across multiple sites is an extension of the single site issue - you need to find the right sites. Unless a business has sufficient cash to try out sites and shut them down, speed of growth can be dictated by the availability of the right sites.

Sustainability, Automation and Trends

From a sustainability point of view, the shop is an interesting place, as on lifecycle studies, the consumption end is a big contributor to the carbon footprint of a cup of coffee. The two main strategies that can be employed to reduce impact at this point of the journey are: to be as efficient as possible with the coffee itself, and to reduce the energy used to brew coffee. There are more and more machines that are focusing on utilising less energy to heat and dispense water. This has the added benefit of reducing the operator's utilities costs.

Whilst specialist shops encourage a barista forward setup, with deconstructed methods that allow the brands and baristas to evolve their coffee making methods and styles, elsewhere advanced automated systems are being used more often to represent specialty coffee in non-barista led environments. Nowadays most specialist shops are starting to look at devices that automate parts of the brewing process, as both training and speed of production can be sticking points in these business models.

Even though shops are mostly focusing on a fast transaction of a house coffee supply, the narrative of coffee's origin continues to take more and more prominence in the café environment. This is also increasingly becoming the case on the menus and offers of larger mainstream coffee operators. The branding in the coffee shop space continues to evolve year-on-year as some semiotics become the norm, and new branding ideas and concepts are introduced. Coffee shop designs can represent cultural spaces and form part of a locality. The industry attracts creatives as customers and employees, and this is borne out in the variety of shop design that we see around the world, even if there are still some threads of similarity most of the time.

The drink formats themselves are, as is the whole supply chain, a mix of established staples and new trends or concepts. In the UK market cold brew has done quite well, but the majority of drinks served in cafés are still steamed milk and espresso combinations. The percentage of these drinks that are made from alternative milks has grown massively.

Boutique shops around the world are adding freezer menus to their offering that allow them to offer a list of "cellared" coffees. Specialty boutique coffee shops may have a north star of offering high-quality crafted specialty coffee, but the exact execution and menu offering is something that is always in a state of flux and consideration.

As with the roasting part of the supply chain, the act of selling a cup of coffee in an environment can take many forms, and as it is such a key connection point with customers, see *Physical Experiences - The Value of Bricks and Mortar*, many coffee brands throughout the supply chain have begun to operate their own coffee shops, allowing them to control the customer engagement point of their coffee business. In these cases, producers and roasters can also focus on using the shop as a retail space for a variety of their coffee products. The market for specialty coffee shops continues to show growth, and even with high competition and challenging trading environments, I do believe these hospitality businesses will continue to show significant value.

HoReCa and Offices

This term technically stands for Hotels, Restaurants and Catering. The Ca is also interpreted as cafés in many definitions. In coffee we tend to talk about cafés separately and instead include catering in the definition. Essentially it ends up being a catch all for all b2b coffee sales where coffee will be prepared for customers on site. These businesses are not really coffee businesses per se, as their primary trade is not coffee. In fact, they are probably better described as "channels" for coffee business. The line is blurry though, as for a catering company, coffee may be a core product, and something they sell as a service.

This arena of business is full of different commercial agreements, and it isn't typically a core market for specialty coffee, although there has been growing success for specialty coffee in these environments.

The business of coffee in these environments is driven by some specific considerations, mainly commercial procurement relationships and coffee delivery solutions. When coffee is "free" to the customer and part of a wider experience or service, this creates an obvious dynamic around price. Namely that the price needs to be low, as the product is seen as a potential loss. Of course, this is an approach that doesn't consider the importance of the customers' complete experience in the space. Everything on offer contributes to an overall experience. This dynamic is often recognized as a failing point of many great restaurants, and has often been commented on by those in the specialty boutique industry, although this too has been changing.

The pandemic tripped up the trend, and had coffee brands all looking to the online opportunity, but interest from specialty coffee in these environments has returned post pandemic. With the café scene still growing, but also becoming more competitive in terms of supply, some coffee roasters and brands have turned their attention to HoReCa environments, which are places where people spend large chunks of their lives.

You may think an office would buy its staff the cheapest coffee, (and sometimes this is true,) but in many sectors, finding and retaining the best talent in an industry has become difficult. Providing a good coffee offering has been one part of many company's wider strategy to create and maintain a desirable working environment. In co-working spaces and offices the coffee can be part of the draw that brings people into the space, or helps keep them happy. All the same, these environments aren't usually places where highly unusual micro lots pop up, and there is still a pricing strain.

A major influence on the transition of specialty coffee into these spaces has been changes in brewing technology. As coffee is a secondary product in all of these environments, it usually makes little sense to have trained baristas on staff. The question of how to brew and deliver the coffee in the environment is integral to its success. Batch brewing systems often are the culprit of the worst brews in HoReCa businesses, as low volume sales cause the coffee to be left on the hotplate for too long, or to get stewed in the Thermos. Batch brewers also still require a degree of operator optimisation to provide a great coffee.

In these environments, systems like fully automatic bean to cup machines and coffee capsules can shine. The change here is twofold: technology in these systems has been constantly improving, and specialty coffee companies have started to embrace the idea of utilising a wider variety of brewing methods to showcase their coffee.

There was a time in the not too distant past where there was rigid dogma around what could and could not be used to brew good coffee. This hasn't gone away entirely of course, but the orthodoxy has greatly diminished. At its genesis the attitude came from a sensible place, as coffee companies wanted to make sure their coffee was presented in a way that optimised its flavour.

The movement that exists surrounding the theory of coffee brewing, which has long been a central part of the specialty coffee movement (geeking out over the minutiae) has, I think, actually reduced the dogma, as the true drivers of cup quality have repeatedly been shown to be the raw ingredient quality plus good roasting and water. Some key brewing fundamentals show themselves. In other words, get the basics right and you can brew some nice coffee on a wide variety of equipment.

There are now some extremely impressive bean to cup machines that can brew very good coffee. They just need to be kept clean and supplied with filtered water in a reasonable mineral zone. Pods too can produce a very nice drink that showcases specialty flavour profiles well, although the strength isn't the familiar espresso strength, but rather a medium concentration brew.

Just as the pandemic showed that coffee was important to people at home, it follows that specialty coffee culture will be in demand in multiple environments, which creates various business opportunities in the space.

If a business moves into catering and office supply, they are likely to be working with larger organisations that are highly structured. For many boutique coffee companies, this sales channel requires more compliance and traceability than they are used to. It also often requires increased operational complexity in terms of managing purchase orders and delivering to fulfilment centres.

As this space is mostly inhabited by larger organisations and structures who have developed strong CSR and procurement policies, it is also a sales space where conversations around the certifications, audits and supply chain verification come into play more so than other channels. The transparency initiatives that I questioned in *Part Four* provide sales value in these scenarios, as of course do any of the initiatives that a coffee brand/supplier is undertaking that the HoReCa client puts an emphasis on as part of its procurement criteria. Certification requirements tend to be more sought after in this channel as well as recognition of company development work such as B Corp and associated commitments.

The exact service relationship can vary wildly from a simple product supply to a full barista or coffee catering service. An area of business in HoReCa that still provides a sweet spot challenge is the smaller client type. Capsules can be a solution for a small office, as can a domestic style coffee set up for offices where team members enjoy manually brewing coffee. However, in many of these environments, and also in many medium and larger style businesses, there is still a coffee solution challenge, as coffee is not a primary focus. To be fair, this is a hurdle in all coffee preparation environments. The challenge is that the most suitable solutions are automated solutions as there is no barista on staff. However, the solutions that achieve a high cup quality require a big capital expenditure, and usually necessitate regular cleaning and handling, with additional costs of yearly maintenance contracts. The lower amount of coffees sold or served doesn't stack up well against the investment. This feels like an area where technological developments will allow specialty coffee companies to better serve this situation.

With all of this chapter in mind, this area of the industry still provides a challenge for boutique specialty coffee companies, and when push comes to shove the specialty companies who usually win these tenders are doing so with their lowest-priced coffee. However, as specialty coffee companies continue to explore the commercial opportunity of their propositions, and as the audience for boutique specialty coffee grows, this area of the industry will likely grow as a part of the specialty coffee business landscape.

Businesses that Orbit Coffee

There are many businesses that orbit the journey of the coffee bean. They are very much part of the business of coffee, and even though they may not handle the beans themselves, some are literally coffee companies, and the coffee market is their sole domain.

Some of these companies very much channel the old Levi's gold rush story in their inception. During the California gold rush Levi Strauss and Jacob Davis didn't pan for gold, instead they made and sold riveted pocket work trousers that we now know as jeans. They also sold other tools such as shovels and wheelbarrows. The saying "don't dig for gold, sell shovels" originates from this story.

For each of the individuals panning for gold the chance of success was slim, and the majority would not hit the jackpot. However, they all needed the tools and clothing to take part. By selling the tools for the endeavour, the success of the individual had no bearing on Levi and Jacob's success, what mattered to their business was that a lot of people took part and joined the rush.

This same story has played out in the specialty coffee industry over the last few decades. Granted, starting a coffee company has a much better risk profile than panning for gold did back then, but it also doesn't have the same quick jackpot potential. The specialty café movement has led to great business for the machine manufacturers who were able to develop and produce machines and brands that resonated with the movement, and thus become the "tools" of the market.

This part of the marketplace is not made up of as many

companies, but for those who have got it right, it can be great business. There are a range of equipment companies vying for both the commercial customers and the growing at home specialty coffee market that boomed during the pandemic. These businesses are much more driven by R&D, Innovation and Technology than businesses handling the bean itself. The equipment businesses in the supply chain can either support in company processes, such as pruning technology on a farm, milling equipment, roastery machines or grinders and brewers. Software and AI can also be a part of developing the whole supply chain. The weather teams that large exporters or importers have could soon be usurped by AI and the service of such analysis could be opened up to many many more businesses of differing sizes.

Each of these businesses is desperate to understand the marketplace to be able to spot areas of values and trends that they can develop products for. All of these businesses have to prioritise a product pipeline, as is typical in a technology product-driven industry. Some of the areas don't actually require constant change, but the market is keen to roll and move. Often the drivers behind this circumstance are wear, and the desire to keep things current. Coffee machines are often treated more like a leased car, leading to an ongoing market appetite, fed by periodic changing of equipment. Often the new equipment in the market is providing an improvement in an area, but sometimes it is just a different take on an idea.

The surprising complexity of the coffee industry and also the variety of trends and preferences at play mean companies need to work hard to understand what motivates sales and engagement in the market. As we have explored, there are many segments in coffee, and different user experiences to service and also importantly, to evolve, change or create. As we looked at in the *Innovation* chapter the ability to see these opportunities and to create products that address a known or unknown need are keys to success. In these businesses there needs to be the balance between invention, engineering and coffee knowledge and approach. The companies typically have the challenge of combining R&D and manufacturing behaviours and cultures.

These types of businesses require significant funding, not only to get started but to keep growing and fueling a product pipeline. This then needs to be supported by the ability to fund working capital and global distribution. Along with the mechanics of designing and manufacturing products and equipment there will be a significant risk profile. Some of the R&D projects will never end up in a product at all, or will be launched to lower than expected market sales or success because they don't hit the right value spot or are ahead of their time or lose out to a competitor product.

It is an interesting space, as we all learn more about coffee we also move the goal posts in terms of what we are looking for equipment to achieve. This means our judgement criteria moves over time. In some cases this has meant not only the development of new products that achieve success against these criteria, but also the revisiting of older technologies and products that we now realise were achieving something we want. A lot of the goals we are looking to achieve haven't actually changed that much, and companies are continually working on incremental improvements to reach those goals.

As you would expect, in this world of invention and R&D, we see more intellectual property at play, as companies look to protect their intellectual property. We looked at this topic in detail in *Intellectual Property* in *Part 3* of the book.

Software companies are interwoven into the coffee industry as they now are in all industries, whether a stock management system, an e-commerce platform or marketing tools. Most of these systems work across multiple industries, so coffee is just one of the spaces they are active in. But, there are specific software platform companies like Cropster and Algrano who are using digital business concepts to directly serve the coffee industry. With software there is often a very sticky adoption dynamic at play, whereby the market leader typically takes all with maybe a few smaller competitors. Once a company builds their operations around these softwares there is a lot of friction involved in changing or moving to another solution. This is good business but also leaves less market opportunity for multiple players.

Other businesses that fit in here are not technological at all, such as milk. The coffee industry in somewhere like the UK is almost as much about milk and alternative milk as it is about coffee. Boutique dairies can and do target specialty boutique coffee as a key or main market opportunity, and more and more alternative milk is marketed and branded around the concept of the barista. The same can be said for packaging formats and takeaway or reusable cup brands. There are many other product categories that intersect with the coffee industry.

From a marketing and branding point of view, these businesses have many of the same levers impacting success. In many cases the core target client to appeal to and convince is a coffee professional of some kind. This could be a barista, a trainer, a green buyer, a roaster, a producer and so on. These customers will be heavily critical and have high expectations of what they want from products and services. There is a much wider customer base who will be happy to be led by the behaviour of other coffee professionals and brands.

As I have mentioned elsewhere in the book, there are many operators, both new entrants and existing companies, who are looking to others to inform their buying decisions. Coffee is complex and it makes sense to seek different forms of verification when trying to assess what to buy and use in your business, but also in your home. For these reasons there is a lot of word of mouth and buying behaviour based on who has adopted the products and services to achieve their business goals.

For companies selling to the coffee industry, but who don't have a specific technological USP, an ability to build a brand that speaks to and connects with an aspect of the community is likely to be their most important marketing dynamic. This is not to say that the product quality is not important, but just that the ability to resonate with the semiotics and community of the market is very powerful. This is true for all of the brands looking to succeed in the space. For this reason, industry events, parties, coffee community events and educational engagement are just some of the marketing activities that are utilised.

A focus on sustainability is relevant to all companies, and has many specific dynamics, depending on the company type and its product. The legislation plans in Ireland to ban single use takeaway coffee cups by 2026 will see a boom in bring your own cup and reuse schemes, and the business dynamic will change significantly.

The technologies utilised at farm level will be affected by both the goal to create more sustainable growing environments and by the EU deforestation laws that will require new activities in the supply chain to be carried out utilising technology. Roasters will need to become more energy efficient, as will brewing devices.

The specialty market is not only growing, it's evolving, and this creates a range of business opportunities for businesses that orbit the journey of the bean from seed to cup.

Part Eight. Thoughts & Questions Posed

Introduction to Part Eight

I started writing this book with a few motivations in mind. My goal was to pen something that was able to add value, afford insight and contribute towards an understanding of how the coffee industry functions as a collection of businesses, with a focus on what we currently term specialty coffee. Writing something down is very different to simply exploring the idea in your head or discussing it with other people. It forces you to really test, expand and refine your own understanding.

When it comes to complex topics, the goal isn't, and in my opinion shouldn't be, to simply offer reductionist answers. The goal is rather to contribute to the discussion so that we all can ask better questions. With something as contextual as specialty coffee, you can only really discuss the different levers and frameworks at play. You can then understand each situation and context by applying these levers.

When it comes to subjects around coffee I often find myself channelling my curious side, asking questions, and critically assessing topics. I think it's easy for this to sometimes feel negative, as the process involves breaking things down and finding faults, but my goal is to do this with a growth mindset. My ambition is always to improve things, to question how they can be done better. You can't do this unless you properly understand the way things work. Great ambitions and idealistic outcomes may abound, but if they aren't accompanied by a realistic and accurate understanding of the frameworks and behaviours at play, then they may end up being a well intentioned but ineffective pursuit.

"In the beginner's mind there are many possibilities, but in the expert's mind there are few."
– Shunryu Suzuki, Zen Mind, Beginner's Mind

The longer I am in coffee the more I worry about this quote. It can be easy to observe patterns and spend a lot of time pointing out where ideas are wrong. However, I also want to maintain the open mind of the beginner, this can be combined with the wisdom and knowledge of the expert.

It is also important to note that while much can be improved and progressed, some things already work very well. There can be a danger of creating a cycle of "out with the old and in with the new" as a matter of course, but with no benefit. Specialty coffee, as an indie small company movement has come to slowly realise this, and has started to take a more nuanced view on what is being achieved and by whom.

In this last part of the book I aim to pick out some of the overarching themes of the book, as well as to pose some questions about how the future of business in coffee may look.

Singing the Praises of Specialty Coffee

My process of trying to critically assess and understand the coffee market can at times feel quite negative and I sincerely hope this book is not, on balance, overly negative. Yes, it definitely was my intention to address misconceptions surrounding the business of specialty coffee and explore some challenging questions, but I also hope I have achieved a balanced and pragmatic assessment of the space. My goal is to contribute to what I see as a very special industry. We improve by identifying things that can be improved.

I am personally very grateful to the world of specialty coffee and the opportunities it has afforded me, since I stumbled across the burgeoning movement in Melbourne. I have felt lucky to engage with the industry as it has continued to grow and evolve and I continue to be fascinated by coffee, its complexity and the connection it affords.

From a business perspective, coffee provides a variety of opportunities. The boutique sector allows for a lot of small businesses to find their customers and to build their tribe. Businesses are able to pursue a mission and product they are proud of, something that they personally have a passion for and feel the reward of delivering to a high-quality and standard.

There are really wonderful businesses to be built in specialty coffee, businesses that focus on bringing people together through a shared experience around coffee. Great coffee experiences usually do represent a series of people and businesses working together and contributing to the final success. Boutique coffee can be a place of creativity and innovation. It can, and has, set trends and values for the wider market.

There are limits to the total impact that a boutique space can have, but that doesn't mean that the businesses and experiences are not valuable. It just means that caution should be taken when making claims about impact, and that there needs always to be a consideration of the wider market. Seeking to do something well is valuable, that is true even if it is small and contained. The wider industry will continue to be a mix of large and small operations.

Coffee as a crop may have its challenges, but it does still provide a valid cash crop with potential in rural, subtropical economies looking to utilise agriculture to develop. The global macroeconomic landscape means that growing and harvesting coffee in certain places and at certain scales is not very sustainable, and in those circumstances, perhaps coffee isn't a suitable crop any longer. Maybe a political situation will prevail that can recreate the International Coffee Agreement. In the meantime, there are examples of specialty coffee creating more value at an agricultural level, and business relationships in the supply chain that are partnership based, such as fixed price commitments and multi-year contracts.

Coffee as a subtropical crop has the opportunity to be a shining example of a sustainable crop. This isn't easy to achieve, but it is a crop that naturally lends itself to diverse, canopy covered ecologies. The crop can benefit from being part of a diversified ecosystem.

The boutique space is creative and explorative in coffee. Many people build businesses that allow them to pursue their own curiosity and value in coffee, which can of course mean different things for different people. Although we have work to do to address inequity and inequality, we also have a diverse industry. People from different backgrounds, cultures and identities come together and connect through coffee.

Many people who come to coffee from other industries explain how unique it is, and how much more open and collaborative it is than other industries. The thing with seeking improvement, is that you focus on areas that can or need to improve. This is valid and useful, but we also have a lot to be grateful for and proud of in our interesting industry.

We live in a grey and complex world. A cup of specialty boutique coffee, carefully crafted and touched by many hands can be a magical moment in a person's day. Being involved in businesses that form part of this proceeding can be highly rewarding, and it explains why so many of us are drawn to doing business in this industry.

Lean Margin Frameworks

It is often quipped amongst those working in coffee that they didn't choose the industry as an easy way to make money. This is perhaps particularly apt for boutique independent businesses.

As we have seen in this book, the typical business model throughout the chain is relatively lean on net profit targets as a percentage of revenue, and larger cash profits are only really achieved at scale. In venture capital business evaluation, you would question if this was "high-quality revenue." In simple terms, revenue is great and everything, but what is the profit and cash flow of that revenue? Although revenue growth, even with losses, can create companies of sizable value, the long term value will be linked to repeatability and profitability, as opposed to just growth.

All this is to say that coffee businesses are, by their nature, predominantly made up of four industries: agriculture, financing and logistics, food manufacturing and hospitality. There are well established economic norms that you would expect in each of those industries. Because coffee is an engaging, exciting space, it can be easy to think that it is different. Throughout the book I focused quite a lot on the micro and macroeconomics at play in an industry fundamentally based on the global trade of an agricultural product.

When building and running businesses in these spaces, it is vital to tie strategy to an understanding of this foundation. On the whole, it means that businesses will need to grow relatively organically and within their means. If the business is funded, valuations tied to EBITDA or a small multiple of revenue will inform the growth rate in the same manner.

These fundamentals do benefit larger businesses that have

scaled. 10% of the revenue of a small business is very, very different to 10% from a large business. This means that what's possible in coffee is distinctly different to the likes of tech start-ups.

The realisation that lean profit is shared by all actors throughout the supply chain, also informs the discussion around what is possible within the seed to cup journey. Available profit is directly linked to the ability to undertake new initiatives.

This dilemma is particularly apparent in smaller boutique businesses who have ambitions to explore what's possible in coffee. The business may be interested in alternative supply chain relationships, or product R&D, or want to put revenue into outreach and brand building capacity. For a micro roaster or small shop owner to be explorative and achieve this kind of progressive programme their price per gram of coffee or per drink would need to be a lot higher than the market average.

This in turn really supports the idea that even specialty boutique coffee needs to be built around achieving a certain level of scale. There are often assumptions made around the impact of scale on quality, and they come from a valid place. There are many scenarios whereby quality becomes less of a necessity at larger scale, and pure commercials take over, even though the loss of quality can also hurt that business.

It is worth remembering that even very small operations are leveraging scale somewhere in the chain, whether through export and import, or the financing of these activities. It is also useful to note though that throughout the supply chain, achieving high-quality at a very small scale with a limited set of resources and a restricted set up is also possible. To contextualise this point, depending on what your coffee business's goal is, there will be certain scale goals that allow you to better pursue your mission. The lesson really, is that you need to understand the optimal scale points for what you are doing (or want to do) in coffee.

This lean industry framework, with costs that scale alongside revenue growth, also means, and perhaps this is the most vital point, that all businesses in coffee need to be very well run. They need to be effective and efficient at what they do. This may sound like an obvious point, but it is worth stressing. There is not enough buffer in the margins or profit for a lot to go wrong. This also means that, like the restaurant industry, it is an industry where a lot of businesses won't last the course. For everyone working in coffee, there has to be a focus on capability and execution. I mean, this is probably a fair point in most business.

I believe it is right to seek excellence in what you do, and in the world of business this needs to be tied not only to creating excellent products and experiences, but also to ambitiously pursuing the idea of running an excellent business.

The Fifth Wave, Can You Scale Quality?
Quality is contextual. Which means that some qualities are easier to scale than others. In its most simple form, this is a question about whether you can make more of a thing, which is dependent on its attributes. Perhaps the hardest thing of all to scale is human-driven experiences.

A single shop operation, in which the founders are on the floor most days, interacting with staff and customers alike, will not continue to be a feasible mode if the business expands to have five sites. It may still be a business that can deliver a quality product and experience, but the experience won't be the same. When I asked Stephen Morrissey (Chief Commercial Officer at the Specialty Coffee Association) what he thinks most about when considering marketing in coffee, he said "the challenge of scaling human relationships and interactions." He noted how much of the business in the industry revolves around emotional connections and human relationships. When Stephen was running the coffee programme at TED, back in the day, he spoke to the author Seth Goden about the challenge of communicating a vision to customers. Seth simply said "tie it to a person, that's the way to do it."

The exact qualities that a business strives to achieve throughout the supply chain will be subjective, which means that individuals making decisions around quality are also directing quality throughout the entire supply chain. Changes in personnel also change the specific product and experience outcomes that the company produces.

The fifth wave is a term that Allegra strategies (based in London) has coined. The idea follows on from the much-parroted narrative of three coffee waves. Allegra has speculated that a fourth took place over the past decade and saw a focus on the science of coffee, and there is now a fifth wave, which is focused on the business and scaling of specialty coffee. You could say that this wave is very much aligned with the title of this book.

Many of the businesses that make up what I have termed the specialty boutique industry have matured and grown significantly since their inception. However, it is also worth noting at this point that for something to be boutique, it can't really be enormous. So in this regard, the boutique aspect of specialty coffee cannot be scaled by a single company, and the scale of the boutique sector is coming from a large collection of boutique businesses working in the same space. Market sizing and opportunity vary in different global markets, but show growth everywhere. As well as this, there are new contenders regularly joining the fray, from small independents to funded entrants, all looking to capitalise on a proposition that has shown great potential. It is worth noting that many larger, existing non-specialty coffee businesses have also implemented aspects of what is typical in specialty boutique coffee into their already scaled-up operations.

Questions of scaling the quality of the coffee itself (rather than the experience) can be broken into two supporting questions. Firstly, can you scale boutique quality? And secondly, is there the consumer appetite to support this growth and scale?

From a supply perspective, high-priced, boutique experimental coffees have limited scale potential due to the price point that matches their craft processes. Now, scale is of course relative. Is there room for more of these coffees? Absolutely. It appears that we are still finding out and realising the extent of the growing appetite for higher-priced boutique coffee with varying flavour profiles across markets. However, in each market these coffees are part of the niche end of the market, and nothing would suggest that these will become the mainstream option, perhaps due to both flavour and price.

There are inherent limitations around growing and producing

boutique coffee. One of the biggest challenges in mountainous areas, where coffee needs to be handpicked, is that a bigger farm requires more labour at the time of harvesting. It is hard to maintain the same level of quality at large farming scales without the addition of expensive post-picking technologies, which are only really affordable or sensible if the farming business is substantial. This does mean that although quality can be achieved at scale it is more likely to be achieved by small to medium-sized farms. Improvements in agronomy, cultivars, processing and technology all allow for better coffee to be produced more regularly.

Access to finance at a producing level remains one of the biggest inhibitors, as farmers cannot maximise the quality potential of their crop if they are not able to utilise all of the possible inputs that can make a harvest as good as possible. Larger scale again means more requirement for debt to maximise quality.

Climate change, combined with existing weather occurrences will always create variability around coffee quality from year-to-year. Interestingly though, from speaking to farmers, I have found that some already experience a challenge in moving their volume of higher-priced coffee. This suggests that it may not be a shortage of good coffee that's currently an inhibiting factor in growing quality coffee for consumers, but rather an access to market and demand dynamic.

I think that Allegra's notion of quality at scale is not about specialty becoming the norm or taking over from commercial coffee, but more about moving beyond the domain of independent subculture businesses. There is a clear dynamic of independents exploring an ambition to grow their brand and new entrants to the market who have scale-driven growth strategies.

In most cases the specialty boutique movement is driven by low to mid-80 point coffees that find their way into the hopper as a house blend. From a coffee shop point of view, you could say there has been an impressive and widespread change and adoption of specialty brewing techniques, which does represent scale. When I spoke with Michael Phillips, director of education at Blue Bottle Coffee and 2010 World Barista Champion, he told me how, when he was starting out as a home barista, he was shocked at how poor the drink preparation was in well known cafés at the time, and he pointed out how far things have now come.

Coffee competitions, combined with a growing barista culture, and training programmes across companies and curriculums, have allowed the industry to come a long way, and the average standard has clearly increased dramatically. Of course, technology has also played its part, and continues to do so, as parts of coffee preparation can be supported with tools and devices.

There are well prepared drinks made in a huge variety of businesses and at scale both across independents and in larger multi-site operators. This change is driven by a combination of people, education, technology and a business focus on quality. It is quite amazing when you think about the change that has happened, and how quickly it has occurred.

In fact, the open source nature of shared experience and education in boutique coffee, has popularised a proliferation of quality-driven techniques and shared learning, leading to a great increase in quality across the industry.

We considered, in the *Technology* chapter, how automated technologies are interesting for their ability to deliver a specialty drink in a non-barista led environment. It may be worth reframing this idea of scaling quality, at least partially, as achieving growth through diversification by coffee brands. Coffee brands can grow by operating in more different environments and utilising contrasting formats and technologies to do this. This can allow the coffee brand to achieve scale and growth through diversification. This is absolutely a trend that has been taking place in boutique coffee.

Technology and product developments have helped improve coffee at scale in various ways in the supply chain. Milling and drying improvements and storage improvements all make it possible to have better coffee, and coffee that stays better for longer, which of course contributes to the ability to achieve quality at scale.

While there have been many developments that have allowed quality coffee to proliferate throughout the supply chain, it is not all plain sailing. There are still multiple challenges when it comes to scaling quality, as appears to be the case in most fields.

In volume driven, commercial environments there is commonly a battle between quality, and volume and efficiency. As I have mentioned again and again, quality is context driven. To frame this point more specifically, there is often conflict between achieving certain qualities and volumes, and economics. This can clearly arise in the picking, processing and milling techniques used at origin, but this dynamic can be witnessed through the supply chain all the way downstream to the client.

In his article, *Mother Ethiopia*, Christopher Feran detailed the following scenario, "By 2019, in order to grow their production volumes, most of the cooperatives I visited in the West employed the same tactics: collecting more cherry with looser sorting requirements; pulping it faster while removing 80-100% of the mucilage; fermenting less; and drying their coffee in full sun in 4-6 days to just 12-12.5% moisture content.

But the strategy they'd pursued—producing more coffee in the hopes of selling it at high prices through the union to deliver a dividend to members—didn't go according to plan. In the tension between quality and volume, volume won; and when quality lost, specialty buyers didn't show".

This quality scenario is not just about growing a larger audience for a quality product, but also about achieving an increased volume within a set of constraints. The solution in this case was to cut corners. The incentive to maximise yield can be found throughout coffee, and is present in most industries.

A good café should be trying to produce drinks as fast as it can, whilst maintaining quality. This is less about scale and more about the challenges any individual coffee shop might face. They may opt for a batch brew to allow quicker filter coffee service, but then if the product does not sell fast enough, stewed, lower-quality brews are served at points throughout the day. Quality loses out again here.

The same can be said for roasteries when it comes to their manufacturing efficiency. It is not so much that quality cannot be achieved as a company increases in scale, but more that certain qualities are more achievable within a scaling structure that will need to increase in line with volume, whilst maintaining a minimum quality.

I have mentioned in the book, on occasion, that within a business context, being tiny is not typically the best platform within which to pursue quality. There actually appears to be a sweet spot of scale, in which team, size, equipment and buying all help to optimise quality. I would however also say that it is currently easier than ever to achieve good quality on a small scale, as boutique equipment and sales channels that support nano and micro operations are becoming more available. This is a really interesting phenomenon. The barrier to entry to play with very high-quality coffee has definitely reduced, representing an opposite trend to the title of this chapter.

The human challenge I mentioned at the beginning of this chapter is real. Companies need coffee professionals to guide and oversee their quality aesthetic. Salaries may increase in scaled companies, but many in coffee are also looking to be in a company culture that is boutique and specialty, and larger companies often mention the challenge of finding, developing and retaining great team members to drive and contribute to quality.

Alongside the personnel challenge is the sales challenge. If a company's sales are driven by trying to appeal to broader audiences, then the approach to quality moves from curated to reactive. The company may end up looking to produce a more commercially accepted version of quality. Coffee companies of all sizes tussle with the balance of whether they are trying to please everyone or prefer to stick to a strong product concept. This becomes more and more apparent as a business scales.

With all of this in mind I would say that to grow and or scale a quality-driven coffee operation requires a company to have a clearly defined approach to quality as one of its "whys." If quality is a north star for the business to return to as a core sign of success, then it will hold strong as the company scales. From a business perspective, this exploration of scaling quality is both fascinating to watch and be a part of.

In the coming years we will see how things play out and return back to the questions at the beginning of the chapter.

1) Can you scale the quality itself? And 2) is there market appetite and demand to support that scale? These aren't questions that will be asked and simply answered, and the book is closed. They are ongoing for an industry like coffee, as the concept of quality itself evolves. However, we can safely acknowledge that there is scaling taking place in the specialty coffee industry and consumers have shown an increasing demand for quality-driven products and experiences in the market.

Industry Trends
A Flavour-Oriented Drink
As well as being a caffeine and aroma filled drink, coffee also occupies a social and cultural space in our lives. As coffee has emerged as a culinary beverage and not just a commoditised stimulant, it has been tempting to start drawing parallels with other such industries. As with all comparisons and analogies, some aspects of the comparison hold true, whilst others don't translate.

The flavour trends in boutique coffee are clear to follow and the comparison to wine here seems apt. This is a drink from a single source ingredient, (let's not talk about additives) fermented and consumed as a beverage. Granted, caffeine is not nearly the psychoactive drug that alcohol is, but still.

In the wine marketplace, a huge swathe of people drink it, showing a varying interest in the product. There is a mass-consumption end and a pointy end, with segmentation in-between. There are also scoring structures, which aim to chronicle and judge the quality of the product. There are focuses on different varieties and cultivars of vine and there are more (or less) established producers whose reputations impact their sales. Terroir is valued, and methodologies are often changed, challenging the status quo or simply expanding the experience and variety present.

The specialty end of coffee has very quickly walked a similar path. Flavour trends circle around scarcity and novelty, intertwined with more established norms around quality. Specialty coffee is seeing a high-level of exploration in terms of species, cultivars and processing techniques. Tensions surrounding what constitutes flavouring is also not unique to coffee.

Brewing Technology
Where the similarities in consumer behaviour and trends don't cross over, is the making aspect of coffee. The brewing and delivery of coffee is quite different to pouring a liquid from a glass bottle sealed with a cork or a metal cap. The need to brew coffee presents both an opportunity and a problem depending on the customer and the context.

The making phase is a huge part of the business of coffee and the consumer experience. There is a sliding scale of what is asked of the customer, from easy and convenient through to complex and involved. You could go so far as to say that coffee brewing can be difficult on purpose. There are game mechanics at play here. A person could express the desire to engage with the intricacy of preparation as a meditative ritual. I am also sure there are customers who are struggling to get the damn espresso to pour correctly, running through a bag of coffee, who would say the experience is anything but relaxing.

Theories of game mechanics propose that much of what we engage with in life comprises a set of unwritten rules that can define our engagement and sense of reward as we search to achieve goals within different frameworks. In this way, the challenge and the craft can have value, and something that is a hassle for some customers, can be part of what others enjoy. The boom in budding home baristas would support this theory, but there is also no way to get around the fact that this appeal is limited, and that convenient and automated systems are what many, arguably the majority, in mainstream coffee are looking for.

A higher percentage of specialty boutique coffee customers are open to using less straightforward methodologies. A certain result in the cup matters more to this customer cohort, so they are willing to undertake additional preparation requirements.

There is a sliding scale of formats that require varying amounts of customer involvement and input. Specialty grade coffees have popped up in a wider range of these formats than ever before, which means that customers looking for a premium quality do not need to belong to a single brewing cohort. There will continue to be trends and innovations across brewing formats that are adopted by boutique companies and customers, and I do believe that brewing coffee will continue to be an area of value that businesses are keen to explore.

The Branding Blur
The branding and marketing trends in specialty coffee are very interesting to follow. The semiotics attached to the boutique independent movement are not singular, even if there are commonalities that flow through the majority of brands. Boutique brands are always reacting to and positioning themselves in reaction to the larger branded chain and the mass coffee market. The large mass coffee brands are, at the same time, keeping a keen eye on product and marketing trends in the independent space. The larger branded chain market clearly considers which organic trends in the independent market may be worth integrating into their own offering and marketing.

All of the coffee businesses in the space, from big to small, are thinking about their position in the market, and their differentiation in relation to the market and importantly, to their competitors. The messaging gap between independent market and the mass market brands has shrunk in the past decade. Some call this the "blur" or the "merge" between the two spaces. Obviously, there are plenty of independent businesses not telling a specialty coffee story as well.
Innovation and Technology
The whole coffee space demonstrates a desire for exploration and novelty, whether through an interest in "new" or "re-emerging" origins and new cultivars and processing techniques, or through novel retail packaging, new tools and equipment, or new drink recipes and formats. The products that represent a new trend can either become established or lose traction, making way for the next new thing. The scarcity aspect of specialty boutique coffee is a moving target, and many factors affect the specific trends at play. At the same time there are many aspects of specialty boutique coffee that feel quite foundational and ingrained.

The trend of research and technology in the market appears to have legs. There is a growing demand at the consumer end of the market for coffee-driven technology and equipment ideas. This is accompanied by continued developments in research and innovation throughout the coffee supply chain, as different companies look to explore and introduce new ideas and concepts around process and flavour.

At the same time, a lot of innovation and development will continue to be focused around the commercial side of coffee. As coffee is a lean margin industry, it makes sense that there is incentive to improve the ability to be commercially successful through the utilisation of innovation. This innovation in the supply chain is not just about efficiency and yield but can be directly tied to quality. So long as quality can be tied to commercial value, it is directly related to potential profitability.

All actors in the supply chain up to, and including the roaster, have conversations tied to the commercial assessment of cup quality. Innovations that make it easier, more likely or more cost effective to hit a certain quality are valuable and will continue to be explored as they have always been in coffee. The boutique specialty end is showing an appetite for further innovation in this regard.

Sustainability

Research and technology will play an important role in what is another growing focus of the market - sustainability. Sustainability developments in coffee will continue to be driven by a mixture of behavioural change and technological change. At the consumer end, the carbon footprint of brewing coffee is really high, and flash heating or induction systems among other solutions are popping up more and more as a means to reduce carbon footprint and energy costs.

Efficient grinding technology and coffee preparation can reduce waste and coffee usage. Arguably, this is less good for the upstream businesses who lose volume, but it also improves the carbon footprint per drink. Importers are focused on upcoming anti-deforestation regulations, but are also exploring different supply chain structures, information chains and software to tell the story of the work they do around the world.

At a farming level, more easily achievable verification, which is attainable through software and technology, appears to be on the horizon. Verification throughout the supply chain will become more demanding and necessary, a subject I looked at in *Greenwashing*. Many boutique producers are already sustainability driven, and this trend will continue, but the sustainability propositions need to also support the economics of the business and the business models in the whole coffee industry need to support sustainability improvements.

New Experiences

Experience is a huge part of coffee. I think that we will see trends around experience in boutique specialty continue to spread all the way through the supply chain. We will continue to see brewing equipment that is based around results but also experience, and consumer brewing formats that combine experience and product quality.

I anticipate more focus on coffee producers. As the trend has been in wine, coffee farms now are able to cater to agrotourism, offering hospitality experiences. This has already begun to take off, especially in Latin America and Indonesia.

We will also see coffee and experiences that challenge preconceptions and concepts of quality. This is happening right now with heavily interventionist processing, in which bacteria and yeast cultures are used to create highly specific flavours. The movement is fascinating to watch, although I really don't like the highly synthetic flavours, which remind me of soap or shampoo. They are proving popular with some baristas and roasters, more so than end customers. As we have explored elsewhere in the book, it is these tastes that drive many trends in specialty coffee. The upfront and masking nature of these processes seems unlikely to hold a position of revered quality once the dust settles, and I think a more nuanced combination of terroir and human intervention will win out, but let's see. There is a lot happening in coffee across the world and across the supply chain.

Part Eight. Thoughts & Questions Posed

Specialty at Scale

Whilst the space is engaging, complex and evolving, it is also clear that much about the coffee industry is based on the four fundamental established industries that we have noted several times in this book: agriculture, finance and logistics, food manufacturing and hospitality. In this way, even with innovation and moving trends the underlying business mechanics are typically quite stable and constant.

Perhaps the biggest business model innovation in coffee in the past fifty years is Nespresso. This end-to-end business model has been referred to as the Apple of coffee. Nespresso has disruptive technology, a mass premium brand and dedicated brand interaction points in its forward-looking boutique stores. Not to mention, the business model bucks the norm for bottom line profit. Utilising a scaled up vertically integrated business model that was able to maintain prices through protected technology the business was able to hit 20% plus EBITDA results from multi-billion-dollar revenue. In recent years Nespresso has seen a drop, but results remain very high for the coffee industry.

Boutique specialty coffee models tend to show innovative ways of approaching product or customer propositions, but potentially over-egg the ease with which a profit can be made, or simply do not truly consider the business model that supports the innovation. I think that the consideration of the business of specialty coffee will only grow as a trend, whether through more business-minded individuals and companies entering the space, or through existing operators prioritising the pursuit of sound and effective business mechanics to support their companies and their vision. I hope my book is able to contribute towards the evolution of the boutique specialty market.

Exits & Consolidation

Quick growth or easily scalable businesses are not common in the industry, and the market looks very different to the start-up, "grow it and flip it" culture that we have seen in the tech world. At the same time the specialty market has been growing fast and continues to do so. This naturally creates interest in the business, and investment opportunities in the industry. There have been some strong success stories, and there have been some businesses that haven't worked out. In any market where there is both a growing market and high business activity, consolidation is also common.

When businesses in the space look to raise money or to exit, the drivers of the highest valuations will be brand and intellectual property. It is both of these things that create perceived and real value in coffee businesses. The other market position that can create a higher value is market coverage. This can allow a company to gain market share by buying a company that has established some significant market coverage in a specific territory, or that has a particular strategic positioning of value obtainable through purchase or majority ownership.

The challenges in growing a substantial business in the space, and the investment needed versus the EBITDA goal of the industry, means that coffee is typically more alluring to private equity and other larger established industry players than it is to pure venture capital. There are also many hybrid investing models and incentives. Of course, a lot of independent businesses in coffee are also started with the help of angel investors or friend and family money, as well as the odd bank loan.

Despite this, there is still venture capital in coffee. Typically venture capital is associated with the start-up and early phase of a company, and has a higher risk appetite. The higher the risk, the higher the potential upside will need to be to counter balance that risk. Venture capital exists based on this foundational principle. Venture capital is attracted to industries and business models that can achieve rapid growth and scalable success, which can be valued highly. Typically, funding will come in tranches, and the funding will be attached to high valuations that allow for multiple raises, creating room for multiple investors at different stages.

Blue Bottle Coffee's journey would be the ultimate example of a successful VC journey in the specialty coffee market. The business reportedly sold a majority stake of 68% for $500m. This was a liquidity event that saw a very high valuation applied proportionality against a much lower revenue and profit in the business. The value was much, much higher than the benchmarks typically found in the space, and represented a number of market conditions occurring across large commercial coffee companies with competing portfolios, as well as a perfectly timed and developed brand proposition by Blue Bottle. In this instance, the investors that bought in before the majority sale, saw a very successful investment return.

At the time of writing this book, coffee brand La Colombe in the US has received $300 million for 33% of their business from Keurig Dr Pepper, valuing the company at roughly $900 million. This is around a 10 x revenue valuation. Not as high as Blue Bottle's multiple, but still very, very high for the space, and in a more challenging economic time. Businesses that have managed to grow to a high revenue position do start to see higher valuations than those that are somewhere between small and big. This large food industry investor is typical of the investment and consolidation cycle in the food and drink sector. It makes a lot of sense that as a company grows, and hits a significant size, that it becomes attractive to the large multinational operators.

It is Ric Rhinehart's (executive director of the SCA) view that the big VC opportunity has mainly come and gone in coffee, and that the business climate at the time that allowed that huge exit was not a precedent, but a moment in time. This had also been my assumption. There are also benchmarks and herd mentality at play, which are fed by appetite for the purchase of a company. The precedent set by previous successes in the market will feed into future appetite. If there is a frenzy, and some companies in a space sell for a high valuation, but then don't turn out to deliver on the investment for the new owners, then it stands to reason that ongoing appetite for those models will be diminished. This is especially true if the buying market for businesses is a relatively small group of larger industry businesses.

There is, however, clearly more interest and investment in consumer coffee brands following the success of brands such as Blue Bottle and La Colombe, and multiple businesses are building models with these as their example. It should be made very clear that these are businesses that have managed to navigate from inception, through early stage and to a large scale before their large value transaction. There clearly continues to be success for scaling coffee businesses to achieve investment or consolidation into a larger industry player.

The larger coffee market will naturally be interested in keeping an eye on the specialty industry as it is a faster growing global market. They will develop their own products and brands to address this market opportunity, but also look to invest in and consolidate specialty brands that have broken past the boutique stage. These could be quicker growth businesses or relatively well established organic growth businesses, as was the case in the purchase of Intelligentsia coffee and Stumptown Coffee in 2015 by Peets and JAB holdings.

All of these examples are American, the biggest value coffee market in the world. All markets around the world are interesting for specialty, the astronomical growth of Luckin Coffee in China has been quite something to watch. The company was definitely never boutique, but from the start they have been using specialty coffees and narratives.

In the UK we have a much smaller industry than America, but a significant specialty market has still emerged. Many companies here are looking to take a similar route but none are really yet to finish that journey. Examples would be Grind Coffee, Black Sheep and Watchouse, amongst others. Generally in the UK, businesses start to raise awareness and interest for larger investment vehicles or larger FMCG business when they hit and pass £10 million annual revenue. A subject we considered a few chapters back in *The Fifth Wave. Can You Scale Quality?* Was that boutique specialty coffee cannot inherently be scaled, as it won't remain boutique, however aspects of what ecompass the boutique coffee movement can be. As well as this, specialty grade coffee itself is already utilised across a variety of coffee businesses in size and market position. These funded growth models are exploring the opportunity for specialty brand narratives and products to move beyond boutique and to achieve a significant commercial position and exit.

Of course exits and consolidation aren't just a conversation for large companies, but can apply to companies of any size. The valuations will simply be more conservative at the smaller end of the boutique market. As the majority of the market we are discussing is made up of these businesses, rather than the successful outliers, it is my observation that exits in the space on the whole will be based around the benchmarks in the underlying business types that sit across most food and hospitality businesses. This will be a multiple based on EBITDA rather than revenue as we looked at in *Ownership, Investment and Valuation* in *Part Two* of the book. As the "quality" of revenue in coffee businesses is a concern for potential buyers, the EBITDA or underlying net profit is a stronger driver of valuation discussions. The appetite for the exact multiple will vary depending on macroeconomic and industry wide factors, but a good goal, for a well run successful business, would be 8 x EBITDA. If this, for example, this is a multi-shop operation hitting 15% EBITDA then this would represent a 1.2 x multiple of revenue. These kinds of goals would be ambitious but achievable depending on multiple factors, and what comes out about the specifics of the business in the due diligence process. There will be a few unicorns that far outstrip these numbers, but there will also be many businesses that don't manage to achieve anything like these numbers.

Consolidation is not inevitable across the market, in fact there are and will continue to be many founders and operators who don't want to sell. They chose to start a business that allowed them to be their own boss and build something around a topic they are passionate about. These businesses can become a huge part of people's lives.

The sales numbers we talked about just now can be sizable if the business has achieved a reasonable revenue, but for many small businesses, the multiples won't be enough to walk off into the sunset. If they enjoy the business, and it provides a sustainable living, they can rightly choose not to sell. For the serial entrepreneur who loves starting new things, the exit is natural. For those who are looking to build something over time, it makes less sense. You can build a significant, sustainable business over time that provides decent profit and return, making the idea of an exit at a competitive valuation less desirable.

Speaking of founders and entrepreneurs, the personal nature of many of these businesses can be a concern for buyers or potential investors. Entrepreneurial types are often strong characters who build things with enthusiasm and sheer will. They also commonly build things around themselves, and the businesses can become highly reliant on them.

From an exit point of view, if there is not a strong company structure and culture, the buyer will be concerned that they are paying for a business that they won't get. By this, I mean that the buyer is reliant on the founder, as the business is built around them, but they are also paying to remove that founder. It is for this reason founder-led businesses often get bought with a crossover period. The key personnel are contractually obliged to stay in the business for a period of time, normally three years or so. The purchase deal will often have split incentives. This could be that the payment for the business is spread across this time, incentivising the outgoing team members to contribute to a successful transition period. This is all easier said than done, and even with this period of transition it can be extremely hard to keep the company's DNA when the founding team leaves.

Finally, consolidation often happens not because of a profitable exit but through an opportunity to exit a business that isn't working. In any movement that sees a lot of entrants, this outcome is inevitable. Each time the market gets squeezed, industry peers start wondering which business will go into administration or be bought next.

The Price of a Cup of Coffee
If all the world's coffee was to get more expensive, and the price increased for both commercial and specialty coffee tomorrow, at what price would people start drinking less coffee each day? This is a thought experiment that is hard to tackle. I am sure there are economists who could use an anthropological model that categorises the potential price elasticity of consumer buying behaviour to predict this number by country and demographic. Even then, this would only be a model, a prediction, and we would only really know the answer if it were to actually happen.

The current pricing dynamic and the way people respond to a given coffee's price is in the context of the wider market. All premium coffee is premium coffee. This means that it has a higher price point to other coffee and is viewed through this lens. This also means that specialty boutique coffee is regularly positioned not as a staple, but as a treat in the space.

Part Eight. Thoughts & Questions Posed

Karl Weinhold, who wrote *Cheap Coffee*, relocated to Portugal after working with coffee in Colombia. He is now embarking on academic studies regarding the C Market and the true influences on coffee's global pricing. He mentioned that when he was in coffee, as is the case for all of us in specialty coffee, he had access to premium coffee every day. It is with this privilege that we make assumptions that the price average customers pay should just go up. Now that he is on a research salary, his perspective has changed. Now for him, premium speciality coffee is the occasional cup, and not the staple, and he sees things from a different perspective.

My team at the roastery were discussing which of their personal subscriptions to cancel as the cost of living rises and inflation soars. "Do I get rid of Disney Plus or the craft beer monthly box?" I asked the team a question, "if you didn't work in coffee, but you had the same salary working in another industry, would you sign up for our coffee subscription?" This question can be asked in a café or indeed throughout many businesses in coffee. The answer was different for different people, but it was interesting that in many cases, it was mentioned that they would treat the coffees as a less frequent purchase and combine it with a lower priced coffee. In other words, they wouldn't sign up for the subscription. For many of us, working in specialty coffee affords us the opportunity to drink premium coffee every day as part of our jobs, which means that after years in coffee, we can become distanced from the perspective of the customer.

Customers who buy premium coffee as their staple, are a demographic with enough disposable income to do so. How we each decide to divvy up our salaries is an individual choice. There will be one person who wishes to dedicate a higher percentage of their earnings to coffee compared to another person who would like to spend this on something else.

It is often easy to think of a specialty customer as a person that is fully committed to the space and is anti-commercial coffee. This customer profile does exist for sure, but there's also a huge swathe of customers who exhibit a variety of coffee purchasing habits. We know that varied behaviour in coffee formats is prevalent, and a customer can very happily embrace both a convenience method and a slow manual format, depending on time of day, the environment and their needs at the time.

In the paper *Market Work and the Formation of the Omnivorous Consumer Subject*, Anissa Pomiès and Zeynep Arsel outline that coffee presents an example of an industry whose consumers have omnivorous taste. They describe a journey that begins with individuals gaining an "appreciation for coffee with primary socialisation and they enjoy the energising and socialising functions of lowbrow coffee."

It is suggested that they then "develop a formal appreciation of coffee later in life as a result of market work conducted by market professionals." The market work and market professional concept is made in reference to the influence that professional coffee businesses have on consumer understanding of coffee. This could also be termed "sensemaking," which is something that we looked at in *Part Five* of the book.

The point here though is that the customer can have multiple tastes and frameworks for coffee at a moment in time, and can be a consumer of very different coffee products simultaneously. This "omnivorous" customer is interesting from many points of view, and in this case it presents an interesting pricing consideration. The suggestion that customers can move between a variety of coffee price points, means that any squeeze in the cost of living will likely shift their customer profile around, therefore changing their buying habits.

Most of what I have written about so far in this chapter has been in relation to retail coffee products, whether pods, beans or instant. An equally interesting price dynamic is at play in coffee shop pricing, especially in the dynamic between branded and independent coffee drink pricing. At the time of writing this book, (2023) the average price of a flat white or other typical menu item in the UK market is often higher at a branded coffee chain than at a specialty or independent shop in the same area.

It is clear that the costs that drive a café's price are not solely linked to the price of the coffee. As we have seen in this book, the costs of running the environment and staffing it outweigh the ingredient costs. But, of course, with the net margin being lean, a change in coffee costs can still have a significant impact.

My knowledge of the different supply chains would strongly suggest that the margin will be better in the branded chains. I think that both Starbucks and Costa are really interesting brands, as they are mass premium brands in the space, and this supports their high price point. It is easy for an independent specialty shop to not realise this. Saying this, I still think that an indie focusing on specialty coffee should aim to at least match, or better surpass, the price point of these brands. Otherwise, they are leaving value on the table.

When I have talked to indie operators, they often express a lack of confidence in pricing. This further supports the narrative that this is an independent, alternative business, rather than a premium or luxury alternative. However, the same specialty shops are selling retail beans at significantly higher prices per bag of coffee than the branded chains. The brands have achieved a high value when selling drinks, so whilst the independent operators seek to differentiate, they also feel the available audience is more price sensitive.

The branded chains are clearly extremely large. This suggests to me that indie operators' pricing concerns are an illusion driven by listening to the loud feedback of a vocal minority, who push back on price. Doing this means that specialty coffee businesses are likely leaving money on the table with their per cup pricing, which is hindering potential improvements in raw ingredients, their teams and the sustainability of their annual profits.

Branded chains are comparable to a typical indie coffee shop in that the model is similar. They both have a focus on selling cups of coffee. Less similar are the chain operators in the food sector, who offer coffee alongside food. They shift a lot of coffee, but price it as an accompanying product and part of a larger ticket price.

I once performed a blind tasting for a TV programme and compared drinks from some of the largest UK coffee providers, which included the likes of Greggs and McDonalds, as well as the major coffee chains. Blind, I chose the McDonalds coffee as the best coffee, (these were all black coffee offerings) and it also was sold at the lowest price of the drinks that I tasted. The Lavazza coffee offering at Wetherspoons is another good example. Coffee in these environments is part of a wider play. The price point is lower, as coffee is used as a conversion tool to accompany the business's more profitable offerings.

Coffee sells through many other channels of course. Specialty coffee brands all boomed during the pandemic, and have since focused more on e-commerce. It is clear however, that the pricing sweet spot is not with the super premium and high-priced coffees and that these have a limited audience. As the price goes up, most brands see the number of sales reduce. I think that the last couple of years have highlighted the potential lack of elasticity in coffee pricing throughout the chain.

The 2021-22 price rise in the C Market, also coinciding with inflation, has resulted in many roasteries and many coffee brands looking at alternative origins or lowering the quality and price point of the green that they source. During challenging squeezes in a high inflation market most coffee businesses will aim for a reduced net profit, which would be single digit pre-tax numbers for consumption businesses. For many independents this can mean moving to break-even or even going out of business entirely if they are not well positioned to take the hit. Increased inflation globally will impact prices throughout the supply chain unless there are other ways to find the lost profit through efficiency or through big FX movements. Boutique companies can often be less affected by these big macroeconomic changes if their customer base is small and shielded.

Historical data and behaviour suggests that the consumption companies throughout the industry will compete to a point where they can make a lean profit, and in most cases avoid losses (unless they have some specific IP or USP to drive a higher profit). The relatively free coffee market will effectively drive towards the most competitive point.

For consumers around the world, their cup of coffee gets more expensive if costs rise throughout the supply chain, and at the end point, companies cannot suck up the difference. This could be container shipping prices, the cost of finance, utilities, labour, inflation, or another of many variables. At the agricultural end, where the C Market is most impactful, the two big impactors on price will mostly be a supply shortfall or a regulation/policy change in multiple large producing countries, such as the end of ICA, (International Coffee Agreement) which we explored earlier in the book.

There have been periods of stability in the recent past, but we see events such as these, all of the time in the market. However, with multiple industry factors at play, which create risk and volatility, we may well be able to answer the question at the beginning of this chapter through our own experience. The next chapter explores some of these market dynamics through the possibility of a potential coming divergence in coffee farming.

Is There a Coming Divergence in Coffee?

Throughout the writing of this book I have been lucky to talk to individuals throughout the industry who all have had unique experiences and could pass on different perspectives. This means that it stands out when I hear a consistent thread echoed through the thoughts shared with me.

One such thought that resonated through the conversations was a sense of a coming divergence in coffee production, particularly in Latin America. Many have observed what could be a growing delta between the incentive to produce volume-based, commercial coffee or small lot, premium coffee.

It is clear that there are many challenges that face the business of coffee, and that the risk exposure is higher at a farming level. This risk is particularly high outside of Brazil and Vietnam, and relates to scale and market pricing. Too small is risky, and as Pedro of Pergamino in Colombia points out, being larger has its own risks also. It is challenging to make the business of growing coffee work. This combined with a "greying" farming population in many countries, and the onset of climate change, has created a recipe for change.

With the viability of growing coffee as a sustainable livelihood long in question in multiple growing areas, the thought process works as follows: younger generations are pursuing economic possibilities away from coffee and away from rural locations, whilst their parents or grandparents continue to run the coffee farm. The time will come that the land and the coffee production is due to be inherited by the younger generation, but do they have any incentive to keep focusing on coffee production?

The younger generation that inherits the land, does not live on the land any longer, and would therefore be unlikely to see the benefit of returning to coffee farming at the expense of the work and life they have built elsewhere. In many countries land is continually split between descendants and this fuels the issue by creating smaller and smaller plots, not viable for production. The land ownership structures in somewhere like Ethiopia are completely different, but the challenges of an ageing farming population, and climate change, are just as applicable in Africa, with projects in various countries designed to encourage the uptake of coffee farming within youth and female populations, to curb overall industry decline.

James Hoffmann has been wondering for some time "when are we going to start seeing the consolidation" that this dynamic is likely to create. There is likely to be significant intention to sell the land. What the land will be used for will be dependent on the country, but in many cases it is likely to not be coffee. There may be some producers who take the opportunity to expand their coffee growing operations, but overall coffee production will decline in this scenario. It is also possible that the land will stay in the family, but will be converted to longer term crop investment, such as hard wood. The challenges presented by climate change as well as other macro economic factors are likely to fuel this decision making process, as annual coffee yields have become more volatile due to erratic weather events.

There is a counter to this thought process. The market has faced many such challenges, and supply continues to be achieved. Coffee remains to have benefits, namely that it is a very liquid cash crop, and there are those in the industry who think that the market will continue to exist with little change. A degree of self-regulation will occur as different countries take up the slack, and as value changes in different regions. This does already occur of course, however, it also feels like this perspective is fuelled by what has been a relatively consistent status quo for a long time, and potentially shows a lack of recognition of ongoing systemic changes that haven't yet reached their conclusion.

Part Eight. Thoughts & Questions Posed

This thought experiment, and current trends, suggest that less coffee will be grown in future. In the specific instances that we are discussing this is true, but there is a compelling argument that global supply will adapt, especially in terms of who is meeting the demand. Countries such as Brazil and Vietnam, where suitable infrastructure and scale allow commercial coffee to be profitable, are likely to fulfil some requirement. Vietnam is known for its Robusta production and it would appear likely that Brazil will also start producing more Robusta. On this same thread, as Robusta gains more of the market, there are also many further locations that can be suitable Robusta growing regions. It should however, also be noted that Robusta is affected by drastic weather events as well, and climate change will still affect all coffee production, commercial and specialty alike.

The conversation around coffee supply within the industry is generally pretty biassed. We are all typically incentivised to expand some aspect of coffee. For commercial coffee this is volume and price, whilst for specialty, it is quality and variety at certain price points, as well as volume. There are of course other projects that encourage different impacts, but on the whole, the above is true. Effectively, without even realising it, the incentive flowing upstream has become about maximising coffee opportunity. This can come from many different angles, including businesses such as roasters and exporters, or local and national governments. The suggestion may be to maximise yield, or plant different coffee trees, or invest in processing, communication and access to market. These are all essentially business development discussions.

However, if this is considered from a different perspective, and if you approach the piece of land as a management consultant project, whereby the different potential uses of the land are assessed in the context of the different economic possibilities for the individuals who own the land, would the same recommendation be made?

What does this mean for specialty Arabica? The prediction is that the boutique premium segment will become more separated from the mass coffee market, and this will lead to an increase in price. This will mimic other industries that have followed a similar track. As a business you want to be at either end of the range, but you don't really want to be in the middle. Many have commented to me that this process is already happening.

Pedro Miguel Echavarría of Pergamino in Colombia, has been exploring different forms of vertical integration. The business now consists of several parts: coffee farms that they own, an exporting business for their own and other local Colombian coffees, a roasting business in Colombia, and now they have eight coffee shops in the country as well. He explained to me how they have been playing around with each part of the business over the past ten years, seeing which bits can show profitability and which cannot. They are continuing to pursue a diversified strategy that spreads risk and opportunity, but they want to reduce the coffee they are growing on their own land, focusing on small lots that they can sell to their own roastery at a premium, or export at a premium, whilst reducing the production of larger lots. He expects their exporting business to be focused on their allied producer programme, in which they work with farms in the three-to-five hectare window and provide access to market for their coffees. The land that they own will change function, and will be used to support agritourism with experience of the coffee brand, inspired by the vineyard tourism model, with lodges and visitor experiences. This will sit alongside the retail outlets and roastery. This case study is fascinating and it touches on so much of what we have explored earlier in the book around business strategy and analysis.

I chose this example to demonstrate the evolving potential of specialty and premium coffee, but also to demonstrate the decision making around what to do and not to do with coffee. In parts of their business they are growing and expanding, and in others they are reducing and stopping activity entirely. Coffee is a competitive and challenging business landscape and successful business solutions won't simply revolve around everyone focusing on tasty coffee.

Less coffee may very well be the right answer in many scenarios. Of course, if we take this idea to its extreme, we can imagine a world where there is a dramatic shortage in supply of coffee versus the demand, and the price of coffee rises triggering a reduction in daily consumption. We explored this in the previous chapter. If one runs with this idea even further you can reach the scenario in which coffee returns to being a less affordable luxury, instead of an affordable daily beverage. This would undoubtedly represent the loss of a whole industry. The hospitality world that revolves around coffee couldn't exist. This would apply to businesses throughout the whole industry, and would lead to huge losses of livelihood across the sector.

But let's not discuss a complete collapse of the industry, rather continue down the train of thought of a divergence of qualities, and a wider price spread. If this change were to happen it would provide a very interesting dynamic at the retail end of coffee. The narrative and aesthetic of specialty coffee is already growing considerably faster than the actual in-cup flavour profile or cost. There is a consumer choice proposition right now, and on the whole, it doesn't require a massive jump to opt in to specialty coffee.

The bulk of what we call the specialty movement is not presently businesses working with very high point scoring coffees. This squeeze grew last year as prices jumped up, and businesses moved their qualities down the 80 point scale to hit commercial prices, effectively trying to find a minimum viable solution, managing quality and cost together. As the business sector that spreads the specialty narrative has become more competitive, this squeeze has been probed more and more. In effect, a lot of business can be won by companies in the specialty sector, at a wholesale level, without asking for a large jump in per unit cost. Whilst their offer is more expensive, it is not several times the price, more like a 20% increase for the client who is transitioning.

The independent boutique sector, alongside those slightly larger businesses who are just growing out of being independent, do not, as we have explored, typically have robust verification processes around branding claims. I posit that, in a divergence situation, there will be more brands that seek to utilise the best commercial grade coffees in their higher volume products, and tell the story of specialty through their low volume, higher priced, showcase products. The likelihood of misleading branding and communications will increase at this point, and I wonder whether this would instigate a new, rebellious movement of coffee brands that would focus on proving that they are actually a "complete" authentic specialty brand, in response.

This idea that less coffee can be good does have legs. If there is a divergence of qualities, it will likely mean that there is less abundantly available quality coffee for specialty coffee. In coffee we are clearly all biassed, and it is interesting to consider how the idea of less coffee is not solely a bad thing. Yes, it will negatively affect parts of the industry, but it could also represent a re-calibration of an industry that needs to see change in the middle. It is particularly interesting and potentially positive if the lost coffee agriculture is due to better economic opportunities in subtropical producing countries.

If this were to happen, large coffee companies would focus on large, commercial supply and increased Robusta production (and possibly other species or cross-species). Super high-end coffee companies would focus on sticking to quality, and would need to explore the business size and market potential that higher prices would dictate. Those in the middle would see the biggest hit. The UK gym market provides a surprising parallel. Following the 2008 financial crisis, a divergence in the market led to growing success for lower priced gym offerings, and the continued growth of super high end, tailored gyms, whilst the middle went out of the market.

I typically don't like trying to predict too far into the future, but this line of thinking does create some important and challenging food for thought. The more I think about it, the more I think this divergence represents a positive outcome in producing countries and a negative outcome for end consumers. I think that whether coffee as a crop has a positive or negative position is almost wholly dependent on context. I collaborate on a project in Africa where coffee is a positive part of a development programme. Where opportunity is limited, in rural communities, coffee can present part of a strategic agricultural business plan. It can be a valuable cash crop in the right circumstances. In multiple economies there also continues to be grants and subsidies that encourage coffee farming.

Without subsidies or regulation, as economies develop and prosper, and alternative economic opportunities present themselves, the incentive to stay in coffee production sits in either going boutique high end or large and more commercial. Yes, there is culture and heritage in coffee that will be lost here. This pattern has played out in many economies as they have developed. In countries like Colombia the specialty coffee market is creating entrepreneurial opportunities, but the question will be about the size of that opportunity. The macroeconomic model of coffee around the world is complex and with so many different contexts in so many different producing countries it is hard to generalise, but these important issues appear to be pointing towards change for the business of coffee.

The Holy Grail - Vision Plus Business

Throughout this book the concept of sweet spots has popped up regularly, whether in optimising bottom-line profit in each phase of growth before investing in the next phase, or the sweet spot of scale for each business, based on its model and position in the marketplace.

When I was speaking to different coffee professionals and entrepreneurs in the industry as I wrote this book, the tussle between vision and commerciality provided a regular talking point. James Hoffmann explained that "specialty coffee in particular had an uncomfortable relationship with the concept of profit, and that the conversation around what a profitable sustainable specialty business model could look like was not common in the space, meaning people didn't know what the business goals actually were" with the focus for many pursuing specialty coffee being around quality, experience and distributed value in the supply chain. These are great goals for a rewarding business in a fascinating industry, and we should support them, however if you can't create a business model that underpins the pursuit you aren't going anywhere.

I grew up around the business of creativity and I witnessed the inherent potential conflict between creativity and business in the world of art. While I recognised that purely pursuing bottom-line profit rarely allowed for or encouraged creativity and artistic values, there is a sweet spot whereby a sound business could feed the creativity. There are obviously limits. If no one wants to buy the art, it won't matter how sound the business model and strategy are.

One of the most extreme examples of building creativity into a business model, is in Dyson, based not far from me in the UK. It took James Dyson 5,127 prototypes to complete the bagless vacuum cleaner that has made his company's name. This experience supported the idea that creative innovation would take time and funding, and he built this into the company moving forward. Their R&D budget is enormous, and teams of designers create 100s of new product ideas every year that make it to the prototype stage, but don't come to market.

If the company had a typical shareholder structure this would without doubt be questioned and reduced. This is a lot of money spent every year on products that don't come to market. The Dyson model believes in this creative process, and that the next great product for their company will be achieved through this approach. This can be accomplished through the value of creating IP, which can support profitable sales prices, and the ability to scale and "own" the technology. As coffee typically does not have the same capacity for IP (excluding the Nespresso example), it's hard to build this kind of business model. However, the lesson is the same - integrate mission and business together.

Noah Namowicz of Cafe Imports gives regular classes on entrepreneurship to students at the University of St. Thomas, Minnesota, and stresses that this is the most important concept to get right. I understood when starting out that my business needed to be profitable to survive, but I didn't fully understand how intrinsic a complementary business model could be in allowing me to pursue a mission over time. If I could go back in time and give myself some advice, the importance of this concept would be what I would lead with. The young me would probably say "yeah, yeah I know I need to make a business that doesn't lose money", and the older me would patiently counter this and say, "sure, but try to think about it as building a business with the structure that allows you to pursue your mission to the point where you can achieve things you haven't even thought about yet".

Acknowledgements

Throughout my career in coffee so far, I have learnt so much from so many people, who have been generous with their time and knowledge. I wouldn't be able to list everyone who has contributed to this book in some way over the years, but here are some of the people I spoke to directly in researching this book.

Nina Marie Braisby, Scott Rao, Ric Rhinehart, Luke Atwood, Jamie Marler, Sam Maccuaig, Lani Kingston, Andrea Otte, James Hoffmann, Colin Harmon, Joanna Lawson, Mandi Caudill, Fernando lima, Andrew Tucker, Pete Southern, James Howell, Ben Palmer, Klaus Thomson, Tim Wendelboe, Christopher Feran, Andrew Bowman, Kyle Ramage, Pedro Miguel Echavarria, Ana Luiza Pellicer, Catalina Gutierrez, James Hennebry, David Balmer, Fiona Dendy, Richard Williams, Stephen Morrissey, Jonny England, Will Little, Stephen Dick, Mat North, Noah Namowicz, Kyle Bellinger, Kieran Masterton, Tom Sobey, Dale Harris, Ed Anderson Brown, Craig Dickson, Lloyd Retzlaff, Josh Tarlo, David Papparelli, Janina Grabs, Jonathan Morris, Paul Arnephy, Sebastian Stephenson, Lesley Colonna-Dashwood, Chris Ammerman, Jeffrey Young, Alexander Robaszkiewicz, James Strong, Heath Jansen, Brenda Alvarado, Alejandro Cadena R., Karl Weinhold, Candice Madison, Mhairi Erskine, Peter Grosvener-Attridge, George Irwin, Ben Stokes, Callum Mousely, Kit Frere, Simon Brown, Raphael Prime, Brad Morrison, Paul Ross, Herbert Peñaloza Correa, Roland Horne, Kane Bodum, Angus Thirlwell, Mike Nunn, Alistair Hines.

About the Author

Maxwell works across the coffee industry, both through his own businesses and through collaborative projects. Maxwell is a three-time UK Barista Championship winner and three time world finalist. Maxwell has co-authored multiple academic published papers on the topic of coffee. In 2015 he co-authored and self-published his first book *Water For Coffee* with chemistry professor Christopher H. Hendon. A second edition will be published in 2024. Maxwell then wrote The Coffee Dictionary which was published by Octopus Publishing. *The Business of Specialty Coffee* is his third book on the subject of coffee.